Pornography in a free society

Pornography in a free society

GORDON HAWKINS
FRANKLIN E. ZIMRING

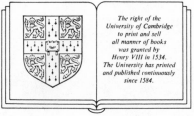

The right of the
University of Cambridge
to print and sell
all manner of books
was granted by
Henry VIII in 1534.
The University has printed
and published continuously
since 1584.

CAMBRIDGE UNIVERSITY PRESS

Cambridge

New York   New Rochelle   Melbourne   Sydney

Published by the Press Syndicate of the University of Cambridge
The Pitt Building, Trumpington Street, Cambridge CB2 1RP
32 East 57th Street, New York, NY 10022, USA
10 Stamford Road, Oakleigh, Melbourne 3166, Australia

First published 1988

Printed in the United States of America

Library of Congress Cataloging-in-Publication Data
Hawkins, Gordon, 1919–
Pornography in a free society / Gordon Hawkins, Franklin E.
Zimring.
p. cm.
ISBN 0 521 36317 9
1. Pornography – Government policy.   2. Pornography – Social
aspects.   3. Obscenity (Law)   I. Zimring, Franklin E.   II. Title.
HQ471.H387 1989   88-17058
363.4'7 – dc19   CIP

British Library Cataloguing in Publication Data
Hawkins, Gordon, 1919–
Pornography in a free society.
1. United States. Pornography. Social
aspects
I. Title II. Zimring, Franklin E.
363.4'7'0973

ISBN 0 521 36317 9

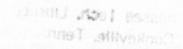

For Michal Patricia
                    –F. Z.

An Earl Warren Legal Institute Study

Contents

List of tables and figures   page viii
Preface   ix
Acknowledgments   xiii

I. **Pornography and the pornography commissions**
    Introduction   3

1. Experts on what? The origins and composition of
    pornography commissions   5
2. On definitions   20
3. The nature and distribution of pornography in the United
    States   30
4. Pornographic communication and social harm: a review of
    the reviews   74
5. Freedom of expression and the public law of pornography   109

II. **Public policy after liberalization**
    Introduction   149

6. Pornography and the subjugation of women: the radical
    feminist challenge   151
7. Pornography and child protection   175
8. Pornography in perspective: social response in the
    noncensoring society   198
9. Notes toward the future   218

References   227
Index   233

Tables and figures

Tables

2.1 The Tower of Babel   *page* 26
3.1 Box office receipts by classification   33
3.2 Number of films in each of the MPA's rating categories, November 1, 1968, to September 30, 1985   34
3.3 Estimated sales of sexually-oriented publications in the United States, 1969   35
3.4 Top-selling sexually explicit magazines: average circulation per month, 1975–84   36
3.5 Video Software Dealers Association annual market survey, 1984   39
3.6 Video Software Dealers Association survey, September 6, 1985   40
3.7 Full-time and part-time exploitation theaters, 1970   51
3.8 Wholehearted consumers of pornography in Sweden   56
3.9 Users of pornography by age in Sweden   56
3.10 Age of patrons, by location: adult theaters and bookstores in the United States   57
3.11 Frequency of viewing sexually explicit films in movie theaters and on video, by age   58
4.1 Behavioral effects: sex crime   75
4.2 Behavior finding   78
4.3 Attitude   80

Figures

3.1 Percentage of men and women recently exposed to erotica, by age   57
4.1 A model of the impact of pornography   87
4.2 Sex and violence   104

Preface

We think Professor A. W. B. Simpson, who was a member of the British Williams Committee on Obscenity and Film Censorship, got it right when he described pornography as "a subject which, though it has its importance, can hardly be viewed as standing in the forefront of the problems of the world" (Simpson, 1983:34). But if it is not one of the most important policy problems that Western democracies face, it is one of the most interesting ones.

Pornography is interesting both as a topic that divides citizens in American society and as a way of studying how such conflicts are deflected and resolved in government and society. Those who wish to study the key elements and tensions in American culture have much to learn from the tug-of-war over pornography, and students of the relationship between social character and the operation of the criminal law encounter a whole curriculum in the recent history of pornography and government in the United States.

In the last years of the twentieth century, pornography has become particularly interesting as a case study in social and governmental change. In the United States and most Western nations, the past twenty-five years have seen a transition from censorship to widespread availability of sexually explicit depictions, which in turn has created a call for reexamining government's proper role in the field.

In America, pornography has been regarded as sufficiently important to justify establishing two nationally chartered commissions within fifteen years. In England, although the Williams Committee in 1977 was the first national body to undertake a comprehensive review of the subject, various aspects of it had in the previous two decades been considered by the Law Commission, two Parliamentary Select Committees, and a Home Office Working Party. In Canada also, the government established in 1983 a Special Committee on Pornography and Prostitution.

When in July 1986 Attorney General Edwin Meese's Commission on Pornography published its final report it was greeted, as was the report of President Johnson's Commission on Obscenity and Pornography sixteen years earlier in 1970, with widespread criticism. But the general tendency of the criticism was rather different in the two cases. This is hardly surprising. One commentator remarked that the report of the Meese Commission was "designed to be the antithesis of its ancestor, the notorious 1970 report of the Federal Commission on Obscenity and Pornography" (Hertzberg, 1986:21).

The two reports are indeed antithetical and the reactions accorded them were similarly contrary in character. The thrust of the storm of protest that greeted the Johnson Commission's report was that it was in effect "legitimizing pornography" (van den Haag, 1971:31). It was subsequently described in the *Reader's Digest* as "The Report That Shocked the Nation" (Keating, 1971:37); and within a month of its publication it was "totally" rejected by President Nixon, who called its conclusions "morally bankrupt" and charged that the commission had "performed a disservice" (Weaver, 1970:1).

The Meese Commission report, by contrast, was denounced for "its glaring and persistent biases in gathering and evaluating evidence"; and its recommendations were said to "pose a serious threat to free expression" (Vance, 1986:76, 77). It was said to reflect "the conservative dialectic that defines the Reagan counterrevolution . . . [and to be intended to be] the signal for a gigantic national crusade, fronted by right-thinking political leaders, against demon porn" (Hertzberg, 1986:21, 23). It was described in a *Time* magazine cover story, "Sex Busters," as "emblematic of a new moral militancy evident in communities around the country and of a willingness of government officials, from federal to local levels, to help enforce traditional values" (Stengel, 1986:12).

The immediate stimulus for this undertaking was the publication of the Meese Commission report and its attendant publicity. Much of what we have to say here is specifically critical of that report, in respect to both its assessment of the evidence and its policy analysis. But it is our view that a single commission's effort can most profitably be judged against parallel attempts. The inherent difficulties of the problem should not be confused with avoidable errors. The errors of one biased view should be contrasted with the shortcomings that stem from the opposite bias. What is needed is a more comprehensive assessment of efforts to grapple with this issue.

This book thus grew out of our interest in looking at the Meese Commission's report in a wider perspective than that of partisan political debate in America. It occurred to us that the report of the Williams Committee, which was also based on a major investigation and carried out during the period between the publication of the two American reports, would provide a useful basis for comparison.

We have not included the Canadian report of the Special Committee on Pornography and Prostitution in our systematic comparative analysis, although we do make references to it in the discussion of various issues. The decision not to treat it in parallel with the other reports was based on three considerations. First, there is a serial continuity between the Johnson, Williams, and Meese reports – with Williams referring back to Johnson and Meese referring back to both its predecessors – from which the Canadian report is excluded. Second, the Canadian committee was concerned not solely with pornography but also with the very different problem of prostitution. Third, we felt a sense of diminishing marginal return. Adding one non–United States commission seemed to us of greater marginal value to the enterprise than adding a second volume. And comprehensive treatment of another report would threaten to bloat this book.

In the pages that follow, we seek first to examine the relationships of pornography and public law in Western democracy by studying the work of three national bodies that engaged in major investigations and filed substantial reports within the past two decades. We then provide perspectives in Part II on a set of problems that have taken on special meaning since the increased availability of sexually explicit communications in the 1960s and 1970s: on pornography and the status of women; on special policies toward children; and on social control of pornography without resort to censorship.

We think we have identified both the reason that the past two decades have been high season for pornography commissions and the function of such commissions in the political history of the topic. The commissions of inquiry, in the United States in 1968, in Great Britain in 1977, in Canada in 1985, and in the United States again in 1985, were part of the process of adjusting to changes in the availability of pornography, changes that had already occurred. We see the reports of these deliberative bodies as ceremonies of adjustment to the social fact of widespread availability. And minor adjustment rather than major policy-innovation is inevitably the recommendation of such a commission.

In discussing this theory with colleagues, we encounter no resistance with respect to the commission reports before Meese. But to call the Meese report an accommodation to widespread pornography is not regarded as self-evident. After all, it is said, the orientation of the members of that commission was profoundly antismut; indeed, the origin of the commission was to serve as a counterpoint to the Johnson Commission, which many conservatives regarded as cheerleading for the increased availability of pornography. Could such a commission as Meese itself be seen as preaching accommodation with the odious?

We think a careful reading of the Meese Commission in its historical context does support such a view. An important distinction must be drawn between complaining about history and trying to change it. The Meese Commission was engaged in complaining about the availability and impact of pornography but did not propose a counterreformation. It sought to remove the governmental seal of approval that social conservatives believe the earlier commission bestowed on pornography and pornographers. But it did not seriously propose an attempt to reverse the revolution in the availability of pornography to adults.

In this sense, both the Johnson Commission report in 1970 and the Meese Commission report in 1986 can be regarded as milestones in the path away from censorship.

We do not provide a solution to the problem of pornography in these pages. Nor in relation to a topic that is, as Harry Kalven said, "freighted with all the anxieties and hypocrisies of society's attitude toward sex" (Kalven, 1960:45) do we anticipate having a great deal of influence on public opinion or on the formulation of public policy. Although this happens to be an area where the advice of scholars is sometimes sought by lawmakers, we believe that the basic contours of public policy toward pornography have been set and are not likely to change soon. In this regard, we think the philosopher Abraham Kaplan stated a worthy ambition when he announced, "My problem is not what to do about obscenity, but what to make of it" (Kaplan, 1955:544). Our attempt in these pages is more to comprehend the problems of pornography in a free American society than to solve them.

Acknowledgments

We began the project that produced this book with a long-term interest in the comparative politics of the criminal law but with no recent history of scholarly interest in the topic of pornography. The particular debts accumulated in the course of this project involve the institutional supports that allowed the enterprise to function and the generosity of scholars who are veterans of the pornography debates.

The Earl Warren Legal Institute, of the University of California at Berkeley, provided Gordon Hawkins with fellowship support in 1986 and 1987, and facilitated Franklin Zimring's trip to Australia in March 1987 – thus, the continuation of our commuting collaboration. The Institute also supported studies of capital punishment and drunk driving policy that provided a model for our comparative approach to the pornography commissions. The wide variety of our administrative needs were in the capable hands of Cathleen Hill. Terrence Meyerhoff provided bibliographic assistance. Karen Chin was both the producer and caretaker of the manuscript.

Five colleagues provided important critical responses to this book. Jan Vetter of Berkeley and John Kaplan of Stanford read most of the manuscript and provided helpful commentary. Robert Post of Berkeley helped illuminate the materials discussed in Chapter 6. Brian Simpson and Frederick Schauer, both of the University of Michigan, provided critical responses to the manuscript that were informed by their scholarly expertise as well as their services on, respectively, the Home Secretary's Committee in Great Britain and the U.S. Attorney General's Commission on Pornography.

I

Pornography and the pornography commissions

Introduction

The twenty years between the mid-1960s and the mid-1980s could, with justification, be called the Era of the Pornography Commissions. After almost two centuries without a federal investigation of the problems of pornography, there have been two federal inquiries in the United States and one in Great Britain, as well as one in Canada dealing with both pornography and prostitution.

Two explanations for this phenomenon deserve attention. First, all these commissions were a response to social changes in the distribution of pornography that had occurred by the mid-1960s in much of the industrialized West. The commissions were responding to a change in availability and the social reaction to that change. They were an effect rather than a cause of widely available pornography. The first of the U.S. commissions was the product of this reaction almost exclusively. The subsequent commissions were a product of both the change in availability of sexual communications and an emulation of the commission on pornography as a political innovation. A commission of inquiry had become, visibly, one of the few things a national government could do about the subject without major cost.

The British and Canadian efforts were inspired in part by the earlier American example. And the Meese Commission was designed as a response to the Johnson Commission. In this last case, it could be said that opposition was the sincerest form of flattery.

Our method of showing the difference in perspective that these reports brought to their subject is to compare the analysis of each document of the core concerns that any pornography commission has to address. This part of the book is organized around these core concerns. It deals specifically with the manner in which they were addressed by the U.S. Commission on Obscenity and Pornography (the Johnson Commission), the Home Office Departmental Committee on Obscenity and Film Censorship (the Williams Committee), and the Attorney General's Commission on Pornography (the Meese Commission). After an introduction to the three bodies in Chapter 1, we analyze the approach of each of them to the definition of the field of inquiry in

3

Chapter 2. Chapter 3 compares the Johnson and Meese Commissions' accounts of the nature and distribution of pornography in the United States. Chapter 4 shows each body analyzing existing evidence on the behavioral effects of pornography. Chapter 5 discusses how each of them deals with the social value of free expression as an issue implicated in making policy about pornography.

Our treatment of these topics is intended both as a guide to the three reports and as an introduction to the issues confronted when considering government policy toward pornography. This general coverage of topics provides a foundation for our consideration of some special concerns in Part II.

1

Experts on what? The origins and composition of pornography commissions

Nationally chartered blue-ribbon commissions, groups of more or less eminent citizens officially charged with the task of considering and then making recommendations for legislative or other action in relation to what is publicly perceived as a national problem, are a much favored political device in Western democracies. It would be ingenuous to think that this is because they have proved notably efficient at problem solving or at producing effective prescriptions for the treatment of national afflictions.

In America there have been, since 1920, nine major national crime commissions under presidential authority or that of the attorney general. When, after his election victory, President Lyndon Johnson responded in 1965 to citizen concern about crime and created the Commission on Law Enforcement and Administration of Criminal Justice, calling on it to "give us the blueprints that we need . . . to banish crime" (Johnson, 1966:983), he was following well-established precedent. But following the commission's report, the crime problem remained certainly unsolved and not even noticeably diminished, awaiting the next round of high-level attention, which was to come before the end of the decade (U.S. National Advisory Commission, 1968; U.S. National Commission, 1969).

The attractions for a government of the commission device are multiple and diverse. An administration told that it must "do something" about a problem can, when it does not know what to do, establish a national commission and seem to have done something. An administration that does not at the time want to do anything about a problem can use the establishment of a national commission as a means of temporization. An administration that seeks endorsement or a rationale for something it wants to do can establish a (carefully selected) national commission. It is also not impossible that a national commission may be established by an administration genuinely seeking information and advice.

It is not surprising that the state of the laws relating to written, spoken, and visual representation of the pornographic should have been the subject of a

5

number of national commissions. Not only are those laws "anomalous, devoid of clear principle or objective and often unenforceable," they are also the subject of continuing debate between those who want stronger and more severe legal controls and those who favor the repeal of all, or nearly all, controls. Governments face constant "pressures – from one direction to clamp down on license, from the other to sustain freedom of expression" (Silkin, 1983:1). When those pressures reach a certain level of intensity, as they had in the three instances we consider here, the appointment of a national commission becomes almost inevitable.

When in October 1967 the United States Congress authorized the establishment of a Commission on Pornography and Obscenity there had been three sets of congressional hearings on the subject during the previous fifteen years (Kendrick, 1987:213). Crusaders against pornography and self-styled civil libertarians had long been engaged in a conflict later described as a "Civil War over Smut" (Witcover, 1970:550). Public concern in the late 1960s was related to the increase in the availability of sexually explicit magazines and films in the United States. The Williams Committee was set up in response to a decade of acrimonious public debate from which there had "emerged a near unanimity of dissatisfaction with the law and its administration" (Simpson, 1983:22). This committee was formed after fifteen or more years of greater availability of increasingly explicit material in Great Britain. The Meese Commission came at a time when great technological developments had affected the transmission of sounds, words, and images. President Nixon had warned in 1970 after the publication of the Johnson Commission report that "if an attitude of permissiveness were to be adopted regarding pornography, this would contribute to an atmosphere condoning anarchy in every other field and would increase the threat to our social order as well as our moral principles" (Kendrick, 1987:219). By 1985 such developments as cable television and videotape recording had, as the Meese Commission report put it, rendered much that the Johnson Commission said about the distribution and availability of pornography "starkly obsolete" (U.S. Department of Justice, 1986:226). And many citizens believed that, in relation to the public portrayal of sexuality, the anarchy President Nixon envisaged had arrived.

The three bodies whose work we review – the U.S. Commission on Obscenity and Pornography (the Johnson Commission), the Home Office Departmental Committee on Obscenity and Film Censorship (the Williams Committee), and the Attorney General's Commission on Pornography (the Meese Commission) – were thus all established in response to what was seen as public concern about an urgent national issue. Yet in no case were their principal recommendations adopted, and their respective receptions suggest that in no case was public disquiet allayed.

The Johnson Commission, which had recommended the repeal of all legislation prohibiting the sale, exhibition, or distribution of sexual materials to consenting adults, was told by an unconsenting President that "so long as I am in the White House there will be no relaxation of the national effort to control and eliminate smut from our national life" (Kendrick, 1987:219). As for the Williams Committee, one of its members, Professor A. W. B. Simpson, wrote, four years after the publication of its report, that the British government had "successfully shelved the Williams Report, and there has never been a Commons debate on its provisions" (Simpson, 1983:57). The overwhelming majority of the ninety-two recommendations of the Meese Commission have been ignored.

The attorney general who appointed the Williams Committee, looking back some years later at "the history – or unhappily lack of history – of what followed" the publication of the committee's report, noted that it was commonly "the fate of august reporting bodies that their reports [are relegated to] pigeonholes" (Silkin, 1983:4). In retrieving three of them from their pigeonholes, or rather the places where they were gathering dust on library shelves, we were concerned not with the fate of their recommendations, some of which were exemplary pigeonhole material, but with the issues they confronted and the processes by which their recommendations came to be made. In this chapter we begin by looking at the genesis of the three bodies, their membership, what they were asked to do, and how their reports were received.

The Johnson Commission

The United States President's Commission on Obscenity and Pornography was appointed in January 1968 to investigate the traffic in pornographic and obscene materials, which Congress had found to be "a matter of national concern" (Public Law 90–100). The purpose of the commission was defined as "after a thorough study which shall include a study of the causal relationship of such materials to antisocial behavior, to recommend advisable, appropriate, effective, and constitutional means to deal effectively with such traffic in obscenity and pornography" (U.S. Commission, 1970:1).

The commission was assigned four specific tasks:

1. With the aid of leading constitutional law authorities, to analyze the laws pertaining to the control of obscenity and pornography; and to evaluate and recommend definitions of obscenity and pornography;
2. To ascertain the methods employed in the distribution of obscene and pornographic materials and to explore the nature and volume of traffic in such materials;
3. To study the effect of obscenity and pornography upon the public and particularly minors, and its relationship to crime and other antisocial behaviors; and
4. To recommend such legislative, administrative, or other advisable and appropri-

ate action as the Commission deems necessary to regulate effectively the flow of
such traffic, without in any way interfering with constitutional rights. (ibid.)

The commission was composed of two women and sixteen men, including
the chairman, Professor William B. Lockhart, who was dean of the University of Minnesota Law School. In addition to the chairman, membership
included five other lawyers: Thomas D. Gill, chief judge of Connecticut
Juvenile Court; Thomas C. Lynch, attorney general of California; Edward E.
Elson, president, Atlanta News Agency; Charles H. Keating, Jr., senior
partner in a Cincinnati law firm; and Barbara Scott, deputy attorney of the
Motion Picture Association of America, Inc.

Three sociologists served on the commission: Joseph T. Klapper, director,
Office of Social Research, Columbia Broadcasting System; Otto N. Larsen,
professor, Department of Sociology, University of Washington; and Marvin
E. Wolfgang, professor and chairman, Department of Sociology, University
of Pennsylvania. There were also two psychiatrist members: Edward D.
Greenwood, M.D., director, Division of School Mental Health of the
Menninger Foundation; and Morris A. Lipton, Ph.D., M.D., professor and
chairman, Department of Psychiatry, University of North Carolina.

Organized religion was represented by: the Reverend Morton A. Hill, S.J.,
president and administrative director of Morality in Media; Dr. Irvin
Lehrman, rabbi of Temple Emanu-El, Miami Beach, Florida; and the Reverend Winfrey C. Link, a Methodist minister who was administrator of the
United Methodist Retirement Home, Hermitage, Tennessee.

The remaining four members were: Frederick J. Wagman, director of the
University of Michigan Library and professor of library science; G. Williams
Jones, assistant professor of broadcast-film art, Southern Methodist University; Freeman Lewis, formerly vice-president of publishing, Simon & Schus-
ter, Inc., and director, American Book Publishers Council; and Cathryn A.
Spelts, assistant professor, South Dakota School of Mines and Technology
and a member of the National Council of Teachers of English.

Professor Lockhart was a distinguished authority on constitutional law and
a leading academic authority on obscenity laws. He had coauthored three
widely cited articles on the subject of obscenity and the law (Lockhart and
McClure, 1954, 1955, 1960). In one article he and his coauthor had made a
strong plea for social scientists to undertake extensive research into the effects
of exposure to obscene or pornographic materials (Lockhart and McClure,
1954:385). "Our obscenity laws," he has said, "are a classic example of how
laws ought not to be made – in the dark" (Lockhart, 1971:210).

Few of the commission's other members had previously shown any particular interest in the subject of obscenity or pornography, or if they had, it is not
mentioned in the biographies of commission members appended to the com-

mission's report. Only in three cases is there any reference to engagement in activity related to the commission's tasks. The Reverend Morton A. Hill's corporation, Morality in Media, is described as an "interfaith organization working to counter the effects of obscene material on the young, and working toward media based principles of truth, taste, inspiration, and love" (U.S. Commission, 1970:635). The Reverend Winfrey C. Link had since 1960 been chairman of the Tennessee Commission on Youth Guidance Subcommittee on Pornography and Obscene Literature. Barbara Scott as a member of the American Bar Association was serving on the association's Committee on Obscenity. In addition, Charles H. Keating, Jr., who was appointed to the commission by President Nixon in 1969, after one of the original members was appointed ambassador to India, and whose biography was not included in the report, was the founder of Citizens for Decent Literature.

The commission held its first meeting in July 1968 and then organized itself into four working panels: (1) Legal; (2) Traffic and Distribution; (3) Effects; and (4) Positive Approaches. An executive director and general counsel were appointed effective the last week in August 1968. The nucleus of the staff, which ultimately numbered twenty, was assembled in September 1968. The commission held public hearings in Los Angeles on May 4 and 5, 1970, and in Washington, D.C., on May 12 and 13, 1970. The final 646-page report of the commission was transmitted to the President and Congress on September 30, 1970. The commission had expended $1,750,000.

The Johnson Commission owed its existence to the initiative of Senator John McClellan (D., Ark.), who in 1967 had steered the resolution about obscenity and pornography's being a matter of "national concern" through the Senate Judiciary Committee and the House to become Public Law 90–100. The same Senator McClellan on October 17, 1970, seventeen days after the commission's report was made public, introduced in the Senate a condemnatory resolution that was passed by a vote of 60 to 5 rejecting the report.

In the years between, the commission's history had not been without incident. In the late fall of 1969, two members of the commission – Commissioners Hill and Link – who were later to describe the majority report as "a Magna Carta for the pornographer" (U.S. Commission, 1970:385), organized "runaway" public hearings in eight cities contrary to the announced policy of the commission. The general tenor of these hearings, which were extensively reported in the press, was "strongly in favor of tightening legal controls" (Packer, 1971:72).

Then, before the publication of the commission's report, a volume was published purporting to be the commission's report and entitled *The Obscenity Report*. No indication of authorship was given and it is not entirely clear what the purpose of the publication was. One observer, Professor H. L. Packer, commented that it "sounded very much like a Birchite document.

Many people thought this document a parody. Among lawyers it was thought to be a hoax perpetrated by law students. Although its provenance is unknown to me, one ought to compare this spurious document with the dissenting views expressed in the genuine report by Commissioners Hill and Link. . . .There is a marked similarity" (ibid.:72–73).

Subsequently the text of the commission's report was prematurely "leaked" by an unidentified commission member to the House Subcommittee on Postal Operations. The subcommittee then conducted hearings mainly given over to the refutation of the unpublished findings of the commission by Professor Victor Cline of the University of Utah, who had been cited by Commissioners Hill and Link, in their joint dissenting statement, as their principal expert on the behavioral sciences (U.S. Commission, 1970:390–412).

The Associated Press obtained a version of the final report that was extensively publicized. Next, Charles H. Keating, who was President Nixon's only appointee on the commission, filed suit to enjoin publication of the commission's report on the ground that the commission had denied him sufficient time to prepare a dissent. He obtained a preliminary injunction but subsequently reached agreement over an extension of time with the chairman of the commission.

It can have been no great surprise to any of the commissioners when President Nixon repudiated the report. Any chance that it might have been was obviated when Ronald Ziegler, presidential press secretary, told reporters without being asked and before the report had been submitted to the President, that the President had views at variance with the report.

The Williams Committee

The Home Office Departmental Committee on Obscenity and Film Censorship, usually called the Williams Committee after its chairman, Professor Bernard Williams (at that time provost of King's College, Cambridge), was formally established on July 13, 1977. Its terms of reference were "to review the laws governing obscenity, indecency, and violence in publications, displays, and entertainments in England and Wales, except in the field of broadcasting, and to review the arrangements for film censorship in England and Wales, and to make recommendations" (Home Office, 1979:1).

The Williams Committee has been described by Samuel Silkin, Q.C., who was the attorney general at the time of the committee's establishment and had requested the Home Secretary to set it up, as "virtually a Royal Commission in character, if not in title." He has since said that what he wanted was "a wide-ranging inquiry by an objective and widely representative group" of the laws in the field of obscenity, indecency, and censorship (Silkin, 1983:3).

The committee consisted of ten men, including the chairman and three women, and included among its members three lawyers: Judge John Leonard, Professor A. W. B. Simpson, and a solicitor, Ben Hooberman. The other members were David Robinson, film critic of *The Times;* Richard Matthews, former chief constable of Warwickshire; Vivian White, secretary of the United Caribbean Association and a youth and community worker in Cardiff; John Weightman, professor of French at the University of London; the Right Reverend John Tinsley, bishop of Bristol; Dr. Anthony Storr, a consultant psychotherapist; Sheila Rothwell of the Equal Opportunities Committee; Polly Toynbee, a journalist; and Jessie Taylor, a headmistress from Manchester.

Professor Simpson says, "How quite we were selected remains a mystery," although "it was rumored that the Archbiship had been given the nomination of a cleric – hence the selection of the Bishop of Bristol, John Tinsley" (Simpson, 1983:24). Professor Williams had earlier served on some similar bodies – the Public Schools Commission (1965–70) and the Royal Commission on Gambling (1976–78). Professor Simpson had been a member of an Advisory Group on Rape.

Professor Weightman subsequently wrote that being selected to serve on a committee of inquiry, such as the Williams Committee, "is rather like being summoned for jury duty. An official letter arrives out of the blue, and in due course you find yourself closeted with a varied group of fellow citizens whom you have probably never met before. . . . Juries of course are picked at random, whereas, someone must choose committees in the name of the minister concerned. . . . But who this is you are not told. The question – why me? – is left unanswered . . . I could only suppose that I had been roped in as the statutory literary academic, who had also happened to be writing film and theatre criticism" (Weightman, 1979:10).

Two members had previously publicly shown some interest in the committee's subject matter. The chairman, Bernard Williams, and the psychiatrist Anthony Storr had both publicly defended the publication of Hubert Selby's *Last Exit to Brooklyn,* published in 1966 by Calder and Boyars, who were prosecuted at the Old Bailey in 1967. As film critic of *The Times,* David Robinson presumably possessed a professional interest in the working of film censorship; otherwise no members of the committee had exhibited any particular interest in the subject. The appointment of Bernard Williams was the subject of some protest at the time, both from the Festival of Light, on the ground that he was not a believing Christian, and from a group of peers and MPs.

The committee met for the first time on Friday, September 2, 1977, and held thirty-five meetings in all. The last was on Wednesday, October 31, 1979, for the formal signing of its 270-page report, which was unanimous.

The cost to the British government was just under £100,000, of which £38,692 was the cost of printing (£100,000 being equivalent to U.S. $220,000 at that time).

Just as the Johnson Commission report was the legacy of a previous administration of a different political persuasion, so the Williams Committee, having been appointed by a Labour government, submitted its report to a Conservative Home Secretary. There is no doubt that this had something to do with what Professor Simpson calls "the decision to kill the report." He believes that there was a clear indication in a ministerial statement made four months before the report appeared that the government "was not going to act on the report and proposed to adopt the standard techniques for burying it" (Simpson, 1983:47–48).

As with the Johnson Commission, there were indications long before the report appeared, indeed, not long after the committee had been appointed, that there would be considerable opposition to its recommendations. In November 1977 an article appeared in the London *Times* saying that "the Williams Committee is quite likely to produce (if the views of some of its membership are anything to go by) a flabby and 'progressive' document minimizing the gravity of these problems in false perspectives in the cool 'rationality' of comittee prose" (Butt, 1977).

Cool rationality was certainly not the keynote of the reception that the report received, which began (and again the similarity to the fate of the Johnson Commission's report is striking) when leaks occurred before publication day. It was scheduled to appear on Wednesday, November 28, 1979, but three days before, on November 25, the *News of the World* ran a front-page story on it, headlined "It's Too Blue for Maggie."

Prior to publication, there also occured a curious echo of Commissioners Hill and Link's denunciation of the Johnson Commission's report as "a Magna Carta for the pornographer" (U.S. Commission, 1970:385). Professor Simpson reports that Mrs. Mary Whitehouse, a prominent antipornography campaigner, "did not trouble to await publication, believing no doubt that mere ignorance should never stand in the way of confident expression of opinion, [and] roundly denounced what she called the 'pornographers' charter'" (Simpson, 1983:45).

Some time after the publication of the report, *The Times* published an article entitled "Pornography: Does a Committee Know Best?" accusing the Williams Committee of proposing that "virtually all real restraints on pornography should now be swept away altogether." Among other things, the article states: "The Williams report is written with great subtlety and cleverness, and the danger is that its style will be taken as a justification of its substance. But the closer it is examined, the clearer it becomes that the report is throughout suffused by formalistic logic chopping, low-grade philosophizing . . ." (Butt, 1980:16).

The government, however, never explicitly repudiated the report. It was simply allowed to fade away. One of the committee's members, the journalist Polly Toynbee, wrote two years later: "Our bone has been buried for us. It looks as if we were useful in keeping the thorny problem of pornography out of the way of politicians for a few years. It's a subject that could hardly be called a vote winner. The Government has not produced a reasoned argument as to why nothing has been or will be done about our recommendations. We do not even know whether the Home Secretary has bothered to read it" (Toynbee, 1981).

The Meese Commission

The Attorney General's Commission on Pornography was established in February 1985 by the then attorney general William French Smith at the specific request of President Ronald Reagan. The formal mandate of the commission was contained in its charter. In that charter, the commission was asked to "determine the nature, extent, and impact on society of pornography in the United States, and to make specific recommendations to the Attorney General concerning more effective ways in which the spread of pornography could be constrained, consistent with constitutional guarantees."

The charter included the specific mandate to "study . . . the dimensions of the problem of pornography," to "review . . . the available empirical evidence on the relationship between exposure to pornographic materials and antisocial behaviour," and to explore "possible roles and initiatives that the Department of Justice and agencies of local, State, and Federal government could pursue in controlling, consistent with constitutional guarantees, the production and distribution of pornography" (U.S. Department of Justice, 1986:1957).

On May 20, 1985, Attorney General Edwin Meese II publicly announced formation of the commission and the names of its eleven members. Four of the members were lawyers: Henry E. Hudson, U.S. attorney for the Eastern District of Virginia, who was the commission's chairman; Edward J. Garcia, a federal district court judge in Sacramento, California; Tex Lezar, a Dallas lawyer and counselor to former attorney general William French Smith; and Frederick Schauer, professor of law at the University of Michigan. Park Elliot Dietz, who was professor of law, behavioral medicine, and psychiatry at the University of Virginia, was not a lawyer but a psychiatrist with degrees in medicine, public health, and sociology. The panel also had a psychologist on a medical school faculty, Dr. Judith Becker, associate professor of clinical psychology in psychiatry at Columbia University's College of Physicians and Surgeons and Director of the Sexual Behavior Clinic at the New York State Psychiatric Institute.

The other five members were as follows: James C. Dobson, founder of Focus on Family, an organization dedicated to the preservation of the home that produces a nationally syndicated radio program, had served for fourteen years as associate clinical professor of pediatrics at the University of Southern California School of Medicine; Mrs. Diane Cusack, a market research analyst, was serving her seventh term as president of the Maricopa County Board of Health; Ellen Levine, editor-in-chief of *Woman's Day* magazine, was a graduate of Wellesley College, where she majored in political science; the Reverend Bruce Ritter, a Catholic priest, had a doctorate in medieval dogma and was founder and president of Covenant House, an international childcare agency; and Deanne Tilton was president of the California Consortium of Child Abuse Councils.

The commission biographies, which constitute the first chapter of the report, do not indicate any particular interest in the subject of pornography on the part of the majority of its members. However, Dr. Becker's major research interests are described as "in the field of sexual aggression, rape victimization, human sexuality, and behavior therapy,"and it is noted that she had presented her research before the International Academy of Sex Research and the Society for Sex Therapy and Research. Dr. Dietz had conducted "research on sexual offenses" and was recipient of the 1986 Psychiatry Section Krafft-Ebing Award of the American Academy of Forensic Science. Professor Schauer had published two books, *The Law of Obscenity* (1976) and *Free Speech: A Psychological Enquiry* (1982), and had also "lectured at universities, conferences, and other gatherings throughout the world" on a variety of subjects including "the legal and philosophic aspects of the regulation of pornography."

The commission held public hearings in six cities (Chicago, Houston, Los Angeles, Miami, New York, and Washington) and also "public working sessions" in all those cities (with the exception of Chicago) and in Scottsdale, Arizona. The commission, which was required to produce a report within a year of its creation, had a budget of $500,000. The two-volume, 1,960-page final report was presented to the attorney general on July 8, 1986. In the report it was noted that "taking into account the changing value of the dollar, the 1970 Commission had a budget nearly sixteen times as large as ours."

The Meese Commission report also met with some unfavorable prepublication publicity. One commentator wrote:

The 1986 commission has been stacked to prevent unwelcome surprises. Its Meese-appointed chairmen, Henry Hudson, is a Virginia county prosecutor who conducted an avid campaign against adult bookstores, and who once told the *Washington Post*, "I live to put people in jail." While serving as chairman, Hudson was angling for a job – for which he has since been nominated – as a U.S. Attorney. Of its 11 members, six have well-established public records of supporting government action against sexy books and films. One of the commissioners, for example, is a Franciscan priest who has condemned Dr. Ruth Westheimer, the chirpy radio sex adviser, for advocating orgasms in premarital sex. Another is a religious broadcaster whose best-selling book, *Dare to Discipline* – a title that would not be out of place in the bondage section of an adult bookstore – advocates corporal punishment of children. A third is a University of Michigan law professor who has argued in law review articles that pornography is not constitutionally protected. The Meese commission lacked the financial and staff resources of its predecessor, but since its conclusions were preordained, it didn't really need them. The Meese report will recommend a long list of stern measures. (Hertzberg, 1986:21)

As early as January 1986, six months before the commission's report was published, the National Coalition Against Censorship (founded in 1974) held a public information briefing in New York "to protest and publicize the bias of the Commission and its likely outcome." Author Kurt Vonnegut, actress Colleen Dewhurst, and feminist Betty Friedan were among the fourteen speakers, from Planned Parenthood, the American Booksellers Association, the Feminist Anti-Censorship Task Force, and other organizations. "We are deeply concerned at the direction the commission is taking," said NCAC executive director Leanne Katz. "Censorship, with all its dangers, seems inevitable" (National Coalition Against Censorship, 1986:1).

But the Meese Commission, unlike the Johnson Commission and the Williams Committee, had not sought to avoid publicity. An article entitled "The Meese Commission on the Road" described its progress as follows:

The commission's 300-plus hours of public hearings and business meetings featured zany, if unintended, comedy: vice cops, born-again Christians and prosecutors thundering indictments of pornography and its progeny – divorce, premarital sex, sexual "deviation" and family destruction – in a 1950s-style epiphany of prurient righteousness. . . . The list of witnesses invited to testify was no more open than the commissioners' minds: 77 percent supported greater control, if not elimination, of sexually explicit material. Heavily represented were law-enforcement officers and members of vice squads (68 of 208 witnesses), politicians and spokespersons for conservative antipornography groups like Citizens for Decency through Law and the National Federation for Decency.

Of the "victims" of pornography, many told tales of divorce, promiscuity, masturbation and child abuse – all, in their view, caused by sexually explicit material. For these born-again victims, the remedy for complex social problems was found in renouncing pornography and sexual sin. The vice cops on the staff energetically recruited the alleged victims to testify, assisted by antipornography groups and prosecutors. (Vance, 1986:1, 77)

The commission also became involved in two lawsuits. The staff director sent a letter on Justice Department letterhead to twenty-three large bookstore chains, book sellers, and convenience stores stating that it had "received testimony that your company is involved in the sale or distribution of pornography" and that the final report would list "identified distributors." Southland Corporation, owner of the 7-Eleven chain, decided after receiving the letter that it would no longer carry *Playboy* and *Penthouse*. The magazines and the American Booksellers Association filed suit.

On July 3, 1986, Federal District Judge John Garrett Penn ruled against the commission in the *Playboy* case, giving the Justice Department five days to write to all the companies it had contacted and explain that the original letter did not mean to imply their publications were obscene or to threaten a blacklist. Another lawsuit against the commission – to counter the staff's attempt to withhold a draft of the report and all its working papers available to the public under the Federal Advisory Committee Act – was filed by the American Civil Liberties Union. The commission's staff withdrew its claim that possession of these documents in the hands of organized crime might constitute a threat to itself, and settled before getting to court.

Nevertheless, despite all the publicity, including the *Time* magazine cover story referred to earlier, which spoke of "a spirited crusade to reassert family values"(Stengel, 1986:12), the Meese Commission report appears to have had little more impact than its predecessors. None of what the American Civil Liberties Union referred to as its "panorama of unconstitutional proposals" (ACLU, 1986:3–4) has been enacted. A ten-lawyer task force in the Justice Department is the only testament to the importance of pornography to the current national administration. This is significant because there has been no change in government that explains the lack of impact that greeted the prior two reports. And the two Meese volumes have gone to join Johnson and Williams on library shelves.

Patterns of commission selection

The experience that members of the various commissions have brought to their duties is an intrinsically interesting topic. It also helps us determine the kinds of experience the political actors who appoint these commissions think is useful, and it may explain differences in tone and outlook that have emerged from the different commissions.

Three common themes are apparent when one examines the personnel of the Johnson, Williams, and Meese commissions. First, those who appointed all three bodies felt the need for a wide variety of backgrounds ranging from law and academic disciplines to psychiatry and the ministry. Those who selected the members of commissions of inquiry on pornography, unsure of what constituted expertise, recruited a wide variety of experts.

But it still seems that one must have had to be an expert on something to be appointed to any of these commissions. Thus, all forty-two individuals serving on these three panels brought professional credentials to the task that were arguably relevant to the assessment of the social impact of pornography and that could be used as the basis for explaining their presence on the commission. Only in the case of the Williams Committee was a layperson appointed as a layperson to one of the pornography panels. No participant was recruited from a lobby who did not also possess professional credentials.

A third common element in the selection of pornography commissions was the dominant role of the legal profession on all three panels. Six of the eighteen members of the Johnson Commission, including the chairman, three of the thirteen members of the Williams Committee, and five of the eleven members of the Meese Commission were lawyers. On each commission there were more lawyers represented than any other single profession. The only significant contrast among commissions was a tendency for the two American commissions to be even more concentrated in their reliance on lawyers than their British counterpart.

The contrast among the commissions is less striking than the similarity in backgrounds, but no less important in explaining variation in the final product. The Johnson Commission, at least numerically, was more dominated by the professoriat than either the Williams or Meese commissions. No fewer than six of the Johnson commissioners were active on college and university faculties at the time of their appointments, including the chair. In contrast, just three professors were appointed to the Williams Committee (but this included the very influential chairman) and three to the Meese Commission.

With respect to the social sciences, the contrast is more substantial. Three of the Johnson commissioners were Ph.D.'s in sociology, a discipline that was not represented in the backgrounds of any commissioner in the two later panels. The relatively high concentration of academics and the cluster of empirically oriented sociologists on the Johnson Commission will prove crucial in our account of the patterns of emphasis in that report as compared to either the Williams or the Meese analyses.

The hallmark of the Johnson Commission report is optimism regarding the potential of social and behavioral science to investigate questions about the impact of pornography combined with a willingness to rely on empirical research. We believe this attitude can be traced to the cluster of academics and, more particularly, the social scientists who functioned as a core group in the larger commission and were the sole working body for the Panel Report on Effects. But it should also be said that, at that historical moment, the attitude was widely shared.

The Johnson Commission deplored the lack of relevant research and expressed the hope that its own "modest pioneering work in empirical research . . . will help to open the way for more extensive and long-term research based on more refined methods" (U.S. Commission, 1970:49, 141).

The Williams Committee "considered very carefully whether this was a matter on which it would be useful to commission fresh research" and decided to make do with "the vast amounts of research that exist" (Home Office, 1979:3–4). "There is," said Williams in a later comment, "already a gigantic amount of research material on these subjects" (Williams, 1981:ix). The Meese Commission decided that "the amount of research conducted in the last fifteen years provides a reasonably sufficient base to reevaluate answers to old questions" (U.S. Department of Justice, 1986:901).

In Chapter 4 we will characterize the efforts of both the Williams Committee and the Meese Commission as "legalistic" in contrast to those of the Johnson Commission. Yet only the Meese Commission, with five lawyers out of eleven members, has a larger relative concentration of lawyers than the six out of eighteen represented on the Johnson Commission. The explanation for this is one of relative dominance. The cluster of academics on the Johnson Commission and, more particularly, the Effects Panel with its social science orientation, effectively counterbalanced the concentration of lawyers. There were no such counterbalances on the Meese Commission or the Williams Committee.

Of all the lawyers on the commissions, only Henry Hudson, the chairman of the Meese Commission, brought a strong law-enforcement orientation to his job and to the work of his commission. Police officers worked closely for and with the Meese Commission staff. This had impact on both the style and the substance of many sections of the report.

For students of commissions of inquiry in general, there were other notable patterns of personnel selection among these three panels. Although one clergyman associated with Morality in Media was appointed to the Johnson Commission and two profamily organization representatives served on the Meese Commission, there was very little explicit consumer representation in any of these commissions, drawn from parents groups, victims of pornography, or other implicated special interests. Some attention was paid, particularly in the 1985 commission, to the presence of women on the panel, but there was apparently no effort to secure a feminist perspective.

The subject of the consumer, incidentally, about which we shall say more in Chapter 3, is one striking respect in which the three bodies had a familial similarity with each other. "A highly visible multi-billion dollar industry" (U.S. Department of Justice, 1986:1353) must have some customers. Yet all three bodies appeared to view with distaste not only the products of that industry but also their consumers. One misses recognition, in any of their reports, of the kind of defense of "hard-core pornography which is orgasmic in intent and untouched by the ulterior motives of traditional art," put by Kenneth Tynan (Tynan, 1970:111).

It is also worthy of note that, with the exception of the Johnson Commission, very little attention was paid to the representation of interests of industries that operate in a regulatory climate affected by the definition and enforcement of obscenity laws. Those who regulate such behavior were represented on all three commissions (attorneys general, police magistrates, U.S. attorneys). Those who are regulated were represented in the Johnson Commission by the director of the Columbia Broadcasting System's Office of Social Research and the director of the American Book Publishing Council. But only the editor in-chief of *Woman's Day* can be seen among the later two commissions as an industry representative, in any sense, and the distance between *Woman's Day* and the regulation of erotic content in magazines seems, to our untrained perspective, considerable.

The absence of industry interests is in contrast to the composition of most commissions of inquiry. More standard is the tendency to ensure the representation of the political views of the governing party on commissions somewhat more faithfully than those of its opposition. All three commissions were appointed as nonpartisan and did not report the political backgrounds of their members. Yet it seems the parties in power established at least some title in their definition of a commission cross section, toward the Democrats in the Johnson Commission, toward Labour in the Williams Committee, and toward the Republicans in the Meese Commission.

What impact these processes had on the finding of these commissions is an open question. As we shall see, however, the contrast in findings is clear and sharp.

2

On definitions

It might seem obvious, althought it has not always been recognized, that an essential preliminary to any discussion of the censorship or prohibition of pornographic material must be some attempt at the definition of pornography. It is not sufficient, although it has in the past been so regarded, to say "I think I can recognize it when I see it" (Allen, 1962:143) or "I know it when I see it" (*Jacobellis v. Ohio*, 378 U.S. 184, 197, [1964], Stewart, J., concurring).

Announcing that we will know "it" when we see it represents an evasion of definition. Even if by means of some kind of intuitive insight we were able instantly to recognize pornography, we would still not be able to say upon inspection what it is that is pornographic about pornography. And unless we can do this, although different observers might agree that a particular work was a piece of pornography, it would be impossible to tell what they were agreeing about. Even widespread agreement would provide no comprehension of the rationale underlying the classification.

Some years ago, a volume of *Law and Contemporary Problems* was devoted to the subject of "Obscenity and the Arts." The editor in his foreword to the volume said: "Assuming there is general agreement that obscenity should be suppressed, the basic problem of definition presents itself: What is obscene?" He then went on, without answering that question, to raise other questions about "the problem of control," the effectiveness of sanctions, and whether the "suppression of obscenity [would] perhaps give rise to even more noxious social evils?" (Shimm, 1955:532).

What is puzzling about this is the assumption of unanimity about the desirability of suppressing some unidentified phenomenon. Clearly the "basic problem of definition" should, if it was going to present itself at all, have had precedence. For unless we know what it is that ought to be suppressed, to say there is "general agreement" tells us nothing. Even if all know it when they see it and are united in agreeing that it should be suppressed, how do we know that the agreement is not totally illusory?

What about the U.S. Treasury Department official who judged photographs of the paintings on the ceiling of the Sistine Chapel to be obscene (Haight, 1978:12)? Then there was the "cultivated Chinese gentleman" who found the pronounced and regular rhythms of the Sousa march "The Stars and Stripes Forever" played by the Marine band "almost unbearably lascivious and suggestive of coitus" (La Barre, 1955:536). As Walter Allen says in an essay in a volume devoted to "original studies in the nature and definition of 'obscenity,' " "we find ourselves floundering in the morass of the subjective" (Allen, 1962:143). This may not matter very much in the context of literary or artistic discussion, but it is of crucial importance in relationship to policymaking.

The importance of such theoretical considerations and the emphasis on the necessity for definition received striking confirmation in the career of the Meese Commission. In this case, the failure to agree about what is pornographic about pornography meant that the commission could not for this reason properly evaluate the evidence on the impact of pornography. But this is to anticipate.

For purposes of exposition, we here set out seriatim the findings of the three commissions on the subject of definition of terms. This is done by identifying the different interpretations of the key terms – obscenity, pornography, and erotica – offered by each, as well as by indicating which term each commission regarded as central to its inquiries.

The Johnson Commission

The Johnson Commission deals with the question of definition summarily in the preface to its report, where it is noted that "the area of the Commission's study" had been "marked by enormous confusion over terminology." The area of the commission's study was described as "a wide range of explicit sexual depictions in pictorial and textual media." The commission explained its use of terms and defined the subject of its investigation in a brief footnote. As to obscenity, the report notes that "some people equate 'obscenity' with 'pornography' and apply both terms to any type of explicit sexual material." It goes on to say simply that "in the Commission's Report, the terms 'obscene' and 'obscenity' are used solely to refer to the legal concept of prohibited sexual materials" (U.S. Commission, 1970:3 n.4).

The emphasis given to the definition of pornography is one of the important contrasts between these three reports. The Johnson Commission, although the word "pornography" appears in the title of its report, deals with the term briefly and dismissively. Having noted that some people use the terms "obscenity" and "pornography" interchangeably, and others "intend differences of various degrees in their use of these terms," it concludes: "The term 'pornography' is not used at all in a descriptive context because it appears to have no legal significance and because it most often denotes subjective disapproval of certain materials rather than their content or effect" (ibid.).

The discussion regarding the use of the term "erotica" in these reports seems a matter chiefly of connotation. The Johnson Commission did not define erotica expressly, but by implication indicated that it should be regarded as identical or coextensive in sense and usage with "sexually explicit." Thus, "the Report uses the phrases 'explicit sexual materials,' 'sexually oriented material,' 'erotica,' or some variant thereof to refer to the subject matter of the Commission's investigations" (ibid.:3,4). It is notable that the report of the commission's Effects Panel, which takes up 125 pages of the commission's report, is entitled "The Impact of Erotica."

The Williams Committee

The Williams Committee Report states that "obscene" is a term that expresses certain reactions such as repulsion and disgust, or even outrage, that an object or work arouses "rather than telling one what kind of thing actually arouses those reactions." It deals at considerable length with the legal usage of the term but concludes that "we suspect that the word 'obscene' may now be worn out, and past any useful employment at all. It is certainly too exhausted to do any more work in the courts" (Home Office, 1979:103–104).

By contrast, the Williams Committee found that pornography was "a rather more objective expression referring to a certain kind of writing, pictures, etc." Pornography was defined as follows:

The term "pornography" always refers to a book, verse, painting, photograph, film or some such thing – what in general may be called a *representation*. . . . We take it that, as almost everyone understands the term, a pornographic representation is one that combines two features: it has a certain function or intention, to arouse its audience sexually, and also a certain content, explicit representations of sexual material (organs, postures, activity, etc.). A work has to have both this function and this content to be a piece of pornography. (ibid.:104)

For the Williams Report, the term "pornography" is regarded as central to its analysis. Although "pornography" appears neither in the title of the Williams Committee Report nor in its terms of reference, the word is used deliberately and repeatedly. Thus "in the course of Chapter 7, we have referred almost all discussions to pornography rather than to obscenity. This emphasis was deliberate" (Home Office, 1979:103). It may be added that in defining pornography as an objective expression rather than as denoting subjective approval or disapproval the Williams Committee enjoyed the support of both the *Oxford English Dictionary* and *Webster's New World Dictionary of the American Language*.

That the Williams Committee's definition is consonant with the dictionary definitions is, of course, not accidental. The expression "as almost everyone understands the term" refers to ordinary usage, and lexical definition is also derived from ordinary usage. In this connection, there is a distinction commonly recognized between what is called lexical definition and stipulative definition: the former referring to "the customary or dictionary meaning of a word" and the latter, to "establishing or announcing or choosing one's own meaning for a word" (Robinson, 1950:19; see also Morris, 1960:30–32). We mention this distinction here because, as we shall see in Chapter 6 when we come to deal with what has been called the "radical feminist critique" of pornography, it assumes some importance.

With regard to "erotica," the Williams Committee begins by noting that the term "erotic" is sometimes used as an alternative to "pornographic," being milder with regard to both the content and the intention. The content by this interpretation is described as being more allusive and less explicit, and what is intended is not strong sexual arousal but some lighter degree of sexual interest.

But the report adds that there is another interpretation of the term "erotica," "under which the erotic is what *expresses* sexual excitement rather than causes it – in the same way as a painting or a piece of music may express sadness without necessarily making its audience sad. . . . In this sense an erotic work will suggest or bring to mind feelings of sexual attraction or excitement. It may cause some such feelings as well and put the audience actually into that state, but if so that is a further effect" (Home Office, 1979:105).

The Meese Commission

The Meese Commission report devotes some five pages to "Defining Our Central Terms." With regard to "obscenity," it is noted that the word "has taken on a legal usage." Accordingly:

We will here use the words "obscene" and "obscenity" . . . to refer to material that has been or would likely be found to be obscene in the context of a judicial proceeding employing applicable legal and constitutional standards. Thus, when we refer to obscene material, we need not necessarily be condemning that material, or urging prosecution, but we are drawing on the fact that such material *could* now be prosecuted without offending existing authoritative interpretation of the Constitution. (U.S. Department of Justice, 1986:230)

As to pornography the Meese Commission decided that "the appellation 'pornography' is undoubtedly pejorative." The Williams Committee definition was criticized as not reflecting "modern usage." "To call something 'pornographic' is plainly, in modern usage, to condemn it." Pornography, the report says, "seems to mean in practice any discussion or depiction of sex to which the person using the word objects." Accordingly, the commission decided to try "to minimize the use of the word 'pornography' in this Report" (ibid.:227–228).

Whereas the Johnson Commission used the term "erotica" freely and the Williams Committee found the term "erotic" helpful to mark "significant and useful distinctions" (Home Office 1979:105), the Meese Commission rejected it. The reference to the term "erotica" in that commission's report runs as follows:

> It seems clear to us that the term as actually used is the mirror image of the broadly condemnatory use of "pornography," being employed to describe sexually explicit materials of which the user of the term approves. For some the . . . word "erotica" describes any sexually explicit material that contains neither violence nor subordination of women, for others the term refers to almost all sexually explicit material, and for still others only material containing generally accepted artistic value qualifies as erotica. In light of this disagreement, and in light of the tendency to use the term "erotica" as a conclusion rather than a description, we again choose to avoid the term wherever possible. (U.S. Department of Justice, 1986:230–231)

Key terms

With respect to what are regarded as key terms in its analysis, each commission follows a separate path. The American commissions use a legal definition of obscenity: material that could be prohibited under prevailing constitutional standards. The Williams Committee speaks of obscenity as expressive of the reactions of an audience, which conforms with the dictionary definitions. All three reports deal with the term in a conclusory fashion, and none of the reports identifies obscenity as a centrally important term in the inquiry.

For the Johnson Commission, "erotica" and "sexually explicit material" are used interchangeably as the most important terms. The problems of denoting what is sexually explicit are considered minimal, and for good reason. The Williams Committee considers the term "pornography" central and devotes substantial energy to its definition.

The Meese Commission rejects each term – "obscenity," "pornography," and "erotica" – as a central term with a fixed, formal, and approved definition. With each, reasons are given, although it is never suggested that none of the terms requires definition. It is hardly surprising that the commission finds that "questions of terminology and definition have been recurring problems in our hearings and deliberations" (U.S. Department of Justice, 1986:227). The Meese Commission rejects the approach of the Williams Committee report in two respects. The specific definition of pornography is disputed, and the function of pornography as the central term in the inquiry is disavowed.

The Canadian Special Committee on Pornography and Prostitution, incidentally, thought that the Williams Committee definition encompassed "a great deal, if not most, of what the ordinary person would think of as pornography" but expressed "reservations about the definition for purposes of the criminal law." In the end, although "very conscious of our debt to those who have struggled with the question of the meaning of pornography," the committee decided that it would "not formulate our own precise working definition of pornography" (Canada, 1985:52, 54, 59).

Later in the committee's report, however, we are told that "perhaps the most central issue of all which requires attention is that of defining what it is that makes material pornographic, " and that the question of what pornography is . . . needs careful and systematic consideration" (ibid:103). But although the term is used freely throughout the report, this "most central issue" somehow has escaped further attention.

The Tower of Babel

A panoramic view of the findings of the three commissions on the subject of definition of terms is presented in Table 2.1, where we have italicized the key terms.

The Babelish confusion of tongues in respect to definition offered by the three commissions can hardly be said to have done a great deal to alleviate "the enormous confusion over terminology" complained of in the Johnson Commission report.

Conclusion

Although all the terms employed in this context are commonly used with meanings that are equivocal and overlapping, there is no doubt, as the report of the Williams Committee pointed out, that "there are significant and useful distinctions to be made here, and these words can be helpfully used . . . to mark those distinctions" (Home Office, 1979:105).

The most appropriate method for selecting the key terms to be employed in discussions of this matter is a process of elimination. It seems clear to us that the term "obscenity," which was rejected by all the commissions except in its "legal usage," and even in that context rejected by the Williams Committee, cannot serve to facilitate discussion or make any significant distinction. We add our own concurrence to the rare unanimity of the three reports on this issue.

Nor is the expression "explicit sexual materials," preferred by the Johnson Commission, much more satisfactory. It is itself explicit as to content – the representation of sexual material – but it denotes nothing in respect to func-

Table 2.1. *The Tower of Babel*

	Obscenity	Pornography	Erotica	Key term
Johnson Commission	"The terms *'obscene'* and *'obscenity'* are used solely to refer to the legal concept of prohibited sexual materials." (U.S. Commission, 1970:3 n.4)	"The term *'pornography'* is not used . . . appears to have no legal significance . . . most often denotes subjective disapproval of certain materials rather than their content or effect." (U.S. Commission, 1970:3 n.4)	"The Report uses the phrases 'explicit sexual material,' 'sexually oriented material,' *'erotica,'* or some variant thereof to refer to the subject matter of the Commission's investigations." (U.S. Commission, 1970:3 n.4)	*Explicit sexual materials*
Williams Committee	*Obscene* is a term which expresses certain reactions such as repulsion or disgust . . . may now be past any useful employment . . . certainly too exhausted to do any more work in the courts." (Home Office, 1979:104)	"A *pornographic* representation combines two features: it has a certain function or intention, to arouse its audience sexually, and also a certain content, explicit representation of sexual materials (organs, postures, activity, etc.)." (Home Office, 1979:103)	"The *erotic* is what expresses sexual excitement rather than causes it . . . an erotic work will suggest or bring to mind feelings of sexual attraction or excitement. It may cause some such feelings . . . but if so that is a further effect." (Home Office, 1979:10)	*Pornography*
Meese Commission	"We will here use the words *'obscene'* and *'obscenity'* . . . to refer to material that has been or would likely be found to be obscene in the context of a judicial proceeding employing applicable legal and constitutional standards." (U.S. Department of Justice, 1986:230)	"*Pornography* seems to mean in practice any depiction of sex to which the person using the word objects. . . . We have tried to minimize the use of the word 'pornography' in this Report." (U.S. Department of Justice, 1986:227–228)	"The term *'erotica'* is employed to describe sexually explicit materials of which the user of the term approves. We again choose to avoid the term wherever possible." (U.S. Department of Justice, 1986:230–231)	No key term

tion or intention, which is an essential conceptual element and the basis for special treatment of this category of material. To distinguish content and ignore the author's or artist's intention or purpose is to miss that aspect which is of central significance in this context. For we are not here concerned with textbooks of human biology or marriage guidance manuals that deal explicitly with sexual techniques.

With respect to "erotica," the two American commissions define the term only insofar as it refers to sexually explicit material. The Williams Committee distinguishes another interpretation of the term "erotic" as that which refers to material that *expresses* sexual excitement rather than arouses it. Assuming for the moment that such material may suggest or bring to mind feelings of sexual excitement without actually stimulating or causing such feelings, this distinction clearly rules out "erotica" as an appropriate key term for policy. We should be here concerned with provocative rather than evocative reference, and public policy concern relates to material that is both sexually explicit *and* has sexual arousal as its primary objective.

Thus, the most suitable and apposite term is evidently "pornography," and the Williams Committee definition of the concept of pornography brings out the essential fact that it is a category of both content and function: A "pornographic representation is one that combines two features: it has a certain function or intention, to arouse its audience sexually, and also a certain content, explicit representations of sexual material" (Home Office, 1979:104).

It seems clear that however a liberal Western democracy may decide to deal with pornography, any modern secular government will seek to permit sexually explicit communication to adults on the same basis as it permits communication about a wide variety of other topics. What seems to be of special concern to governments and communities is a combination of sexually explicit content and the sexual provocation, arousal, or excitation of an audience, from which it is assumed sexual activity will follow.

The Williams Committee's identification of "pornography" as the key term in the discussion of this matter and its definition of it are examples of the kind of work that should have made the task of later commissions considerably easier. That committee identified, we think, what is pornographic about pornography.

Having said that, we confront one of the puzzles of the Meese Commission report: that is, its failure to recognize the centrality of the concept of pornography and its rejection of the Williams Committee definition of the term as an example of "analytic purity" that does not reflect "modern usage" (U.S. Department of Justice, 1986:228). The result of this rejection was, as we document at length in Chapter 4, a profound muddle in relation to the issue of the effects of pornography.

It is remarkable that having adopted a definition of the word as a perjorative or derogatory term and having declared that it would "minimize that use of the word 'pornography' in this Report," the commission found itself unable to avoid its use. Indeed, it recurs constantly throughout the report.

Moreover, it is explained that "where we do use the term . . . in this Report a reference to material as 'pornographic' means only that the material is predominantly sexually explicit and intended primarily for the purpose of sexual arousal." In the same context, but in relation to "hard core pornography," the report states:

If we were forced to define the term "hard core pornography," we would probably note that it refers to the extreme form of what we defined as pornography, and thus would describe material that is sexually explicit to the extreme, intended virtually exclusively to arouse, and devoid of any other apparent content or purpose. (ibid.:228–229)

Thus having criticized the Williams Committee definition of "pornography" because of its "analytic purity" the commission then, for the purpose of exposition, adopted a definition virtually identical to its own rendering of the Williams Committee definition: "The Williams Committee in Great Britain several years ago . . . defined pornography as a description or depiction of sex involving the dual characteristics of 1) sexual explicitness; and 2) intent to arouse sexually" (ibid.:228).

What was the reason for this extraordinarily equivocal posture? Perhaps lawyerly caution about *proving* the elements of pornography identified in the Williams Committee definition, in a court of law, held back some members of the commission from wholehearted and explicit acceptance of that definition. For this was a commission that sought to avoid narrowing the boundaries of governmental control over sexually explicit communication. And the central issue that lay behind this effort was concern with *provocative* sexual communication.

How is it possible to prove that material was intended, or is likely, to trigger impulses to engage in sexual activity? Clearly, one can understand the attempt to avoid definitions that would place obstacles in the way of any expansion of control. Yet the sexually provocative aspect of pornography is absolutely necessary to its existence as a separate topic for governmental concern.

A subsidiary issue is whether the message sent must be intended as provocative for the communication to be regarded as pornography or whether sexual explicitness with the effect of arousing the audience is sufficient. The issue is confused somewhat by the tendency of those accused of pornographic communication to deny provocative intent, even when the circumstances strongly corroborate the awareness of provocation. Certainly if any special social or legal judgments are to be attached to pornography, we believe that the sender's knowledge of provocative impact or reckless disregard of the strong likelihood of such an effect should be required.

We have dealt at length with issues of definition because they matter, as we shall see in Chapter 4 when we turn to the vigorously contested if muddled debate on the effects of pornography.

3

The nature and distribution of pornography in the United States

According to Andrea Dworkin, "In the United States, the pornography industry is larger than the record and film industries combined" (Dworkin, 1981:201). This statement has been cited by one of Dworkin's critics as an example of the kind of "bizarre assertions unlocated in time or space, and presented without the least attempt to justify them rationally," that are characteristic of her style of exposition (Simpson, 1983:74).

In fact, Ms. Dworkin's assertion reflects a long-standing tradition. In the literature dealing with pornography, accounting commonly takes the form of dubious quantitative impressions and largely notional statistics. What Max Singer called "the vitality of mythical numbers" (Singer, 1971:3) is here, as in relation to some other social problems such as drug abuse and illegal gambling, a perennial feature.

This is in part inevitable. One effect of the operation of the criminal law in these areas is that although it may be unable to suppress the activities themselves, it is often remarkably effective in discouraging open documentation or public recording. It may not be true that it is impossible to regulate behaviors that are prohibited, but even partial prohibition can make it very difficult to measure their extent. The Meese Commission found that "compiling information on the production and distribution aspects of this industry was a very difficult task. Much of the detailed information was closely guarded . . . and was thus unavailable to the Commission" (U.S. Department of Justice, 1986:1367).

This, of course, has never discouraged confident dogmatism. But when the Johnson Commission undertook its work in 1968, it "could find no satisfactory estimates of the volume of traffic in obscene and pornographic materials." Articles appearing in newspapers, magazines, and in other reports had variously estimated the traffic in the pornography industry "to be between $500 million and $2.5 billion per year," but these were "almost always without supporting data or definitions which would make such estimates meaningful" (U.S. Commission, 1970:4).

The commission therefore decided that its "first task" must be to determine the scope of the subject matter of its investigation. Thus, the first chapter of Part I of its report deals with its findings on the volume and patterns of the commercial traffic and distribution of sexually oriented materials in motion pictures films, books, and periodicals. In addition, three volumes of the commission's technical reports deal with various aspects of the marketplace for sexual materials; the industries that publish and distribute them; and the retail outlets and their customers (U.S Commission, 1971–72, vols. 3, 4, and 9).

The Meese Commission also reported that it "spent much of our time investigating the nature of the industry that produces, distributes, and sells sexually explicit materials." Volume 1 of the commission's report contains a brief chapter giving a general overview of the market and the industry. In volume 2 a much longer chapter on the production and distribution of sexually explicit material provides a historical overview and what is described as "an in depth discussion of the industry today" (U.S. Department of Justice, 1986:1367), describing the various sexually oriented materials and services, and how and where these products and services are produced and distributed.

In this chapter, we attempt to summarize and critically analyze the information provided in those two commissions' reports and in such other reports as we have been able to find. This is done initially under two headings: varieties of pornography and places of display. We then deal with the consumers of pornography, pornography and collateral activities, and recent trends.

This survey provides the foundation for assessing the impact of recent developments on the social context of pornography in the United States and for our discussion, in Part II of this book, of regulation in the future and its impact.

Varieties of pornography

According to the Meese Commission, the pornography industry has grown considerably over the past thirty years by continually changing and expanding to appeal to new markets. "In the last several decades," their report states, "the industry has gone from a low yield, covert business to a highly visible multi-billion dollar industry" (U.S. Department of Justice, 1986:1353). But, as the Johnson Commission pointed out in 1970, there is no monolithic pornography industry; "rather, there are several distinct markets and submarkets which distribute a variety of erotic materials. . . . These industries vary in terms of media, content, and manner of distribution" (U.S. Commission, 1970:7).

Traffic and distribution

The Johnson Commission was assigned inter alia "to ascertain the methods employed in the distribution of obscene and pornographic materials and to explore the nature and volume of traffic in such materials" (U.S. Commission, 1970:1). Accordingly it appointed a Traffic and Distribution Panel to concentrate on the study of this subject. The report of that panel, authored by John J. Sampson, and published as volume 3 of the commission's technical reports represents the first comprehensive analysis of the traffic and distribution of sexually oriented materials in the United States.

In the introduction to that volume it is noted that no comprehensive estimate of the pornography industry is made because any single overall estimate of the market for sexually oriented materials would be relatively meaningless in view of the extremely diverse materials constituting the market. Such estimates as had been made in the past, it is said, were valueless because they lacked specific definitions and, moreover, were "based on pure speculation rather than on investigation of the facts" (U.S. Commission, 1971–72, 3:4).

Because of the broad and diverse range of materials involved, the panel decided to limit its investigation to the media causing the greatest concern. These were specified as motion pictures, books, and periodicals, and certain additional materials such as sexual devices, 8mm films, and photo sets. The panel did not include in its investigations live performances such as burlesque shows, nightclub acts, or stage plays. Nor did it deal with radio, television, or newspapers except for "the small segment represented by the 'sensational' or 'underground' press" (ibid., 3:3). The panel report is divided into four parts, each dealing with a separate category of material: motion pictures, books and magazines, mail-order sales, and "hard-core" or under-the-counter materials.

Motion pictures

In the panel report, motion pictures are divided into six categories: general release, art, exploitation (or skin flicks), hybrid, new genre, and 16mm films. As for general release films, the report notes that in the previous two years the sexual content of such films had greatly accelerated in respect of theme, activity depicted, and degree of nudity. Few areas of sexual conduct had not been the central subject of widely distributed general release films, including adultery, promiscuity, abortion, perversion, wife swapping, orgies, male and female homosexuality, and so on.

Sexual activity depiction had also become much more graphic. Scenes of simulated intercourse were increasing and other sexual acts including masturbation, fellatio, and cunnilingus were sometimes suggested and occasionally simulated. Partial nudity was common, full female nudity was increasing, and a few general release films had shown both sexes totally nude. Art films were defined as those that treated sexual matters with a degree of explicitness not found in general release films in the 1950s. But it was reported that by 1970

Table 3.1. *Box office receipts by classification*

Rating		1970 projected receipts (millions)	Percentage of receipts
General	G and GP	594	54.0
release	R	262	23.8
	X	72	6.6
Nonsex, unrated		16	1.5
Art		35	3.2
Exploitation		65	5.9
Hybrid/ new genre		56	5.0
Total		1,000	100.0

Source: U.S. Commission (1970:12).

only "foreignness" or limited audience appeal set such films apart from many general release movies.

Exploitation films were defined as low-budget films that concentrate on the erotic. But it was said that the increase of sexually related themes and the incidence of nudity in general release movies had blurred the distinction between general release and exploitation films so that there was no longer a clear line of demarcation. Hybrid films were defined as those combining the sexual explicitness of exploitation films with the distribution patterns of general release films. New genre films were highly sex-oriented and graphic films – the most sexually explicit of all motion pictures. Finally, there were 16mm films that featured such things as females displaying their genitals and graphic depictions of sexual intercourse and oral–genital contact and apparently little else. These were said to be as yet a minor factor in the traffic of sexually oriented materials.

The acceleration in the sexual content and explicitness of films coincided with the initiation in 1968 of a movie-rating system for the guidance of viewers. This system, which contained four classifications, provided rough guidelines for judging the sexual content of films. "G"-rated films contained little in the way of sexual matters and "GP"-rated films were limited to moderately explicit indications of sex. "R"-rated films could contain virtually any theme, a wide range of sexual behavior, and full female nudity (genitalia). "X"-rated films were distinguishable from R-rated films by the quantity and quality of the erotic theme, conduct, or nudity contained in the film.

Table 3.2. *Number of films in each of the MPA's rating categories, November 1, 1968, to September 30, 1985*

Rating	Number	Percentage
G	900	12.9
PG	2,523	35.9
PG-13[a]	60	0.8
R	3,190	45.2
X[b]	363	5.2
Total	7,036	100.0

[a]Introduced in July 1984.
[b]This number represents a small portion of films advertised as "X" rated. The remaining "X"-rated films were self-designated and are not reflected in the 363 figure.
Source: U.S. Department of Justice (1986:1381).

At the time when the panel investigation was conducted, many of the films being shown had been released before the ratings system went into effect. But on the basis of trade journal reports, the panel calculated projected receipts for 1970 for the principal categories of film in their classification system. The results are shown in Table 3.1. The panel noted, however, that

within the past two years, the increase in sexual content of widely distributed motion pictures had made labeling and categorization of many sexually oriented films almost impossible. Certain pioneering films and their imitators have, in effect, smashed the neat classifications of general release, art, and exploitation films which formerly existed as yardsticks for analyzing the sexual content of movies. The industry recognizes that something unique is happening, but the creation of any commonly recognized labels for these new "sex" films has not yet occurred. (U.S. Commission, 1970:84)

In addition to the materials referred to above, the Johnson Commission reported that in 1970 a very limited amount of material defined as "hard-core pornography" in the form of "stag films" consisting of reproductions of sexual intercourse depicting vaginal, oral, or anal penetration were being made. It said that "the stag film production is primarily a localized business with no national distribution . . . there are no great fortunes to be made in stag film production. It is estimated that there are fewer that half a dozen individuals who net more than $10,000 per year in the business" (ibid.:18).

The Meese Commission report does not provide the information necessary to make possible a direct comparison with the Johnson Commission data. It does, however, contain a curious table, reproduced in Table 3.2, the point of which is unclear, showing the number of films rated in each of the Motion

Table 3.3. *Estimated sales of sexually oriented publications in the United States, 1969 (in millions)*

	Mass market	Adults only
Books	—[a]	45–55
Magazines	123	25–35

[a]Impossible to arrive at total sales figures.
Source: U.S. Commission (1970:14, 17).

Picture Association of America's categories from the inception of the rating system on November 1, 1968, through September 30, 1985.

Apart from this, the only other relevant information given, under the heading "Sexually Explicit Motion Pictures," runs as follows:

At present, there are approximately twelve to twenty-four production companies involved in making sexually explicit theatrical release sixteen millimeter or thirty-five millimeter films. These films are sold to distributors who in turn sell or rent the films to "adults only" pornographic movie theaters across the country. In 1985, approximately one hundred full length sexually explicit films were distributed to nearly seven hundred "adults only" pornographic theaters in the United States. These theaters sold an estimated two million tickets each week to their sexually explicit movies. The annual box-office receipts were estimated at five hundred million dollars.

In addition it is said that sexually explicit 8mm films are distributed to "adults only" pornographic outlets throughout the country but they are described as not being a "major influence in today's market" (U.S. Department of Justice, 1986:1384–1385).

Books and magazines

The Johnson Commission classified sexually oriented publications into two categories: sexually oriented mass-market books and periodicals; and "adults only" publications. Estimated sales of these materials for 1969 are shown in Table 3.3.

The Meese Commission did not produce directly comparable figures. As far as sexually explicit books are concerned, the report deals only with paperbacks. No sales figures for these are given. Indeed, the only information provided runs as follows:

The volume of sexually explicit paperback books which have been published is tremendous. The 1970 President's Commission on Obscenity and Pornography estimated that approximately five thousand new "adult" titles were published each year. Recent studies of this segment of the industry suggest that while it is doubtful that five

Table 3.4. *Top-selling sexually explicit
magazines: average circulation per
month, 1975–84*

Year	Average circulation
1975	14,084,961
1976	15,450,702
1977	15,814,086
1978	14,984,420
1979	16,104,180
1980	16,470,221
1981	15,406,458
1982	13,981,162
1983	12,189,909
1984	10,617,482

Source: U.S. Department of Justice (1986:1409–
1411).

thousand sexually explicit paperbacks are still published each year, the actual number published is still large. (U.S. Department of Justice, 1986:1451)

In regard to magazines, the Meese Commission report gives the average monthly circulation figures for the thirteen top-selling mainstream sexually explicit magazines from 1975 to 1984. The magazines included are *Cherie, Chic, Club Magazine, Club International, Forum, Gallery Magazine, Genesis, High Society, Hustler, Oui, Penthouse, Playboy,* and *Playgirl*. The growth in the circulation of these magazines during the 1970s appears to have halted in 1980, since when there has been a significant decline. Figures for the total circulation of all the magazines over the period are shown in Table 3.4.

The Meese Commission report also says that in addition to the thirteen magazines just mentioned, it was estimated there were "currently between fifty thousand and sixty thousand different sexually explicit magazine titles available in the United States"; and also that "hundreds of new titles come out each month." The source of both pieces of information is given as "Interview with Sergeant Donald Smith, Los Angeles Police Department (March 9, 1986)" (U.S. Department of Justice, 1986:1413).

Mail-order sales

The Johnson Commission's third category of sexually oriented materials comprised books, magazines, 8mm home movies and photo sets, sexual devices and pseudomedical products, and such miscellaneous items as strip-poker cards, sexy lingerie, and rubber or leather wearing apparel, sold through mail order. The commission estimated that the total volume of sexually oriented mail was approximately forty-five to forty-eight million letters during fiscal year 1969 and that the retail sale value of sexually oriented material bought through mail order "probably did not exceed $12 to $14 million" in that year (U.S. Commission, 1970:18).

The Meese Commission reported that sexually explicit magazines were distributed to mail-order companies "in most large cities such as Los Angeles, New York, and Chicago as well as some small cities" through "a sophisticated nationwide network." The commission said that at least half the retail sales of sexually explicit magazines were made by pornographic outlets and the remainder of these magazines were sold by mail order. But no estimate of the volume of sales was given. It also reported that approximately 50 percent of the sales of what it called "sexual device and paraphernalia products" were distributed through mail-order operations, although once again no estimate of sales was made (U.S. Department of Justice, 1986:1413, 1450).

Under-the-counter or hard-core materials

The Johnson Commission's fourth and final category, hard-core pornography, was not very precisely defined. The Traffic and Distribution Panel report stated that "in this report the term [hard-core pornography] is used as a synonym for 'under-the-counter' or covertly sold materials" but it noted that "at present, distinctions between materials sold openly and those sold covertly have become extremely unclear."

Nevertheless, it said that "there is one genre of sexually-oriented material which is almost universally sold under-the-counter in the United States: wholly photographic reproductions of actual sexual intercourse graphically depicting oral, vaginal, or anal penetration" (U.S. Commission, 1971–72, 3:179). This type of material was available in the form of stag films, already mentioned in the section on motion pictures, hard-core photographs and photo sets, and hard-core magazines and brochures.

The panel reported that the nationwide traffic in and distribution of hard-core pornography was only a small part of the total traffic in sexually oriented materials. It said that "an estimate of a retail market in the range of $5 million to perhaps $10 million seems reasonable but actual sales could very well be considerably less than $5 million nationwide" (ibid., 3:201). But it noted that imports of such materials from Scandinavia appeared to be increasing.

It is not possible to compare the findings of the Johnson Commission with those of the Meese Commission with regard to this category of material, for two reasons. In the first place, at the time when the Johnson Commission's Traffic and Distribution Panel reported, in many metropolitan areas the kind of material classified as "under-the-counter" was being openly exhibited and openly sold. So that, as the panel noted, "at least to some extent" this "made any discussion of the 'under-the-counter' concept passé" (ibid., 3:179). By the time the Meese Commission was established in 1985 there no longer existed any material that was "almost universally sold under-the-counter."

In the second place, the Meese Commission, as we have seen, adopted its own classification system for sexually explicit material. It noted that the definition of the term "hard-core pornography" was "problematic." It defined the term tentatively as referring to "material that is sexually explicit to the extreme, intended virtually exclusively to arouse, and devoid of any other apparent content or purpose" (U.S. Department of Justice, 1986:229). But it is not used anywhere in the commission's report in a way that would make possible comparison with the Johnson Commission's findings.

Videotape cassettes

Videocassette recorders (VCRs) were first introduced into the American market in 1975. When the Meese Commission reported in 1986, it was estimated that VCRs would be in 38 percent of American homes with television sets by the end of 1986 and 85 percent of those homes by 1995. Sexually explicit films were first put on videotape around 1977. The commission cites a Merrill Lynch report that in the late 1970s, X-rated videotapes, which were retailing for more than one hundred dollars, constituted over half of the prerecorded industry sales (U.S. Department of Justice, 1986:1389).

The commission's report includes a table prepared by the Video Software Dealers Association (VSDA) in 1984 showing the range of video programming consumed by the public, and the percentage of the market taken by each type of material identified, as shown in Table 3.5.

It is pointed out in a footnote that current estimates (at March 1986) "place the figure for 'Adult' video tape cassettes at no more than nine percent" (U.S. Department of Justice, 1986:1388). The report, however, goes on to say:

The thirteen percent of the video market identified by the industry as "Adult" *excludes* most of the sexually violent material that the Commission found to be the most harmful form of sexually explicit material. The categories labeled "Action/Adventure," "Science Fiction," and "Horror," which together comprise more than half the market, include many films that contain scenes of rape, sexual homicide, and other forms of sexual violence. The harmfulness of these materials is not lessened by the fact that the breasts and genitals are covered in some scenes, nor the fact that these films are not given an "X" rating by the Motion Picture Association of America, nor the fact that the industry does not consider them "Adult" materials. Indeed, all of these features increase the availability of these materials to minors. Moreover, the "music video" category, which includes many sexually violent depictions, is specifically marketed to young people. (ibid.:1389)

Table 3.5. *Video Software Dealers Association annual market survey, 1984*

Type	Percentage of market
Action–adventure	25.2
Science fiction	19.6
Adult	13.0
Children	10.4
Comedy	8.8
Drama	8.6
Horror	8.0
Music video	2.9
How-to	2.7
Foreign	0.8

Source: U.S. Department of Justice (1986:1388).

Insofar as that is correct, what the commission has to say about the distribution of sexually explicit videotape cassettes presumably does not apply to, or include, "the most harmful form of sexually explicit material." The information given is in any case not very detailed. It is said that "recently, the major sexually explicit film distributors have rapidly entered the national video tape market" and also that "the sexually explicit video industry's profits are in the hundreds of millions of dollars annually" (ibid:1392–1393). But accounting at this level of imprecision serves little useful purpose.

Finally, on the subject of sexually explicit videotapes, the commission reported the results of a survey of its members, conducted by the VSDA in September 1985, regarding the retail of "adult" videotapes. The response to that survey is reproduced in Table 3.6.

There are a number of problems regarding the interpretation of the figures in this table. In the first place, the term "adult" was not explained or defined in the survey. It is therefore uncertain what type of material participants included in this category. To what extent that which the Meese Commission called "the most harmful form of sexually explicit material" was or was not included is unknown.

In the second place, the VSDA is a national trade association whose regular membership consists of approximately two thousand retailers and wholesalers of video software throughout the United States. But the extent to which they may constitute a representative sample of the estimated twelve thousand general video retail outlets in the United States that distribute sexually explicit videotapes (U.S. Department of Justice, 1986:1394) is unknown. More-

Table 3.6. *Video Software Dealers Association survey, September 6, 1985*

Number of individual stores that responded to survey: 2,279

Number of companies that responded to survey: 705

Stores that carry "adult" product:

	Yes	No
Number of stores	965	1,314
Percentage of respondents	42	58

The following questions were answered by retailers who carry "adult" products:

1. What percentage of your gross dollar volume is in "adult" product?

% of "adult" product	% of respondents
0–5	13
6–10	23
11–15	25
16–20	19
21–25	8
26–35	11
36–90	1

2. What percentage of your daily transactions are in "adult" product?

% of "adult" product	% of respondents
0–5	18
6–10	25
11–15	25
16–20	16
21–25	6
26–35	9
36–90	1

3. What percentage of your total inventory is in "adult" product?

% of "adult" product	% of respondents
0–5	15
6–10	45
11–15	19
16–20	11
21–25	5
26–35	4
36–90	1

Source: U.S. Department of Justice (1986:1397–1398).

over, sexually explicit videotapes can also be obtained in "adults only" pornographic outlets.

Although the Meese Commission reported that there could be little doubt that there had been "a dramatic increase" in the production of sexually explicit videotapes and other material (ibid.:284), the information provided on the nature of the increase is minimal. The commission conducted an investigation of currently marketed materials in six cities: Washington, D.C.; Baltimore, Maryland; Miami, Florida; Philadelphia, Pennsylvania; New York, New York; and Boston, Massachusetts. But the only relevant quantitative data derived from that investigation, presented in the report, is a forty-page list of 2,370 film titles.

Cable and satellite television

Cable television is a subscription service that first appeared in the United States in the 1940s to serve areas where broadcast television signals could not be received. In 1986 there were over 6,500 cable television systems serving more than 40 million subscribing households in the United States. While broadcast television stations are required to be licensed by the Federal Communications Commission, cable systems are not and they operate on a contractual agreement or franchise with a state or local government body. In addition to cable there are several other types of television services including Satellite Master Antenna Television, Over-the-Air Subscription Television, Backyard Satellite Receiving Dishes, and Multipoint Distribution Service.

Individual local cable operators control what programming is offered on their systems and usually offer at least one "pay television" channel, which includes "adults only" programs for which the subscriber pays an additional fee. The Meese Commission found that analysis of the various forms of television transmission disclosed that, "while a significant amount of material appeared on network television that qualified as "the type of sexual violence that the Commission has found to be the most harmful form of pornography," "most of the sexually explicit programs appear on 'pay television' " (U.S. Department of Justice, 1986:1421–1422).

It reported that channels that carried R-rated programming reached in excess of 14.5 million homes over 6,900 cable and satellite systems. In addition, both cable-transmitted pay television channels and direct satellite channels carried exclusive "adult oriented," "X," and other sexually explicit movies. It noted, however, that "most operators limit such programming to the late evening hours and transmit the material in scrambled mode to ensure against inadvertent reception by nonsubscribers" (ibid.:1427).

Dial-A-Porn Services

The recorded messages known as Dial-A-Porn began in 1982 after the Federal Communications Commission ruled that providing information by recorded messages was a service beyond the permissible scope of the telephone company's authority. After deregulation, some telephone companies began holding lotteries to select providers of recorded messages on dial-it services. One company, Dial-A-Porn Services, was a winner in the lottery conducted in New York State and by February 1983 was offering services over three telephone lines.

There are two types of Dial-A-Porn calls. The first involves customers dialing a number and carrying on a live conversation with performers who will talk in terms as sexually explicit as the callers desire and may encourage them to masturbate during the course of the conversation. Callers are billed on their credit cards for the call.

The second type of Dial-A-Porn call involves the receipt of a prerecorded message consisting of descriptions of sex acts. These are sometimes described as though they were actually occurring during the call, with the callers and performers as participants. Callers are charged for each call to this service on their telephone bills. According to the Meese Commission, "the acts described include lesbian sexual activity, sodomy, rape, incest, excretory functions, bestiality, sadomasochistic abuse, and sex acts with children" (U.S. Department of Justice, 1986:1431).

The commission's report describes a firm called Dial-A-Porn Services as "one of the leading providers" of this type of service. But although it states that there are "many other Dial-A-Porn providers in the market" and refers to "the Dial-A-Porn industry in general," it gives only desultory information about the extent of these operations and the size of the industry. For example, it is said that "Dial-A-Porn recordings are now available locally in New York, Los Angeles, San Francisco, Philadelphia, Denver, Pittsburgh, Baltimore, Washington, D.C., and other major cities across the country. These services generate large numbers of calls . . . Dial-A-Porn providers and the telephone companies realize significant revenues from the Dial-A-Porn services."

Some indication of the size of such revenues can perhaps be inferred from the random items of information that are provided. For example, "in New York City, one major Dial-A-Porn provider earned . . . a total of $3.6 million for the year ending February 28, 1984"; "Pacific Bell estimates that their company earned twelve million from Dial-A-Porn calls between October 1984 and October 1985"; and "one telephone company has refused to offer Dial-A-Porn services at an estimated revenue loss of five hundred thousand dollars per year" (ibid.:1429–1435).

Sexually explicit computer services and bulletin boards

Sexually explicit computer subscription services were described by the Meese Commission as "the most recent advance in 'sexually explicit communications.' " The computer services are in fact similar to Dial-A-Porn telephone services. The report give some details of one such service: an "uncensored erotic" service called SEXTEX. This service offers an array of features, some of which are listed in the report as follows:

(1) conference calls with unlimited parties, (2) a "sex shop" that allows the operator to purchase sexual devices, sexually explicit magazine and video tapes by computer, (3) bulletin boards where the operator can post related messages for other subscribers to read and/or respond to, (4) an electronic mail service which allows one subscriber to send personal notes to other SEXTEX users and to other computer information services, (5) a "Guide" which features articles on sex and travel, and (6) the opportunity to place or answer a personal ad or seek some sexual advice.

There are also a number of sexually oriented national and local bulletin board systems. The Meese Commission cites some examples: "GENDERNET describes itself as an information source for the transvestite and transsexual. ODYSSEY II is designed for nudists and swingers. SYSLAVE is known as the kinkiest in L.A." (U.S. Department of Justice, 1986:1437–1445).

The Meese Commission also reported that computers have emerged as a method of communication between pedophiles about child victims. Specifically on this topic, it said:

Many pedophile offenders and child pornographers have traditionally used the mails as the mainstay of their psychological base as well as the source of information regarding potential victims. Recently, however, pedophile offenders and child pornographers have begun to use personal computers for communications. A person may now subscribe to an information service whereby he or she can contact other subscribers. The services are private commercial enterprises which sell access codes to subscribing members. These services offer everything from "private" communications accessed through individual code words to conference calls. The communication may also take the form of a "bulletin board" message to which any other subscriber may respond. . . .

Investigators have discovered that pedophile offenders use personal computer communications to establish contacts and as sources for the exchange or sale of child pornography. The computer user, after establishing a secure relationship with another subscriber, will arrange for materials to be sent through the mail. The subscribers will identify and describe the types of materials they seek. Respondents will then transmit the material to the designated address.

Pedophile offenders and child pornographers may also use personal computer services to identify particular children who can be used in making child pornography. The subscribers may describe the child physically and give a location where the child may be found. (ibid.: 628–631)

Peep shows

Peep show booths are often situated at the back of "adult" bookstores. The booths are partitioned, four-sided cubicles generally made out of wood or plaster with dimensions on the average of about three by five feet. A customer places coins or tokens into a coin- or token-operated box and a movie or videotape is activated. The movies include homosexual, heterosexual, and a variety of other sexual activities. The viewer may see two minutes of a movie for twenty-five cents. Quarters or tokens must be repeatedly inserted to continue viewing the movie, which may last from ten to twenty minutes.

The Johnson Commission's Traffic and Distribution Panel report devoted only one paragraph to what it referred to as "arcade movie machines, also known as 'peep shows.' " They are described as an "important sideline economically" for many 'adult' bookstores. It is said that "reports of bookstore owners indicate that the 'peep show' business is extremely lucrative," but no estimate of the amount of money involved is given. In this connection, it is noted that "cash receipts are not recorded in a systematic manner (which provides an opportunity to reduce the taxes paid on actual income)" (U.S. Commission, 1971–72, 3:109).

The Meese Commission's report goes into some detail both about the "anonymous sexual relations" and a variety of "sexual activities" alleged to occur in the booths and about the state of the booth's floors and walls: "sticky with liquid or viscous substances including semen, urine, feces, used prophylactics . . . a particularly nauseating smell." Surprisingly, the report says of these insalubrious premises (to which barely 6 out of the report's 1,960 pages are devoted): "It has been estimated that peep shows are the biggest moneymaking portion of this industry. Annual net profits for peep show booths alone have been projected at two billion dollars" (U.S. Department of Justice, 1986:1471–1477). There is no indication as to how this estimate was arrived at.

Sex newspapers or tabloids

The Johnson Commission's Traffic and Distribution Panel reported that what it refers to as "sex newspapers" came into being in 1968. They are described as "composed entirely of sexual material." A New York publication entitled *Screw* is said to be "the first and most famous" of these journals. Circulation figures for sex newspapers in August 1969 are given: "*Screw* had a circulation of nearly 150,000 far outstripping the sales of the *New York Review of Sex* at 40,000 issues, *Pleasure* at 70,000, and *Kiss* at 55,000." It is reported that "gross retail sales for *Screw* in 1970 will be in excess of $2.5 million. None of the other sex newspapers . . . have approached this success" (U.S. Commission, 1970: 103–104).

The Meese Commission refers to these publications as "sexually explicit tabloids." "The best known of these tabloids is *Screw* Magazine." The commission's report devotes two pages to description and examples of advertisements in a tabloid for "sexually related goods and services." Only one other publication, *Hollywood Press*, is mentioned. No details of circulation or retail sales are given (U.S. Department of Justice, 1986:1457–1460).

Other materials

The Johnson Commission's Traffic and Distribution Panel report devotes very little space to what it calls "sexually oriented materials other than books and magazines," although it is said that "*the majority* of 'adult' bookstores" handle them. "Some sell a wide variety of sexual devices, such as artificial vaginas and rubber penises, and a variety of lotions, potions, and elixirs, allegedly designed to improve sexual prowess." Curiously, elsewhere the report says that "sexual apparatus and pseudo-medical elixirs, lotions, balms, and so on are sold only through mail order and in *a few* 'adult' bookstores" (U.S. Commission, 1971–72, 3:109, 131; emphasis added).

The commission contracted for three separate studies of the marketing of "adult materials" in San Francisco, Denver, and Boston; and the operating procedures of retail outlets in those cities are set out in some detail in the contractors' reports (ibid., 4:3–224). But although all three of the studies provide estimates of the volume and value of the market in sex-oriented materials, in none of them is there a breakdown of this type of material from the rest of the merchandise sold in "adults only" retail outlets.

The Meese Commission also dealt very briefly with what are described as "other materials sold in pornographic outlets." Some space in the four pages dealing with this topic is devoted to listing various "sexual devices and paraphernalia" including some twenty-eight different "sadomasochistic sexual devices." The commission reported that "most of the 'adults only' pornographic outlets in the United States carry sexual devices and paraphernalia as part of their general stock," but it provided no estimate of the volume of sales (U.S. Department of Justice, 1986:1446–1450).

Orientation

Neither the Johnson Commission nor the Meese Commission developed any detailed typology or ordered codification of the themes to be found in pornographic materials. Not that the content of the materials was ignored, although the only detailed content analysis, as opposed to descriptions of content, to be found in either of the reports is presented in "A Study of Mass Media Erotica" in a Johnson Commission technical report, which provides an analysis of

366 *Romance* or *Confession* magazine stories (U.S. Commission, 1971–72, 9:99–164). As these stories "are edited for their erotic content and the editors ensure that the language is indirect" and the arousal intended is "emotional rather than sexual" (ibid., 9:103), the relevance of this study to what is ordinarily regarded as pornography is rather remote.

The Johnson Commission report stated in its "Overview of Findings" that "activities most frowned upon by our society, such as sadomasochism, pedophilia, bestiality, and nonconsensual sex are . . . outside the scope of the interests of the average patron of adult bookstores and movie houses" (U.S. Commission, 1970:21). What was inside the scope of the average patron can be derived from the summary descriptions of the contents of exploitation films (or skin flicks) and "adults only" paperback books and magazines, given in the commission's report.

Thus the vast majority of exploitation films were said to be directed at the male heterosexual market. "Relatively few films," the report said,

are produced for a male homosexual audience, but the number of these films has apparently increased in the past year or two. Full female nudity has become common in the last year or two, although full male nudity is virtually unknown except in those films directed at the male homosexual market. Sexual activity covering the entire range of heterosexual conduct leaves very little to the imagination. Acts of sexual intercourse and oral–genital contact are not shown, only strongly implied or simulated; sexual foreplay is graphically depicted. (ibid.:10)

The vast majority of "adults only" paperback books were said to be written for heterosexual males, although about 10 percent were aimed at the male homosexual market and a small percentage (less than 5 percent) at fetishists. "Virtually none" were "intended for a female audience." The sexual content of paperback books published for the "adults only" market was said to have become progressively stronger in the previous decade. "Today," the report says,

the content of "adults only" paperbacks runs the gamut from traditional "sex pulp" books (stories consisting of a series of sexual adventures tied together by minimal plot, in which the mechanics of the sex act are not described, euphemistic language is substituted for common or clinical terms, and much of the sexual content is left to the reader) through modern "sex pulp" (common terms for sexual activity and detailed descriptions of the mechanics of sex act are used), "classic" erotic literature, "pseudomedical" (alleged case-study analysis of sexual activity), illustrated marriage manuals, and illustrated novels (with photographs in which young females pose with the focus of the camera directly on their genitalia), to "documentary" studies of censorship and pornography containing illustrations depicting genital intercourse, and oral sex. Insofar as the textual portions of many of these books are concerned, it is probably not possible to exceed the candor, graphic descriptions of sexual activity, and use of vulgar language in some currently distributed "adults only" paperback books. The pictorial content of some illustrated paperback books similarly cannot be exceeded in explicit depictions of sexual activity. (ibid.:15)

"Adults only" magazines were described as devoted principally to photographic depictions of female and male nudity with emphasis on the genitalia.

Some of these depictions contain two or three models together and some pose both males and females in the same photograph. The posing of more than one model in a single photograph has resulted in a considerable amount of implied sexual activity, either intercourse or oral–genital contact, but neither actual sexual activity nor physical arousal of males is depicted at the present time. Nearly 90% are intended for a male heterosexual audience. About 10% are directed to male homosexuals and feature male nudes. Fetish and sadomasochistic magazines, featuring bondage, chains, whips, spanking, rubber or leather wearing apparel, high-heeled boots, etc., are a rather insignificant part of the total production (less than 5%). (ibid.:16)

The Meese Commission reported that "among the most common inquiries made to the staff of the Attorney General's Commission on Pornography was a request for information on the content of currently available pornography in the United States" (U.S. Department of Justice, 1986:1499). In order to provide data concurrent with the deliberations of the commission, the commission through its staff investigated "the content of currently marketed materials." The investigation (conducted, as noted earlier, in Washington, D.C., Baltimore, Miami, Philadelphia, New York, and Boston) produced the information provided in a chapter of over three hundred pages in the commission's report entitled "The Imagery Found Among Magazines, Books, Films in 'Adults Only' Pornographic Outlets" (ibid.:1499–1802).

What is referred to as "the quantitative data" presented in that chapter consists entirely of a 108-page list of titles. There are 2,325 magazines titles, 725 book titles, and 2,370 film titles (ibid.:1505–1612). As to content, the information provided consists of a one-page summary headed "Results" and a 190-page "review of specific materials and prepared descriptions of selected materials" (ibid.:1613–1802).

The results summary runs as follows:

In all stores surveyed magazines and bookstores with depictions of vaginal intercourse between one female and one male were in a minority among the types of sexual activity depicted.

There were geographic difference in only a very few types of sexual activity depicted on the covers of books and magazines displayed for consumer purchase. Films and magazines which depicted actual photographs of sexual encounters between humans and animals were seen in New York, New York; Philadelphia, Pennsylvania, and Miami, Florida, but not in Washington, D.C.; Boston, Massachusetts, or Baltimore, Maryland. Stores in at least two cities, Boston and Baltimore, had magazines which depicted and featured sexual activities involving one or more persons with amputated limbs. Materials depicting actual scenes of urination and/or defecation were present in some of the locations but not in others. All outlets, with the exception of one store in Baltimore and one in New York City, had paperback books which featured the preceding themes as well as incest and child molestation. Every store surveyed featured magazines with photographs depicting bondage, simulated child pornography and various other paraphillic activity in significant percentages. (ibid.:1502)

The review of specific materials consists simply of detailed descriptions of individual magazines, paperback books, motion picture videotape cassettes, film clips shown in peep show booths, and one "adult" tabloid. The descriptions were written by a Washington, D.C., Metropolitan Police Department detective and an Arlington County, Virginia, Police Department detective. They are prefaced with the statement that "no claim is made that the materials described are the most representative sample that could be found in [that] there is no existing source of information to identify such materials."

It is said that "the materials that were selected however were not to be . . . the 'worst' representative materials found." Without any indication of what the two detectives might have regarded as the worst (or, for that matter, the best) material, it is difficult to know what significance to attach to such a statement. It is said that "all materials had to be available for sale to the general public, over the counter or through mail order," but no indication is given as what proportion of the material available was represented by the items selected (ibid.:1613–1614).

Some of the material described is certainly bizarre enough to raise doubts about the extent to which it represented what the Johnson Commission called "the interests of the average patron of adult bookstores and movie houses" (U.S. Commission, 1970:21). The point is of sufficient importance to deserve illustration.

Thus, one of the descriptions relates to a magazine containing sixty-four four-color photographs accompanied by a text "describing in graphic and nauseating detail the use of urine and feces in sado-masochistic sexual activity." The photographs include such things as "eight close-up photographs of a caucasian female expelling liquid enema and fecal matter from her rectum into a chamber pot" (U.S. Department of Justice, 1986:1632–1633).

Another magazine described, contained twenty-nine two-color photographs featuring a naked prepubescent Caucasian female identified as ten years old and a dachshund accompanied by a text "describing in graphic detail bestial acts involving cunnilingus and masturbation." The photographs described include depictions of the female masturbating the dog; the dog licking the vagina of the female; the dog straddling the girl's back "in a position commonly referred to as 'Doggie style' " (ibid.:1683–1639). Of the ten magazines described, two feature sadomasochism, two feature bestiality, three feature homosexual activities, and none deal with what the Meese Commission defined as "non-violent and non-degrading materials" (ibid.:335).

The one paperback book selected was entitled *Tying Up Rebecca*. The following is an extract from the description provided:

On the cover the title is above an illustrated picture of a red haired female who is nude from the waist up. She has one rope around her neck, another around her body and arms, and her ankles are tied to a bar, spreading her legs apart. She is standing but is bent at the waist from the pull of the rope. She has a ball gag in her mouth, and is wearing a garter belt, stockings, and shoes. (ibid.:1647)

The illustration does not misrepresent the contents of the book as described by the police officer. Again, however, there is no indication as to what proportion of the 750 titles available were of that character.

In the absence of any description of technique for sampling or, indeed, any principles or procedures for selection whatever, it is impossible to attach any significance to what these "trained investigators" (ibid.:1500) produced. There is no way to judge what proportion of the total amount of porno-graphic material available was represented by the items singled out for description. The information provided by this investigation may well be totally misleading.

A passage from the joint statement of two dissenting members of the Meese Commission underlines the crucial deficiency:

We do not even know whether or not what the Commission viewed during the course of the year reflected the nature of most of the pornographic and obscene material in the market; nor do we know if the materials shown us mirror the taste of the majority of consumers of pornography. The visuals, both print and video, were skewed to the very violent and extremely degrading. (ibid.:1499)

Places of display

In 1970 Abelson and his associates carried out for the Johnson Commission a large national survey to provide information regarding the nature of the experience that adults in the United States had had with erotic materials. It was found that 85 percent of adult men and 70 percent of adult women in the United States had been exposed at some time during their lives to depictions of explicit sexual materials in either visual or textual form. It was also found that first experience with explicit sexual materials for Americans usually occurred during adolescence. Movies were found to be the main medium in which people had recently seen erotic depictions. Seeing erotic films was mainly a social activity. Women were likely to have seen such films with their spouses; men, with friends of the same sex (U.S. Commission, 1971–72, 9:7).

The Abelson study has not been replicated. No comparable study was carried out for the Meese Commission. To what extent patterns of exposure have changed since 1970 is largely unknown. The nature and extent of what has been called "the stunning change in the way in which people now receive erotic stimuli" (U.S. Department of Justice, 1986:200) has not been thoroughly investigated. The Meese Commission's investigations, however, did reveal that

technological innovations have created a new delivery system for the consumption of pornographic and erotic materials (notably via home video and cable). Since the home video industry is still young, it is reasonable to assume that the supply and public demand for pornographic materials may increase. Some recent industry figures actually show video purchases and rentals of pornography on the increase. There is, however, a significant corresponding decrease in both the number of adult theaters in this country and the circulation figures of the so-called skin magazines. (ibid.:199)

Homes

Insofar as it is true that "the real proliferation of sexually explicit materials in the United States took place in the 1970s" (U.S. Department of Justice, 1986:1363), the findings of the Johnson Commission may now be of little more than historical interest. Certainly the finding that "the typical adult's experience with specific erotic depictions is . . . only around once a year" (U.S. Commission, 1971–72, 6:12) must now require revision.

To what extent the advent of the "new delivery system" for pornography has changed patterns of exposure is unclear. It is possible that the findings that "both adults' and adolescents' typical experience with visual erotic materials has been in a movie theater" (ibid., 6:24) is no longer applicable. With VCRs in 38 percent of American homes with television in 1986 it seems likely that the home, which in 1970 was the second most frequently cited location for the "most recent" experience with sexually explicit material (ibid., 6:25) will have achieved greater prominence.

In 1985 a Gallup poll revealed that 9 percent of Americans had rented an X-rated videotape in the past year (Gallup, 1985). *Adult Video News* estimated that 1,700 new sexually explicit videos were released in 1985 and predicted that a high growth rate would continue (U.S. Department of Justice, 1986:1390). The Meese Commission, as noted earlier in this chapter, cited an industry prediction that VCRs will be in 85 percent of homes with televisions by 1995 and that home video cassettes will become the dominant entertainment medium by the 1990s. It seems likely, therefore, that by the end of the century the home will be the venue for the most frequent exposure to pornography.

"Adult" bookstores and sex shops

The Johnson Commission reported that there were as of spring 1970 in the United States approximately 850 self-labeled retail "adult" bookstores and 1,425 retail outlets that provided a restricted-access section for "adult" materials, in addition to selling other products in a nonrestricted-access area. Most

Table 3.7. *Full-time and part-time exploitation theaters, 1970*

Number of exploitation theaters			Total all theaters	Percentage of theaters with exploitation policy
Full-time	Part-time	Total		
524	356	880	11,478[a]	7.7[b]

[a]The total number of theaters was derived from the *1967 Census of Business* (Washington, D.C.: U.S. Government Printing Office, 1970).
[b]Not all the theaters believed to be operating in 1967 reported to the Census Bureau. Thus the total number of theaters was understated and the percentage of those with an exploitation policy probably overstated.
Source: U.S. Commission (1971–72, 3:38).

were located in metropolitan areas of 500,000 or more population. It also reported that yearly gross sales for the average "adults only" store were probably in the range of $60,000 to $75,000 with net profits sometimes in excess of $20,000 per store per year (U.S. Commission, 1970:102).

In the brief section on " 'Adults Only' Pornographic Outlets" in the Meese Commission report, no comparable data are provided. The commission toured three of the fifty "adults only" pornographic outlets operating in Houston, Texas, accompanied by "vice detectives." "During this tour, the Commissioners observed the materials available in the outlets, the peep show booths complete with persons engaging in explicit sexual activity – and the generally unhealthy environment posed by the sexual activity and debris in the store" (U.S. Department of Justice, 1986:1485).

The commission reported that "the impact of sexually explicit video on 'adults only' pornographic outlets is uncertain." It said that those who patronize them primarily for the atmosphere and potential for sexual activity, or to purchase sexually explicit magazines, book, or sexual devices, would "undoubtedly not be significantly influenced by the availability of video." But it concluded that "it is unclear at this point what long term effects sexually explicit videos will have on these 'adults only' pornographic outlets" (ibid.:1484).

"Adults only" pornographic theaters

The Johnson Commission reported that the total number of what it called "full-time exploitation theaters" in the United States was 524 (410 indoor theaters and 114 drive-ins) and that in addition a number of other theaters exhibited exploitation features on an irregular basis. Table 3.7 shows the data derived by the commission from the exploitation industry (organized in the Adult Film Association of America [AFAA]) and the Census Bureau.

The commission estimated that the total box office receipts during 1969 for exhibition of exploitation films "fell within a range of $60 million to $70 million, the latter figure probably being somewhat more accurate" (U.S. Commission, 1971–72, 3:53). At $65 million this would represent 5.9 percent of the estimated box office gross for 1970 as shown earlier (Table 3.1).

The Meese Commission reported that in the 1970s, " 'Adults Only' pornographic theaters became more noticeable as they advertised and showed films of better technical quality. Many of the mainstream theaters went out of business in the 1970s and were purchased to show sexually explicit films" (U.S. Department of Justice, 1986:1364). No details or quantitative estimates of this expansion are given in the report.

As to more recent developments, the commission cites a *Newsweek* article ("The War Against Pornography," March 18, 1985) as the source of its report that "in 1985, approximately one hundred full length sexually explicit films were distributed to nearly seven hundred 'adults only' pornographic theaters in the United States. These theaters sold an estimated two million tickets each week to their sexually explicit movies. The annual box office receipts were estimated at five hundred million dollar" (ibid.:1385).

The commission also reported, however, that "the sexually explicit film industry is presently in a state of transition from a theater-centered base to one dominated by video tape cassettes viewed in the Home" (ibid.:1368). It further reported that John Weston, counsel for the Adult Film Association of America, had told the commission "that the 'adults only' pornographic theater business has been declining and will be virtually nonexistent by 1990."

Weston's reasons for making that assertion are summarized as follows:

First, the theaters themselves are expensive to maintain and operate. Second, with the advent of video tape cassettes, Americans are choosing not to go out to movie theaters for their movie entertainment. Weston bases this latter statement on the fact that theater admission costs are higher than video rentals, as well as his belief that an increasing number of people would rather watch movies in the comfort of their own home. (ibid.:1385–1386)

Who sees pornography?

In the Meese Commission report, "the pornography industry" is described as "a highly visible multi-billion dollar industry" (U.S. Department of Justice, 1986:1353). Moreover, as noted at the beginning of this chapter, the commission is said to have "spent much of our time investigating the nature of the industry that produces, distributes, and sells sexually explicit materials" (ibid.:277). Indeed, two chapters of the report, "The Market and the Industry" and "Production and Distribution of Sexually Explicit Materials," comprising some 170 pages, are devoted to that topic (ibid.:277–298, 1351–1498).

The report states rightly that "we do not believe we could responsibly have drawn conclusions relating to that industry unless we became familiar with it" (ibid.:277). Yet a most curious feature of the report is that the nature of the demand for the output of this vast productive enterprise is almost totally ignored. About the supplies of, and about the nature of, the goods and services provided in this large-scale business activity a considerable amount of information is given; about the demand side of the equation, almost nothing. All that appeared in the commission's report is a brief (eight-page) section entitled "Public Exposure to Sexually Explicit Materials" (ibid.:912–917, 919–921).

Yet while production, exchange, and distribution are the means, consumption is the end. Market performance responds to the demands of consumers. The concept of consumer sovereignty as the ultimate determinant of market decisions may be an imperfect guide to economic reality, but without consumers there would be no market. And a multibillion-dollar industry could not exist without a very substantial demand for its products. To concentrate on the supply function and virtually ignore demand is to misconceive the nature of economic analysis.

That the commission did this is odd because in the chapter entitled "The History of Pornography" it acknowledges that "although one task is largely to think about laws and law enforcement, we know that thinking about law requires thinking as well about the social foundations of the practice involved." It also declares itself anxious "to encourage thinking about sexually explicit material as a social phenomenon" (ibid.:236).

In fact, although the first element of the Meese Commission mandate was the assessment of "the dimensions of the problem of pornography" (ibid.:215–216) in order to study the nature and extent of the demand for pornography, it is necessary to refer back to 1970, to the Johnson Commission. That commission devoted one volume of technical reports to *The Consumer and the Community* and a number of studies in other volumes to the consumers of explicitly sexual materials and the patron of pornographic outlets (U.S. Commission, 1971–72, vols. 1, 4, 9). But even there the information provided is sparse and inadequate.

Consumers: by gender

Al Goldstein, the publisher of *Screw* and the producer of *Midnight Blue*, a cable television program, has said, "Once pornography was acceptable only if it was sold in fancy expensive editions that claimed to be 'erotic art' from

India or Japan. To me pornography is what the truck driver wants, what the sanitation man reads, what the bus driver buys" (Goldstein, 1984:32–33). It is significant that the occupations he referred to are predominantly male. For there seems to be no doubt that the great majority of pornographic material is consumed by males.

The Johnson Commission found that the "vast majority of exploitation films are directed at the male heterosexual market. Relatively few films are produced for a male homosexual audience, but the number of these films has apparently increased in the past year or two." It found also that the "vast majority of 'adults only' books are written for heterosexual males, although about 10% are aimed at the male homosexual market." It found, too, that patrons of adult bookstores are "predominantly male." It found that "men are more likely to be exposed to erotic materials than are women" (U.S. Commission, 1970:10, 15–16, 19, 21).

Empirical studies of the marketplace for sexual materials with an emphasis on retail outlets and their customers were carried out for the Johnson Commission in Denver, Boston, and San Francisco. The overall picture in relation to the male–female ratio of customers is remarkably consistent. In Denver, for example, interviews with the owners–clerks of "adult" bookstores elicited estimates that between 95 percent and 98 percent of customers were male. These estimates were confirmed by a week's observations in three stores where 97.4 percent of customers were male and 2.6 percent female. Observation of adult movie attendance in Denver revealed that 93.5 percent of patrons were male and 6.5 percent were female (U.S. Commission, 1971–72, 4:38, 52, 60).

In Boston "information provided by almost all booksellers interviewed" was "to the effect that females composed a minuscule portion of their customers," although "one bookseller differed estimating the percentage of female customers as high as 10%." In San Francisco observations of adult bookstores' patrons revealed that 96.53 percent were male and 3.47 percent were female. Observations of adult movie patrons found that 96.70 percent were male and 3.30 percent were female (ibid., 4:119, 192, 196).

It should be noted in this connection that women customers seem not to have been encouraged in some outlets. For example, in downtown Denver at two arcades housing coin-operated booths featuring three-minute color movies "women customers were not permitted in either arcade." Similarly in Boston a breakdown of data relating to arcade customers revealed that: "Only men are allowed to view films." In San Francisco also "observations of the arcade patrons reveal a male clientele (female entrance is prohibited)" (ibid., 4:31, 176, 192).

The national survey of experience with erotic material revealed that whereas 44 percent of men had seen what were called "stag movies" (shown at private homes or private parties or club meetings), only 9 percent of women had. In relation to skin flicks (shown in movie theaters), while 23 percent of men had seen them, only 7 percent of women had. It was reported that "there is a sex difference with respect to who tends to see these films alone. Fourteen percent of men and 2 percent of women report the last such experience as one in which they saw the film by themselves" (ibid., 4:16–17, 33).

A study carried out for the Johnson Commission on "Urban Working-Class Adolescents and Sexually Explicit Media" in the city of Chicago is of interest in that the findings "conform to the general pattern of findings in such studies: symbolic materials have a noticeably less arousing and erotic effect on women than they do on men." Thus, more than twice as many males as females were excited or aroused by movies of sexual intercourse: 69 percent as opposed to 27 percent (ibid., 9:220, 225). In this connection it is notable that Kinsey and his associates found that pornography which males find stimulating commonly brings no more than minimal response from females (Kinsey et al., 1953, chap. 16 passim).

A study entitled "The Consumers of Pornography Where it is Easily Available: The Swedish Experience," also carried out for the Johnson Commission, similarly reported that a "basic fact to be noted is the much greater consumption and acceptance of pornography by men than by women." This was said to be explained in part "by the fact that most pornography is directed to men" (U.S. Commission, 1971–72, 9:462). It should be added that it is also produced *by* men, for as the Kinsey researchers discovered, although the amount of deliberately pornographic material the human race has produced is quite incalculable in extent, "it is exceedingly difficult to find any that has been produced by females" (Kinsey et al., 1953:672).

Another explanation given for the sex differential in relation to pornography in Sweden is "the generally and traditionally more conservative and restrictive attitudes that women have about virtually all sexual matters." But it was reported also that "rapid change" was taking place and a survey dealing with attitudes to pornography carried out by the Swedish Institute for Opinion Research revealed that "women of the younger generation have a more liberal stand on pornography than the older generation" (U.S. Commission, 1971–72, 9:462). The change is reflected in Table 3.8, which shows the age distribution of these members of the Swedish population classified as wholehearted consumers of pornography. About all these matters, the Meese Commission had nothing at all to say. It did not even comment on the interesting finding in the 1985 Gallup poll that in the eighteen- to twenty-year-old age group the percentage of women who had bought or rented an X-rated videocassette in the previous year was equal to two-thirds of the male figure: 12 percent to 17 percent (U.S. Department of Justice, 1986:920).

Table 3.8. *Wholehearted consumers of pornography in Sweden*

	Percentage	
Age	Men	Women
18–21	37	19
30–60	15	2

Source: U.S. Commission (1971–72, 9:464).

Consumers: by age

In the Swedish study referred to it is said that one of "the popular views about the consumers of pornography . . . shattered by this research" is the notion that "most users of pornography are old men." "Most users of pornography" in Sweden were "in fact younger persons," as shown in Table 3.9.

The national survey carried out for the Johnson Commission in America also found that "the high consumers of erotic [material] tend to be young adults under 30 years of age," as illustrated in Figure 3.1, which shows the ages of those who had had the most amount of recent experience with erotic materials. It appeared that experience with erotica achieved a consumption peak relatively early in adulthood and diminished thereafter in a consistent fashion. The information was derived from interviews with a nationwide probability sample of adults age twenty-one and older and with a sample of "adolescents" (aged fifteen to twenty), including some who lived in the same households as adult respondents and others from households not in the adult sample.

Table 3.9. *Users of pornography by age in Sweden*

Age	Percentage
18–20	33
21–25	42
26–30	31
31–35	28
36–40	19
41–50	10
51–60	10

Source: U.S. Commission (1971–72, 9:-460).

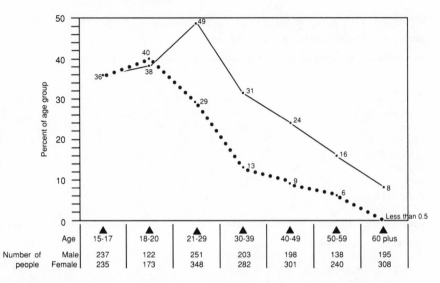

Figure 3.1. Percentage of men and women recently exposed to erotica, by age. Solid line represents men; broken line represents women. Data on 15- to 20-year-old respondents are from the adolescent sample. *Source:* U.S. Commission (1972, 6:40).

Table 3.10. *Age of patrons, by location: adult theaters and bookstores in the United States*

	Age group				
	−18	19–27	28–40	41–60	61+
Mean of nine theaters in seven cities	—	23	30	39	8
Mean of six bookstores in six cities	—	36	39	24	1

Note: All figures are in rounded percentages that may not total 100.
Source: U.S. Commission (1971–72, 4:232).

On the other hand, a study for the Johnson Commission of a variety of demographic and behavioral characteristics of persons paying admission to adult film theaters and making purchases in adult bookstores in a number of communities in the United States revealed a somewhat different age pattern, as shown in Table 3.10. From this table it appears that a substantial majority (69 percent) of the customers of "adult" theaters fell within the twenty-eight- to sixty-years-old range, although bookstore customers tended to be younger than moviegoers.

Table 3.11. *Frequency of viewing sexually explicit films in movie theaters and on videos, by age (Canadian national sample)*

	12–17 (%)	18–34 (%)	35–49 (%)	55+ (%)
Movies				
Never	28	34	48	74
1–2 times/year	22	44	35	12
1/mo. or more	39	12	7	4
Videos				
Never	32	33	50	83
1–2 times/year	22	37	25	7
1/mo. or more	37	23	20	5

N = 1,071.
Note: "Don't Know/No" response not included.
Source: U.S. Department of Justice (1986:921).

It is relevant, however, to note that many jurisdictions prohibited the attendance of persons under eighteen at adult movies and bookstores. At the same time, some bookstores or movie theaters had different age require-ments. "One New York theater has a posted minimum age of eighteen; the very next theater on the same block requires that a patron be twenty-one years of age" (U.S. Commission, 1971–72, 4:233).

A more recent set of data, which *is* noted in the Meese Commission Report, in its short section on "Public Exposure to Sexually Explicit Materials," is based on a national probability sample of 1,071 respondents in Canada. The Canadian results show that adolescents aged twelve to seventeen report most frequent exposure to sexually explicit material. As shown in Table 3.11, two out of five, twelve- to seventeen-year-olds view such material in movie theaters at least once a month and more than a third view similar material with the same frequency on home video. It is not unreasonable to assume that a similar pattern would apply in the United States.

Consumers: by sexual orientation

At the time the Johnson Commission reported there seems to have been relatively little pornographic material available that catered to specialized tastes. The greater part of it was described simply as "sexually oriented." The national survey carried out by Abelson and his associates for the commission noted that the experience that most adults in the United States had had with erotic materials was with "portrayals of sex that conform to general cultural norms" (U.S. Commission, 1970:120).

About "adults only" paperback books, the commission reported that as of 1970 "perhaps 10% or more are directed at the male homosexual market, and less than 5% are specifically written for any of the various fetishes." At the same time, it was reported, there had been some development of male homosexual magazines, although they appear not to have become particularly explicit.

Homosexual magazines through the late 1960s consisted primarily of posed pictures of nude males. The genitals of the models, the focal points of the photographs, were flaccid. Photographs were usually of a single model, although group scenes were not unusual. There was little or no physical contact between models, and sexual activity was generally not even implied. . . . Magazines aimed at male homosexuals have changed somewhat in the last year or two, and self-imposed restrictions on implied sexual activity are eroding slowly. Most homosexual magazines, however, are considerably less graphic than magazines featuring females. (ibid.:96, 97, 98)

In addition, the report continued,

Relatively small quantities of fetish books and magazines were produced featuring uses of items such as rubber and leather wearing apparel, lingerie, high heeled boots, etc. Sadomasochistic depictions or descriptions of bondage, spanking, and "domination" by clubs, whips, etc. were also available in limited quantities. Sexual explicitness in these materials was usually far less than in typical "girlie" magazines. Although quite a number of titles were produced, these magazines were not a major factor in the marketplace. (ibid.:97–98)

With regard to movies, the Johnson Commission reported that "at present, there are few areas of human sexual behavior which have not been explored" (ibid.:77); and also that "between 1964 and 1968 exploitation films moved in a variety of directions" (ibid.:81). They dealt with a considerable variety of themes including forms of fetishism (known as "kinkies"), transvestism, lesbianism, and mixtures of sex and violence (known as "roughies") but there seems, with one exception, to have been little attempt to cater for special groups of consumers.

The Johnson Commission, as we have noted earlier, reported that there were a "few films . . . produced for a male homosexual audience," and that the number of these films had "increased in the past year or two." "A small number of theaters," the report stated, "exclusively exhibit male homosexual films. . . . This market is quite small at present . . . although 'male' films are developing their own producers and theaters" (ibid.:81).

What the Johnson Commission called "hard-core" or "stag" films covered a wide range of sexual activities, but there seems to have been little specialization.

Because pornography historically has been thought to be primarily a masculine interest, the emphasis in stag films seems to represent the preferences of the middle-class

American male. Thus, male homosexuality and bestiality are relatively rare, while lesbianism is rather common. In recent years, there has been an increased emphasis on group sex, usually three or four individuals, but as many as seven have been noted in a single film. Many stag films attack certain forbidden social and sexual themes; for example, taboos against miscegenation, cunnilingus, and fellatio are constantly assaulted in American stag films, while foreign countries with a strong religious base have a significant anti-clerical strain in their stag films. The taboo against pedophilia, however, has remained almost inviolate. The use of pre-pubescent children in stag films is almost nonexistent. (ibid.:115)

The Meese Commission in its "general overview of the market and the industry" deals mainly with the "explicitness of detail" or "unalloyed explicitness" in the products of "the pornography industry" rather than the degree of specialization to be found. Apart from noting that among sexually explicit magazines "in recent years variations aimed at a female audience have also appeared," and that "the material available for viewing in some of the [peep show] booths is frequently oriented toward the male homosexual" (U.S. Department of Justice, 1986:280, 290), there is only one reference to the development of material catering for specific sexual tastes.

Thus, in reference to "adults only outlets or establishments" the commission reported that

the bulk of the stock of these establishments consists of pornographic magazines, frequently arranged by sexual preference. There can be little doubt that the range of sexual preferences catered to by magazines is wider than that of any other form of pornography. As the listing of titles later in this report makes clear, virtually any conceivable, and quite a few inconceivable, sexual preferences are featured in the various specialty magazines, and materials featuring sado-masochism, bestiality, urination and defecation in a sexual context, and substantially more unusual practices even than those are a significant proportion of what is available. (ibid.:291)

In what is described as its "in depth discussion of the industry today" the commission's report provides some more detail about the range of material available. Thus, the sexually explicit magazines primarily available at "adults only" pornographic outlets are said to

portray masturbation as well as group, lesbian, gay and transvestite sexual activities. Actual anal and vaginal intercourse as well as fellatio, cunnilingus, and sodomy are also prevalent. There are depictions of rape, incest, bondage and discipline, sadomasochism, urination and defecation, bestiality, and simulated sexual activity with juveniles. Additionally, they cater to every type of paraphilia which has currently been identified.

In this connection, "paraphilias" are defined as psychosexual disorders where

unusual or bizarre imagery or other acts are necessary for sexual excitement. Such imagery or acts tend to be insistently and involuntarily repetitive and generally involve either: (1) preference for use of a nonhuman object of sexual arousal, (2) repetitive sexual activity with humans involving real or simulated suffering or humiliation, or (3) repetitive sexual activity with nonconsenting partners. In other classifications these disorders are referred to as "Sexual Deviations." – American Psychiatric Association, *Diagnostic and Statistical Manual of Mental Disorders* 266 (3d ed. 1983). (ibid.:1403–1404)

But although material catering for those suffering from these psychosexual disorders is said to be available "in significant percentages," there is no way to judge how significant such percentages are because they are not disclosed. Nor is information provided as to the extent of that "significant portion of what is available" which is devoted to the various "conceivable and . . . unconceivable sexual preferences" said to be catered for.*

With regard to the sexual orientation of videotapes and films, the Meese Commission does not provide any detailed report. As to videotapes, the material available in "adults only" outlets offering them is described merely as "for all practical purposes the same as that which would be shown in 'adults only' theaters or peep shows, and the same range of sexual themes and practices is commonly available" (ibid.:284).

On the subject of "the sexually explicit film industry," the commission's report tells little more about the content of the movies than that the sexual activity portrayed "may include sadomasochistic activities, anal sex, group sex, urination and defecation"; and that "the most important part of the movies is considered to be the male ejaculation scene" (ibid.:1371–1373). There is no attempt at classification or systematic analysis of the sexually explicit movie consumer market.

The only consumer group dealt with at any length by the Meese Commission is that devoted to child pornography. "Child pornography," the commission reported, "had become a part of the commercial mainstream of pornography by 1977, sold 'over the counter' and in considerable quantities." The subject of children's involvement in pornography as both consumers and participants is dealt with in Chapter 7 and therefore is not discussed here in detail. However, it should be noted that on the subject of the extent of the consumer demand for this type of material, the Meese Commission seems to have been confused to the point of self-contradiction. At one place child pornography is described as a "highly organized, multi-million dollar" industry that operates "on a nationwide scale." At another it is said to be "difficult to assess the size of this trade" and that while "there is some commercially produced material . . . the

---

* A footnote in the Meese Commission's report referring to the statement about "significant percentages" runs as follows: "Full formal results were not completed at the time of printing of this final report. The Commission, through its archives, will make such information available to persons conducting future research on this subject" (U.S. Department of Justice, 1986:1503 n. 2258). We were informed that the archives were in the care of Alan E. Sears, who had served as the executive director of the commission. A letter to Mr. Sears (July 16, 1987) and a number of phone calls produced no response.

greatest bulk of child pornography is produced by child abusers themselves in largely 'cottage industry' fashion" (ibid.:410, 600).

Collateral activities and impacts

Pornography and prostitution

Webster gives the derivation of pornography as from the Greek *pornographos*, "writing about prostitutes." Etymology, however, is an unreliable guide to meaning here. For whether pornography is identified by its content or by its function, writing about prostitutes is often singularly devoid of pornographic elements. Moreover, much pornographic material is neither in writing nor does it deal with prostitutes.

Pornography and prostitution, however, are both aspects of what is called "commercial sex." The former relates to sexual excitation or arousal and the latter to sexual satisfaction. Both have been seen as offensive activities or services and subjected to criminal prohibition. Moreover, as Joel Feinberg has pointed out, they have both been subject to controls short of criminal prohibition such as residential restrictions applied to "acts of solicitation, places of assignation, houses of prostitution, adult bookstores and sex shops, pornographic movie theaters and the like" (Feinberg, 1985:43).

In a study entitled "The Traffic in Sex-Oriented Materials in Boston" carried out for the Johnson Commission, it was noted that the heaviest concentration of adult bookstores was in and adjacent to the area of downtown Boston known locally as the "Combat Zone," which had achieved notoriety as the place to go for illicit goods and services. "For soldiers and sailors on leave, or tourists and locals attracted to the mock excitement and the dim glitter of the demimonde, the Combat Zone is perceived as 'where the action is' " (U.S. Commission, 1971–72, 4:104). The "action" included, among other borderline and prohibited activities, prostitution.

Similarly, the study of "The San Francisco Erotic Marketplace" also carried out for the Johnson Commission revealed that the Tenderloin, a seventeen-block area on the north side of Market Street that constituted the "red light" district of the city, was the center for both prostitution and pornography outlets. "The Tenderloin, as it is known, is also the center of street prostitution traffic in the city. Male and female prostitutes – the former white, the latter mostly black – can be found without difficulty at any hour of the day or night. . . . And then there are the bookstores and sex film rooms – fourteen of the former and seven of the latter, in addition to two arcades. The majority of bookstores stay open into the early morning (16 hours a day, until 2 AM) while the film rooms close at midnight" (ibid., 4:160).

The Meese Commission also noted that peep shows, "adults only" pornographic theaters, and "adults only" bookstores "are likely to exist in close proximity to areas in which prostitution exists" (U.S. Department of Justice, 1986:386). But the primary focus of that commission was on different kinds of connection between pornography and prostitution; in particular, the relation between use of pornography and prostitution, and that between pornographic modeling or performance and prostitution.

In regard to the former, the commission reported:

Witnesses who testified before the Commission and individuals who submitted statements reported several connections between pornography and prostitution. One such connection was the use of pornography as instructional manuals for prostitutes. For example, a former prostitute testified: One of the very first commonalities we discovered as a group, we were all introduced to prostitutiton through pornography; there were no exceptions in our group, and we were all under eighteen. Pornography was our textbook, we learned the tricks of the trade by men exposing us to pornography and us trying to mimic what we saw. I could not stress enough what a huge influence we feel this was. (ibid.:797–798, 831)

It also reported:

Yet another connection was the use of magazines to stimulate clientele: When I worked at massage studios, the owners had subscriptions to *Playboy, Penthouse, Penthouse Forum*, and the like. These magazines were arranged in the waiting area of most of the massage places which I worked in. If a girl was not inside with a trick, she was expected to sit out front with the men who were waiting or who were undecided and to look at the magazines with them in order to get them titillated. They used the soft porn to help them work up the courage to try the acts described in the magazine with the prostitutes at the massage studio. (ibid.:798, 832)

These witness statements are both quoted twice in the commission's report, in the first place as examples of the physical harm caused by pornography (ibid. 797–798); and in the second place as exemplifying social harm (ibid. 831–832). Under the "Social Harm" heading, the Meese Commission further reported that women

who are or who have been prostitutes identified pornography as a significant factor in prostitution. These individuals reported that pornography was not only used and made of them while engaged in acts of prostitution, but they stated that pornography is used to perpetuate the concept that women are accustomed to being placed in the role of a prostitute: I am speaking for a group of women, we all live in Minneapolis and we all are former prostitutes. All of us feel strongly about the relationship between pornography and prostitution. Many of us wanted to testify at this hearing but we are unable because of the consequences of being identified as a former whore. This is absolutely incredible to me that prostitution is seen as a victimless activity and that many women are rightly terrified of breaking their silence, fearing harassment to themselves and families and loss of their jobs. We have started to meet together to make sense of the abuse we have experienced in prostitution and how pornography endorses and legitimizes that abuse. (ibid.:832–833)

The other connection between pornography and prostitution identified by the Meese Commission related to performers in pornography. The commission's conclusion on this topic was simply that "pornographic modeling" represented "a subset of prostitution" and is worded as follows:

Modeling and Prostitution. It seems abundantly clear from the facts before us that the bulk of commercial pornographic modeling, that is, all performances which include actual sexual intercourse, is quite simply a form of prostitution. So much was directly asserted by representatives of prostitutes' organizations who testified before us, as well as representatives of law enforcement and effectively denied by no one. Every court which has examined the questions from this standpoint has agreed, reasoning that where persons are paid to have sex it is irrelevant that the act is for display to others. (ibid.:889–890)

Other commercial vice

The question of the relationship between pornography and commerce in other kinds of proscribed materials, substances, and services is dealt with in both the Johnson and Meese Commission reports under the heading "Organized Crime." On this topic they reached what the Meese Commission described as "contrary" conclusions. The contrasting nature of these conclusions can best be shown by brief quotation.

The Johnson Commission's Traffic and Distribution Panel report under the heading "Erotica and Organized Crime" said:

Although many persons have alleged that organized crime works hand-in-glove with the distributors of adult materials, there is at present no concrete evidence to support these statements. . . . The hypothesis that organized criminal elements either control or are "moving in" on the distribution of sexually oriented materials will doubtless continue to be speculated upon. The panel finds that there is insufficient evidence at present to warrant any conclusions in this regard. (U.S. Commission, 1970:117–118)

The Meese Commission, under the heading "The Role of Organized Crime," reported:

We have spent a considerable amount of our time attempting to determine whether there is a connection between the pornography industry and what is commonly taken to be "organized crime." After hearing from a large number of witnesses, mostly law enforcement personnel, after reading a number of reports prepared by various law enforcement agencies, and after consulting sources such as trial transcripts, published descriptions, and the like, we believe that such a connection does exist. (U.S. Department of Justice, 1986:291)

The Johnson Commission's conclusion was based principally on two pieces of commission-sponsored research. The first of these was a survey derived from interviews with police and prosecutors in a representative sample of seventeen major U.S. cities. The authors stated that "police and prosecutors reported strong suspicions that there was a relationship between the distributors of adult books and magazines and organized crime [but] they had no concrete evidence." Responses ranged from "it's too big . . . not to be tied to organized crime," to "neither the police nor the prosecutor saw any connection between the problem of obscenity and pornography and organized crime" (U.S. Commission, 1971–72, 5:42, 47, 60).

The second study dealt with the possible relationships between the traffic in sex-oriented materials and organized crime in New York, Los Angeles, Chicago, Boston, and greater San Francisco. A key passage in the study runs:

If our hypothesis is correct, the black market characteristics of the traffic in sex-oriented materials is likely to attract a relatively large number of "criminal types." The extent to which the industry as a whole, or significant components thereof, may be related to *organized crime systems* is, however, a question which is quite distinct. Whatever inferences may be drawn regarding the life styles of participants in this business, it should be recognized that there is no necessary correlation between individual or collective criminality and "organized crime" as it is used herein. If there was, any cooperative effort by two or more individuals to engage in any activity in violation of law could be regarded as an "organized crime" enterprise. Under such a broad definition, it would follow that any combination of persons associated in the traffic in sex-oriented materials of a legally obscene nature would be engaging in an "organized crime" activity. (ibid., 5:67)

The conclusion that the Johnson Commission drew from this study was that there is

some evidence that the retail adult bookstore business which purveys materials that are not only at the periphery of legitimacy but also at the margin of legality, tends to involve individuals who have had considerable arrest records. The business does involve some risk of arrest and, therefore, would be avoided by persons with more concern for legitimacy and general reputation. Therefore, there is a greater likelihood that persons with some background of conflict with the legal system will be found among "adult store" proprietors. This is not the same, however, as being an adjunct or subsidiary of "organized crime." (U.S. Commission, 1970:118)

The Meese Commission acknowledged that "we reach our conclusions in the face of a negative conclusion of the 1970 Commission, and in the face of evidence provided by the FBI." The FBI evidence was obtained from Director William H. Webster of the Federal Bureau of Investigation. "Director Webster surveyed the FBI field offices throughout the country, and reported to us that 'about three quarters of those [fifty-nine] offices indicated that they have no verifiable information that organized crime was involved either directly or through extortion in the manufacture of pornography. Several offices did, however, report some involvement by members and associates of organized crime' " (U.S. Department of Justice, 1986:292).

More than two hundred pages in the Meese Commission's report are devoted to what is described as "the substantial role which organized crime . . . plays in the pornography business in the United States today." There are frequent references to La Cosa Nostra and "the control of organized crime families in the pornography industry" (ibid.:1043, 1050). Moreover, Henry E. Hudson, the chairman of the commission, was convinced that "most elements of the pornography industry [are] directly controlled by La Cosa Nostra, through its members or associates" (ibid.:32).

In fact, what is called the "cumulative evidence" of the involvement of "the Columbo, DeCavalcante, Gambino, and Lucchese 'families' " consists of a loosely articulated aggregation of rumors, allegations, and unconfirmed reports. And in the end the commission was forced to conclude that although there was obviously some degree of organization in "the pornography industry," there was "nothing that would justify saying that these organizations are La Cosa Nostra or are a part of La Cosa Nostra" (ibid.: 295–296).

The commission continued to claim, however, that major parts of the industry were controlled by organized crime. Yet the only attempt made to substantiate that claim proves on examination to be entirely vacuous. Thus the report states:

In particular, there is strong evidence that a great deal of the pornographic film and video tape distribution, and some of the pornographic magazine distribution, is controlled by one Reuben Sturman, operating out of the Cleveland area, but with operations and controlled organizations throughout the country. Although we inevitably must rely on secondary evidence, it appears to us that Sturman's enterprise is highly organized and predominantly devoted to the vertically integrated production, distribution, and sale of materials that would most likely be determined to be legally obscene in most parts of the country. Of this we are certain, and to that extent we could say that significant parts of the pornography industry are controlled by organized crime." (ibid.:294)

But the references to "strong evidence" and "secondary evidence" are quite irrelevant here. For this is not an empirical claim at all. It is simply a matter of definition that any organized business enterprise dealing in legally obscene materials, whether "controlled by one Reuben Sturman" or by anyone else, would "to that extent" represent "organized crime."

In this connection, the 1986 President's Commission on Organized Crime reported that while "organized crime is generally thought to be involved in many more activities such as . . . pornography," it found nothing to support this other than "anecdotal evidence." Moreover, pornography is not included in the commission's table of estimates of criminal income, which lists the eighteen types of crime that are the principal "sources of income for organized crime" (U.S. President's Commission, 1986:455, 460).

Competition with mainstream business

One problem confronting the Johnson Commission was that of drawing a real distinction between different categories of sexually explicit material. For example, in relation to motion pictures it found that

exploitation films (usually known as "skin flicks"), are low-budget films which concentrate on the erotic. Ordinarily, these films are shown only in a limited circuit of theaters and the film titles, though advertised, are not familiar to most people for lack of publicity. Until one or two years ago, the lines of demarcation between these films and general release movies were quite clear. However, the increase of sexually related themes and the incidence of nudity in the latter have blurred many of the former distinctions to a point where there is a considerable overlap. Today, perhaps the chief distinction between some sexually oriented general release films and exploitation films is that the latter (a) are much less expensive to produce (an average cost of $20,000 to $40,000); and (b) are ordinarily exhibited in far fewer theaters (about 5% of all theaters exhibit such films at least on a part-time basis). (U.S. Commission, 1970:9–10)

The commission also noted that with "the recent acceleration in sexual content of films" the movie-rating system provided only

rough guidelines for judging the sexual content of rated films. "R" rated films can contain virtually any theme. Considerable partial nudity is allowed as is a good deal of sexual foreplay. Several "R" films have contained scenes of full female nudity (genitalia). The chief difference between "R" and "X" rated films is the quantity of and quality of the erotic theme, conduct or nudity contained in the film rather than a set of absolutes which automatically classify a film as "R" or "X." (ibid.:8–9)

The Johnson Commission encountered similar demarcation problems in relation to magazines and books. "The wide range of periodicals makes it difficult to distinguish which publication should be classified as sexually oriented." Moreover, even after some kind of classification was achieved (e.g., "confession" magazines, "barber shop" magazines, and "men's sophisticates") there remained "a special group of sex-oriented mass market magazines which do not adequately fit any of the above classifications. Preeminent among these is *Playboy*" with its "photographs of feminine pubic hairs" and "articles and fiction [containing] a significant degree of sexual orientation" (ibid.:13–14).

In regard to books, the commission distinguished mass-market books from "adults only" books. But it found that "there is an overlap of sexually oriented materials between the mass and the 'adult' markets." Nor could "pornographers" be distinguished from other publishers because some publishers produced materials for both markets. In 1968 two of the top ten best-selling fiction titles were "sexy books" and in 1969 six of the top ten best sellers were "sexually oriented" (ibid.:15).

By the time the Meese Commission was established, this problem had intensified. "More than in 1957," said the commission's report, when the law of obscenity became inextricably a part of constitutional law, more than in 1970, when the President's Commission on Obscenity and Pornography issued its reports, and indeed more than just a year ago in 1985, we live in a society unquestionably pervaded by sexual explicitness. In virtually every medium, from books to magazines to newspapers to music to radio to network television to cable television, matters relating to sex are discussed, described, and depicted with a frankness and an explicitness of detail that has accelerated dramatically within a comparatively short period of time.

The commission found that the pervasiveness of sexual explicitness in society had greatly increased the difficulty in "distinguishing what might plausibly be characterized as 'pornographic' from the entire range of descriptions, depictions and discussions that are more sexually explicit than would have been the case in earlier times" (U.S. Department of Justice, 1986:277–278). Moreover, there was no general agreement as to what distinctions might be drawn or how they might be applied.

Thus, when it considered sexually explicit magazines the closest the Meese Commission came to classification was to obtain "frequency counts" of the advertising, editorial, and pictorial content of twelve of the most widely circulated of them. This produced such findings as that editorial content "varied from being totally or almost totally sex-oriented (*Club International* had one hundred percent sex-oriented content, followed by *Cheri* with ninety-four percent, *Club* with ninety-three percent, and *High Society* with ninety-one percent), to having a greater proportion of general interest topics (sixty-seven percent in *Playboy* and sixty percent in *Penthouse* were on non-sex-related topics)" (ibid.:1400–1401). No indication was given in the report either of the purpose of this exercise or of the significance to be attached to its findings.

When it came to consider videotape cassettes the commission again encountered problems with classification. Thus, as mentioned earlier in this chapter, it found that "*most* of the sexually violent material that the Commission found to be the most harmful form of sexually explicit material" was not classified by the industry as "adult" but included in such categories as "Action–Adventure," "Science Fiction," "Horror," and even "Music Video" (ibid.:1389; emphasis added).

What the Meese Commission seems not to have clearly recognized was that the distinction it drew between "the pornography industry" and the mainstream entertainment business did not reflect reality. It noted that "the major sexually explicit film distributors have rapidly entered the national video tape market" and that "at least twelve thousand of the over twenty thousand general video retail outlets across the United States distribute sexually explicit video tapes" (ibid.:1392, 1394).

It noted also that " 'Adults Only' pornographic outlets are by no means the exclusive retailers of sexually explicit materials in the United States. Sexually explicit magazines rely heavily on single issue sales in convenience stores and general bookstores and newsstands across the country. Some of the mainstream stores now also sell 'X' rated video tapes. Sexually explicit magazines and tabloids are also sold at newsstands. Newsstands often place these magazines in racks alongside non-sexually explicit magazines. . . . Vending machines are also used as a retail outlet for sexually explicit tabloids" (ibid.:1487).

But the commission had nothing to say about the nature or significance of these developments. It reported without comment the Counsel for the Adult Film Association's prediction that the "adults only" pornographic theater business would be "virtually nonexistent by 1990" (ibid.:1386). It did not seem to notice that with "as many as half of all general video retailers in the country" offering material that "would commonly be conceded to be pornographic" (U.S. Department of Justice, 1986:288), the marketing of sexually explicit videotapes was no longer primarily in the hands of "pornographic outlets" but rather carried on by mainstream video-rental agencies. Despite all the evidence, preoccupied with exposing "the true pornography industry" (ibid.:284), the most significant development of all, the institutionalization of the trade in sexually explicit material as legitimate business, went unremarked.

Also ignored was a collateral feature of this development. In its chapter entitled "The Role of Private Action," the commission states that "for citizens to protest in the vicinity of a pornography outlet is fully within the free speech traditions of this country" and says that if people feel that businesses are behaving improperly it is the citizens' "right and their obligation to make those views known" (ibid.:422). It fails to note, however, something of considerable significance in that context: that as the trade moved out of pornography outlets and into mainstream stores it became much more susceptible to boycott and more vulnerable to citizen pressure and protest.

Recent trends

One of the most striking features of both of the commissions' reports we have been considering is the absence from their policy analyses of detailed discussion of recent trends or of where the course of events might be leading. Yet any scheme envisioned for prospective regulation should be founded in some baseline conception of what the future would look like if the laws were not changed.

The Johnson Commission noted briefly such things as "a declining concern with established religions" and "conflicts regarding the responsibility of the state to the individual and the individual to the state" that, it said, "may all be considered to represent changes in the moral fiber of the nation." "To some," it said, "these phenomena are considered to be signs of corroding moral decay; to others, signals of change and progress" (U.S. Commission, 1970:3–4). What these phenomena meant to the Johnson Commission was not revealed.

The Meese Commission was no more specific. "Little in modern life," it observed, "can be held constant. . . . The world changes, research about the world changes, and our views about how we wish to deal with that world change. . . . As we in 1986 reexamine what was done in 1970, so too do we expect that in 2002 our work will similarly be reexamined" (U.S. Department of Justice, 1986:226–227). But apart from the suggestion that it envisioned national commissions on pornography recurring at sixteen-year intervals, the Meese Commission refrained from speculation about the future.

No less important for responsible policymaking than a conception of what the future might hold, absent governmental intervention, is an assessment of the impact of any measures of regulation or deregulation proposed, on the nature and extent of pornographic communication. This is not to require that commissioners be skilled in the practice of divination, but simply that policy proposals should be framed in the light of some estimate of their probable effects. Yet in neither case did the commissions have anything to say about the likely consequences of the adoption of their recommendations or about the role of pornographic communication in the social order of the proximate future.

What are the key trends? What do they bode for the future? The most important change of the last two decades is the integration of sexually explicit communications into the mainstream of the American communications industry. For over the period from 1965 to 1985, all the major forms of pornographic communication became available in the United States through mainstream channels of commerce. The sex magazine became a specialty market of its own, staking out a substantial niche of the corner newsstand rather than the adult bookstore or the under-the-counter mail-order market. Heterosexual and homosexual materials that would have been considered hard-core pornography in 1965 were available in mainstream bookstores and newsstands by 1975.

The career of sexually explicit motion pictures has been more varied. From the mid-1960s onward, the sexual content of general release films increased dramatically, so that what was shown only in sexual exploitation films of the early 1960s was available in the R- and X-rated general release films of the early 1970s. Meanwhile, sexual exploitation films for public advertisement and theatrical release became even more explicit, leaving very little in the nature of heterosexual activity that was unavailable in sex films for theatrical release and therefore the special province of the 16mm and 8mm so-called stag movie markets. Finally, the development of the videocassette recorder and the sale and rental of videocassette films have provided overwhelming competition to theatrical displays of sexually explicit motion pictures. The pornographic movie house is an endangered species. The public peep show does not prove an irresistible attraction for the man who can easily acquire a private edition.

The distribution of sexually explicit communication, including a substantial amount of pornography, is thus increasingly a function of the economic mainstream in the United States. *Penthouse* is sold at the local newsstand and at the local convenience store. Every small city has a videocassette rental shop that offers its customers *Debbie Does Dallas* as well as exposure to *Back to the Future* and Disney classics.

The social correlates and implications for social control of these trends have not been seriously studied. As the distribution of pornography has become a mainstream economic activity, pornography is no longer a distinct subunit of the economy.

However, the producers of pornographic motion pictures and books have not yet become integrated with the larger economy. Even sex magazines have not diversified into other extensive mass-market publication ventures or been acquired by general interest publishing conglomerates.

But the economic isolation of pornography in the United States was mainly evident in its production by 1985. And the use of mainstream economic institutions for the distribution of pornographic materials increases the sensitivity of the distributors of the sexually explicit to the sentiments and tastes not only of those who might buy sexually explicit material but also of consumers generally. The corner sex store is not vulnerable to a consumer boycott by individuals who would in no event ever be purchasing its wares. But the corner 7-Eleven store will worry out loud about the people who ordinarily purchase its cigarettes and soft drinks but who might take their business down the street because of the availability of sexually explicit publications on the 7-Eleven premises.

The past two decades have witnessed not just increasing availability of sexually explicit films, books, and periodicals, but also a change in the focus of pornographic communication. Twenty years ago, pornographic books and magazines were always available for home consumption but were relatively expensive and usually viewed and purchased at a sex shop. Sexually explicit magazines are now widely sold by mail subscription as well as distributed at mainstream newsstands. The availability of rental videocassettes has made the American middle-class living room into a theater of the sexually explicit.

The increasing focus of the home as the arena for sexually explicit communication has a number of further social consequences. Widespread home possession and use of sexually explicit communication might lead to an increased trend toward individuals viewing such materials with other family members. Thus, there may be an increase in shared viewing of videocassettes by adult males and females.

There is almost certainly increased availability of any pornographic materials maintained in home settings to the children who live in that home and their friends. Under these circumstances, the existence of available pornography in one out of seven or one out of ten middle-class homes might make it available to more than half of all adolescents interested in seeing such films. And the relative ease with which rented videocassette materials may be copied is a particular problem here, where it is not all two hours of a theatrical movie that concern an adolescent population but only ten minutes of the "good parts," and where audience standards for picture quality and sound are not high.

As the distribution of heterosexual pornography has been moved into the economic mainstream, there is some dispute about the residual roles of sex shops. The sex shop may have become a residual sexual theater for the homeless, the poor, and the embarrassed middle-class citizen who does not wish family members to know of this aspect of his life. There is also some evidence of increasing specialization in the production of pornography in the 1970s and the emphasis of these specialty materials in sex shops. This is one way in which specialty sex shops might be expected to respond to mainstream competition, but we cannot make confident judgments on the extent of this trend from the random and disorganized documentation provided by the Meese Commission.

Of all the manifold contributors to the social changes surrounding pornography, one deserved special mention. The changing patterns in the distribution of pornography in the United States resemble the classic scenario of middle-stage decriminalization. The social changes that took place between the 1965 and 1975 were in part a reaction by the public to the withdrawal of the threat of criminal prosecution for possession and purchase of sexually explicit books and from magazines, photographs, and motion pictures.

This partial decriminalization has influenced not simply the availability of materials but also channels of distribution and, to a lesser extent, social patterns of use. Our impression, however, is that the social patterns of decriminalization have not been played out to an end state because the production of pornographic pictures, tapes, and movies has not been effectively decriminalized. Although the distribution of pornography has changed in many ways that are symptomatic of decriminalization, the production of pornography has not yet followed suit. Only the sexually explicit magazines have producers in the economic mainstream. Pornographic films and tapes are still made only by old-style pornographers.

The changes in the nature of pornography that might come with competition in production might in turn have further impact on who would consume the new pornography and in what social settings. Thus, the current circumstances in the United States should not be taken to indicate end-stage decriminalization and its social and economic products. Partial decriminalization has produced wide availability but restricted choice. If the production of pornographic films is effectively decriminalized, we can expect new producers and perhaps new kinds of pornography.

4

Pornographic communication and social harm: a review of the reviews

The issue broadly stated is: What are the effects of pornographic communications on their audiences? But that is far too general a question, for the issues multiply when the questions become specific.

The kinds of audiences to be considered in assessing effects vary widely in many characteristics and almost certainly in regard to their responses to pornographic communication. Moreover, the kinds of effects that have been suggested are equally variable. Does pornography induce forcible rape? Does it provoke masturbation? And in addition to possible immediate behavioral consequences of pornographic communication, what about effects on attitudes and long-range behavior tendencies? As we shall see, the spectrum of possible effects discussed in the policy literature goes from extreme sexual violence to rather trivial shifts in attitude-questionnaire responses.

Two preliminary points need to be made before we commence analysis of research into the effects of pornographic communication and the conclusions drawn from it by pornography commissions. First, it would be utterly astounding if pornographic communication, a medium-sized industry in the Western world, had no impact at all on its audience. The billions of dollars expended on pornographic materials by willing consumers testify to the capacity of such material to have some effect on human states of consciousness. The question is thus not whether such materials have any effects but whether they have certain specific effects and what value, positive or negative, we associate with the occurrence of those specific effects.

The second reason why specificity is required in discussion of the impact of pornographic communication relates to the methodology and limitations of empirical social science. Different forms of pornographic communication, different audiences, and different attitudinal and behavioral characteristics of those audiences must be studied one or two at a time. This sort of incremental process of investigation provides a fragile basis for the kind of sweeping generalizations frequently advanced as social science in debates about pornography.

There are two senses in which analysis of the effects of pornographic

74

Table 4.1. *Behavioral effects: sex crime*

Johnson Commission	"In sum empirical research designed to clarify the question has found no evidence to date that exposure to explicit sexual materials plays a significant role in the causation of delinquent or criminal behavior among youth or adults. The Commission cannot conclude that exposure to erotic materials is a factor in the causation of sex crimes or sex delinquency." (U.S. Commission, 1970:27)
Williams Committee	"It is not possible, in our view, to reach well-based conclusions about what in this country has been the influence of pornography on sexual crime." (Home Office, 1979:80)
Meese Commission	"We have reached the conclusion, unanimously and confidently, that the available evidence strongly supports the hypothesis that substantial exposure to sexually violent materials as described here bear a causal relationship to antisocial acts of sexual violence, and for some subgroups possible to unlawful acts of sexual violence." (U.S. Department of Justice, 1986:326)

communication is crucial to the determination of what government might do to regulate it. First, the high value placed on freedom of expression throughout the West places a presumption against regulation in the way of any regulatory scheme. Both the freedom to speak and freedom to hear can be seen as of primary importance in this context. The First Amendment of the Constitution of the United States which provides that "Congress shall make no law . . . abridging the freedom of speech, or the press" is just one embodiment of a larger tradition of liberty that demands some indication of harmful effects – and thus inquiry into impact on behavior – before special regulation would be considered.

There is a second reason why investigation of the behavioral effects of pornographic communication is required. By definition, at least by the definition adopted here, pornography is oriented toward the stimulation of sexual arousal. To analyze its impact on conduct is thus especially appropriate, just as analogously we might wish to investigate the impact of political commercials on voting behavior or advertisements for food on the purchase and consumption of foodstuffs. Indeed, it would be absurd, having defined pornography in terms of its intent to arouse sexually, to fail to investigate its impact on behavior.

The question of harm: no, maybe, and yes

A comparison of the three commissions' reports on the issue of whether pornography causes palpable social harm reveals sharply contrasting postures in both approach and conclusion, as shown in Table 4.1.

The Johnson Commission's evidential basis for reaching conclusions about harm was a series of commissioned psychological and sociological studies and a review of the available research. It came close to summarizing the available evidence as proof of a negative relationship between pornography and sex crime. The Williams Committee, by contrast, took an aggressively agnostic stance that was used to support many if not all of the same policy conclusions as the Johnson Commission without, however, relying on or endorsing the quality of the research.

In fact, on the question of the weight to be placed on existing research the sharpest contrast on one dimension is between the Johnson Commission and the Williams Committee rather than between the Johnson Commission and the Meese Commission. The Meese Commission, relying on a mixture of empirical studies and its own reading of softer empirical data, concluded that what it categorized as a particular subset of pornographic material – sexually violent material – probably caused sex crime. Only the Williams Committee rejected any confident conclusions from existing studies.

Two further points merit mention before examining the reports individually. First, it is important to note that these three efforts did not produce *two* directly opposed conclusions but rather *three* different approaches. It is not simply a matter of different preferences on the ultimate question of censorship predetermining conclusions on the available evidence. Both the Johnson Commission and the Williams Committee favored the unrestricted availability of most pornography for adults, but their treatment of, and reliance on, social science research and field experimental method was quite distinct.

Second, it would be a mistake to review these three clearly distinguishable approaches with a view to determining which was correct. Each assessment has significant weaknesses, which we discuss later in the chapter. In these matters, there are many different ways of making a mistake.

Nevertheless, with such sharp differences in the conclusions reached we should ask whether the evidentiary base assessed at the three different points in time – 1968–70, 1977–79, and 1985–86 – was significantly different. Our own answer to this question is that it was not. Although many more studies were available to the Meese Commission than to the Johnson Commission fifteen years earlier, the principal differences between those commissions relate not to the nature and extent of the evidence but to how the evidence was evaluated and weighed.

No new statistical studies of either the incidence of sex crimes in population areas or the behavior of sex offenders led to the Meese Commission's rejection of the Johnson Commission's conclusions. The new laboratory studies produced between 1970 and 1985 measured attitudes and the willingness to engage in behavior far removed from sex crime. The anecdotal evidence cited by the Meese Commission in 1986 was in abundant supply when the two earlier bodies took evidence.

The contrasting conclusions of the three commissions provide a remarkable instance of the role of social science in the formulation of public policy. Indeed, we have found no more striking example of the drawing of contrary conclusions from the evidence provided by social science research in any area of modern policy debate. We shall now examine how each commission reached its particular conclusion, before returning to a critique of the inferences they drew. Their respective findings are shown in Tables 4.2 and 4.3.

The Johnson Commission

The conclusion of the Johnson Commission regarding the effects of obscenity or pornography in relation to delinquent or criminal behavior was that in sum, "empirical research designed to clarify the question has found no evidence to date that exposure to explicit sexual materials plays a significant role in the causation of delinquent or criminal behavior among youth or adults. The Commission cannot conclude that exposure to erotic materials is a factor in the causation of sex crimes or sex delinquency" (U.S. Commission, 1970:27). This conclusion and the way in which it was reached met with widespread criticism.

The Johnson Commission in statements of this kind and in its endorsement of the consultant and panel reports has been widely read as concluding that "exposure to erotic materials is" *not* "a factor in the causation of sex crimes or sex delinquency." Their report does go beyond the "not proven" posture of the Williams Committee by placing heavy emphasis on the lack of relationship reported in the various studies made and by citing that research with approval.

Yet in a strict sense there is no allegation in the Johnson Commission report that the negative proposition had been proved or was relied on to support the commissions' recommendations. Why, then, was the Johnson Commission regarded by observers, rightly in our view, as implying that there was strong evidence against a causal relation between pornography and sex crime, whereas the Williams Committee escaped this categorization, even while advocating similar social policy based on its conclusions about social harm?

The difference, we believe, reflects the contrast between a lawyer's manipulation of presumptions to determine an outcome and the social scientist's attempt to marshal empirical evidence in support of a policy argument. The Williams Committee put distance between its policy conclusions and the social science data. The Johnson Commission, more committed to the value of the research, gave the impression that it was relying on research evidence.

Table 4.2. *Behavior finding*

	Benign effects	Rape	Aggression	Perversion
Johnson Commission	"Two studies found that a substantial number of married couples reported more agreeable and enhanced marital communication and an increased willingness to discuss sexual matters with each other after exposure to erotic stimuli." (U.S. Commission, 1970:25)	"The Commission cannot conclude that exposure to erotic materials is a factor in the causation of sex crimes." (U.S. Commission, 1970:27)		"In general, established patterns of sexual behavior were found to be very stable and not altered substantially by exposure to erotica." (U.S. Commission, 1970:25)
Williams Committee	"We also received evidence of how pornography had been of help in enabling married couples to overcome their sexual problems: . . . More generally . . . such material is also used in the clinical treatment of sexual dysfunction." (Home Office, 1979:88)	"We unhesitatingly reject the suggestion that the available statistical information for England and Wales lends any support at all to the argument that pornography acts as a stimulus to the commission of sexual violence." (Home Office, 1979:80)	"We consider that the only objective verdict must be one of 'not proven.'" (Home Office, 1979:68)	"All evidence points to the fact that material dealing with bizarre or perverted sexual activity appeals only to those with a pre-existing interest established by the experiences of early life . . . there is no evidence that exposure to such materials inculcates a taste for it." (Home Office, 1979:86–87)

Meese
Commission

"If we take the entire potential rate of 'effects' which could occur as a result of exposure to sexually explicit materials, and if we take the commission of sex offenses to be one extreme of that continuum, then the other end might be represented by beneficial effects. Many have made an argument for such benefits. Public opinion data both in 1970 and 1985 show that a majority believe use of sexually explicit materials 'provide entertainment,' relieve people of the impulse to commit crimes, and improve marital relations. . . . There are also two areas in which sexually explicit materials have been used for positive ends: the treatment of sexual dysfunctions and the diagnosis and treatment of some paraphilias." (U.S. Department of Justice, 1986:1028)

"We have reached the conclusion, unanimously and confidently, that the available evidence strongly supports the hypothesis that substantial exposure to sexually violent materials as described here bears a causal relationship to antisocial sets of sexual violence and, for some subgroups, possibly to unlawful acts of sexual violence." (U.S. Department of Justice, 1986:326)

"In both clinical and experimental settings, exposure to sexually violent materials has indicated an increase in the likelihood of aggression. More specifically the research which is described in much detail later in this Report, shows a causal relationship between exposure to material of this type and aggressive behavior towards women." (U.S. Department of Justice, 1986:324)

"It would be strange indeed if graphic representations of a form of behavior, especially in a form that almost exclusively portrays behavior as desirable, did not have at least some effect on patterns of behavior." (U.S. Department of Justice, 1986:326)

Table 4.3. *Attitude*

	Toward women	Toward rape	Other
Johnson Commission	"One presumed consequence . . . is that erotica transmits an inaccurate and uninformed conception of sexuality, and that the viewer or user will (a) develop a calloused and manipulative orientation toward women and (b) engage in behavior in which affection and sexuality are not well integrated. A recent survey shows that 41% of American males and 46% of females believe that 'sexual materials lead people to lose respect for women.' . . . Recent experiments . . . suggest that such fears are probably unwarranted." (U.S. Commission, 1970:201)		"Exposure to erotic stimuli appears to have little or no effect on already established attitudinal commitments regarding either sexuality or sexual morality." (U.S. Commission, 1970:26)
Williams Committee	"Many of our women correspondents wanted the law to be invoked against the degradation of women in pornography; but the consensus of those parts of the women's movement from which we heard tended to attach greater importance to freedom of expression than to the need to suppress pornography." (Home Office, 1979:88)		"From everything we know of social attitudes, and have learnt in the course of our enquiries, our belief can only be that the role of pornography in influencing the state of society is a minor one. To think anything else, and in particular to regard pornography as having a crucial or even a significant effect on essential social values, is to get the problem of pornography out of proportion." (Home Office, 1979:95)

Meese Commission

"To the extent that these materials create or reinforce the view that women's function is disproportionately to satisfy the sexual needs of men, then the materials will have pervasive effects on the treatment of women in society. . . . We obviously cannot here explore fully all the forms in which women are discriminated against in contemporary society. Nor can we explore all the causes. . . . But we feel confident in concluding that the view of women as available for sexual domination is one cause of that discrimination." (U.S. Department of Justice, 1986:334)

"The evidence is also strongly supportive of significant attitudinal changes on the part of those with substantial exposures to violent pornography. These attitudinal changes are numerous. Victims of rape and other forms of sexual violence are likely to be perceived by people so exposed as more responsible for the assault, as having suffered less injury, and as having been less degraded as a result of the experience. Similarly, people with a substantial exposure to violent pornography are likely to see the rapist or other sexual offender as less responsible for the act and as deserving of less stringent punishment." (U.S. Department of Justice, 1986:326–327)

"These attitudinal changes have been shown experimentally to include a larger range of attitudes than those just discussed. The evidence also strongly supports the conclusion that substantial exposure to violent sexually explicit material leads to a greater acceptance of the 'rape myth' in its broader sense – that women enjoy being coerced into sexual activity, that they enjoy being physically hurt in a sexual context, and that as a result a man who forces himself on a women sexually is in fact merely acceding to the 'real' wishes of the woman, regardless of the extent to which she seems to be resisting. The myth is that a woman who says 'no' really means 'yes,' and that men are justified in acting on the assumption that the 'no' answer is indeed the 'yes' answer. We have little trouble concluding that this attitude is both pervasive and profoundly harmful, and that any stimulus reinforcing or increasing the incidence of this attitude is for that reason alone properly designated as harmful." (U.S. Department of Justice, 1986:327)

The Johnson Commission reviewed the evidence on the question of effects from a great variety of sources, including survey research among youths and adults, psychological studies of normal and criminal sex-offender adults and normal and delinquent adolescents, and studies based on crime statistics.

With very few exceptions, the evidence discussed at length by the Johnson Commission and the research conducted under its auspices focused on the relatively immediate physiological, psychological, and behavioral impact of pornographic communication. Both the immediate and long-term impact of such communication on sexual attitudes and sexual practices are notably absent from the Johnson Commission's research emphasis, although some survey responses concerned these topics; the question of the impact of pornographic communication on attitudes toward women and toward fraud and force in sexual behavior was not emphasized. Only one study was reported on the relationship between exposure to pornography and willingness to use ethically marginal seduction techniques such as alcohol and verbal manipulation. This study was interpreted as suggesting that exposure to pornography had a mild suppressive effect on the approval of the use of those techniques by those disposed to use them (U.S. Commission, 1970:201).

In a review of the Johnson Commission's report, Professor Herbert L. Packer wrote, "the most controversial portion of the Commission's Report is unquestionably the Panel Report on the 'Impact of Erotica.' " He criticized the commission for "relying so heavily and so misguidedly on the behavioral sciences," at the same time acknowledging "my bias that research is the opiate of behavioral scientists" (Packer, 1971:74, 76).

Professor Packer was not alone in being critical of the panel report. Indeed, the commission's report itself includes, in a dissenting statement by two commissioners (Morton A. Hill and Winfrey C. Link), a lengthy "Critique of Commission Behavioral Research" and an evaluation by Dr. Victor B. Cline ("University of Utah psychologist and specialist in social science research methodology and statistics"), who reported that "the empirical research studies . . . reveal of great number of serious flaws, omissions, and grave shortcomings" (U.S. Commission, 1970:390).

Much of the criticism the report provoked was directed at what was called "the Commission's exclusive reliance upon statistical and 'behavioral science' techniques of analysis [and] the implicit claims that the Commission has made for the primacy of its behaviorist methodology over other ways of thinking about social problems and legal principles" (Clor, 1971:65, 76). Even James Q. Wilson, who judged that the research carried out "within the limited framework of each study, was on the whole quite unexceptionable," argued that "the weakness of the Obscenity Commission is that it relied too exclusively on social science research" (Wilson, 1971:61).

In his critique Professor Packer noted, in relation to the Effects Panel, that "of the six members of this Panel only one (Dean Lockhart, sitting *ex officio*) was not a behavioral scientist" (Packer, 1971:74). This was correct: the panel chairman, Otto N. Larsen, was professor of sociology at the University of Washington; G. William Jones taught communications at Southern Methodist University; Joseph T. Klapper was director of social research for CBS; Morris A. Lipton was teaching psychiatry and was director of research development at the University of South Carolina; and Marvin Wolfgang was director of the Center for Criminological Research at the University of Pennsylvania.

But this is hardly surprising. It may be true that contemporary social and behavioral science is subject to many "conceptual and methodological limitations" (Johnson, 1971:199), and that some questions about some of the effects of erotic materials may not be researchable. Yet it seems not unreasonable that a panel assigned to study social effects, in particular the causal relationship of such materials to antisocial behavior, should be composed of social and behavioral scientists.

Some of the considerable critical comment generated by this aspect of the Commission's work does not meet the "hope and expectation [for] careful appraisal of public policy in this emotionally charged area" expressed by the commission's chairman, William B. Lockhart (Boyd, 1970:453). A great deal of it seems to have been animated by the same spirit that led Billy Graham to declare the commission's report to be "one of the worst and most diabolical ever made by a presidential commission" and one that "no Christian or believing Jew could support" (Geyer, 1970:1339). Indeed, the dissenting statement filed by the sole appointee of President Nixon to the commission, which is included in the report, was accurately characterized by James Q. Wilson as "an intemperate unpleasantly *ad hominem* screed in which interesting and perhaps important objections are frequently obscured by a ranting tone" (Wilson, 1971:54).

The nature of the more serious criticism directed at the research conducted by the panel into the effects of exposure to erotic material was ably summarized by Professor Weldon T. Johnson, who was senior author of the panel's report, as follows: "Three issues have emerged. It has been argued that: a) the investigation of effects is irrelevant to dealing with the pornography problem; b) the actual effects of exposure to erotic materials are not measurable within the framework of social science research; and c) the effects, particularly the presumed pernicious effects, are obvious but have not been recognized generally or in the Report" (Johnson, 1971:195). With regard to the first of these issues it seems unnecessary to add to Professor Johnson's own response. He points out that when the commission was established it was *instructed* to undertake "a thorough study which shall include a study of the causal relationship of such materials to antisocial behavior" (ibid.:195). He adds, moreover, that not only was the commission directed specifically to work in the area but also a commission-funded national survey found the question of the effect of erotic materials was "an important one in determining public attitudes" and "of general social concern" (ibid.:197–198).

On the question of measurability of the effects of exposure to erotic materials and the various methodological criticisms of the commission's research program, it is hard to improve on the statement of a member of the Effects Panel, Joseph T. Klapper, which is included in the commission's report:

As a professional researcher in the behavioral sciences, I have long been aware that research answers complex questions only by a series of approximations. The pioneering research which the Commission has been able to accomplish in a two-year period is not and could not be either complete or flawless, not indeed could it have been so if five years had been available. The strengths and limitations of the research bearing on effects are stated at length in the Report of the Effects Panel. Given these imperfections the research is nevertheless remarkably consistent, and it does not establish a meaningful causal relationship between exposure to erotica and antisocial behavior. (U.S. Commission, 1970:373)

In a similar vein is the statement by the two psychiatrist members of the commission, Professor Morris A. Lipton and Dr. Edward D. Greenwood, one of whom (Lipton) was a member of the Effects Panel:

All research, and especially research in the behavioral sciences, initially produces imperfect results. . . . We would have welcomed evidence relating exposure to erotica to delinquency, crime, and antisocial behavior, for if such evidence existed we might have a simple solution to some of our most urgent problems. However, the work of the Commission has failed to uncover such evidence. Although the many and varied studies contracted for by the Commission may have flaws, they are remarkably uniform in the direction to which they point. This direction fails to establish a meaningful causal relationship or even significant correlation between exposure to erotica and immediate or delayed antisocial behavior among adults. To assert the contrary from the available evidence is not only to deny the facts, but also to delude the public by offering a spurious and simplistic answer to highly complex problems. (ibid.:380)

The strengths and limitations of the commission's research bearing on effects are, as Joseph Klapper pointed out, "stated at length in the Report of the Effects Panel." Moreover, although a number of reviews of the state of knowledge regarding the effects of pornography or sexually explicit material reflected in the scientific literature have been carried out since 1970, it remains true, as Maurice Yaffe pointed out in a review carried out for the Williams Committee, that "there does not appear to be any strong evidence that exposure to sexually explicit material triggers off antisocial sexual behavior" (Yaffe, 1978:242).

The verdict of the Williams Committee on the studies undertaken for the Johnson Commission is relevant:

We noted that the American commission, in the light of all the studies undertaken for it, concluded that "empirical research has found no evidence to date that exposure to explicit sexual materials plays a significant role in the causation of delinquent or criminal behavior among youth or adults"; we noted also that this conclusion was criticized in a number of quarters as having been based on a partial examination of the evidence in which ambiguities and certain contraindications were ignored. Without ourselves entering into the controversy about the Commission's methods, we make the comment that the effect of reexamining the original studies in the light of a hostile critique of the Commission's conclusions, such as that put forward principally by Professor Victor Cline, is simply to make one adopt rather more caution in drawing inferences from the studies undertaken. (Home Office, 1979:66)

With regard to the criticism that the presumed pernicious effects were obvious but not recognized in the report because of its orientation toward behavioral science research, it is true that this was the established research orientation of at least six commissioners. But the senior author of the Effects Panel report seems to have had few illusions about the limitations on the utility of behavioral science research in policymaking. He claimed no more than that "behavioral science can contribute to *some* of the issues raised by the concern about pornography, and that potential contribution probably is in the clarification of logical and empirical assumptions underlying various policy strategies" (Johnson, 1971:217).

We would add here what can be called a conditional critique of the Johnson Commission's summary of the evidence, a critique that only applies forcefully if the commission's report is read as asserting that there is strong evidence against the proposition that pornography causes socially harmful behavior. Viewed in that light, the psychological experiments can be faulted on a number of grounds and the crude statistical time series studies on criminal statistics are of limited probative value.

The psychological experiments are early research, and although some of the studies reported in volumes 7 and 8 of the commission's technical reports are impressive, it is also the case that the number of studies, the range of groups, and the variety of types of communication studied are inadequate to sustain sweeping generalization. Frequently the research approach is applied to only one group without replication on another similar group or tests on differently constituted groups. Often only two groups, adults and younger persons, are the subject of experiments rather than special high-risk groups. No psychological experiments, as opposed to questionnaires, seem to have been employed with sex offenders in the commission's research.

A second problem with psychological research among normal populations is the insensitivity of such experiments to changes in low-incidence behavior. A study, such as the commission reports, of the impact of pornography on slightly fewer than two hundred people can statistically measure the impact of the stimulus only on the frequency of activities involving a substantial number of the audience. One can discover how many subjects are sexually aroused; how many of the sexually active had intercourse (if rates of sexual activity are high enough); and how many of the subjects masturbate (if the rate of that activity is high enough). But with respect to forcible rape, incest, or any other sexual practice of low statistical frequency among normal populations, a doubling or trebling of a very low rate of deviation is likely to be invisible.

A third problem with the research review of the Johnson Commission as proof of the negative of the harm hypothesis is the failure to examine separately the impact of all of the widely different types of pornography. Pornographic communications differ along a variety of dimensions: homosexual or heterosexual, the presence or absence of sadistic or masochistic themes, or material involving adults or children. Pornographic communications also vary in regard to additional affective content that does not strictly relate to sexual orientation: for example, and this is considered a crucial influence by the Meese Commission, heterosexual pornography can combine elements of force or violence. And the media of pornographic communication vary from the written word to the large screen. Finally, the contexts in which pornographic communication is projected and received may vary widely.

Of special significance in assessing the impact of pornography on the young is the nature of the peer group context in which pornography is usually consumed. This is a special case of the problem of external validity of sufficient importance to merit special mention in any commission report. Moreover, experimental interventions of the kind described in the Johnson Commission report do not provide opportunities to study the interactive effects of pornographic stimuli with other psychoactive stimuli – for instance, the combination of pornography with alcohol, or with deviant peer group pressure, or with both. It is not simply the inhibitions that are introduced by the observational apparatus of the experiment but also the way in which the experimental environment simplifies and distorts social realities that is troublesome in this context.

With such variation, a general conclusion of noneffect cannot be established on the basis of even one hundred experimental interventions unless variations in the character of the appeal, the medium of communication, and the context in which the message is received can be disregarded as being unimportant. The Johnson Commission did not assert that these differences were unimportant.

The manipulation of aggregate crime statistics at the national level presents its own set of formidable barriers to inferences about the effects of pornography on sex crime. With respect to national aggregates – for example, the United States as a unit, or England and Wales – there are problems, both in measuring variations in the availability of pornography and in controlling for all the other changes that may occur with the passage of time, that may affect the incidence of crime. If sex crimes and street robbery both increase by

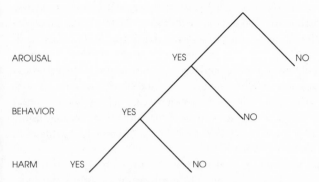

Figure 4.1. A model of the impact of pornography.

similar amounts as pornography becomes more freely available, does this mean that pornography cannot be the cause of the increase in sex crimes? Or does it indicate that the increased availability of pornography along with other factors caused the increase in both types of offenses? Even the Danish studies, which are more specific as to time and more carefully controlled as to other factors, represent a relatively crude method of measuring the short-term impact of sharp changes in the availability of pornography.

All these considerations may not be strictly relevant to the conclusions actually drawn by the U.S. Commission on Obscenity and Pornography. But we highlight these problems in our discussion of the work of this first commission to indicate the problems encountered in regard to the work of each of the commissions considered here.

Moreover, there is one other respect in which the analysis of the Johnson Commission report provides a quite useful introduction to the assessment of the work of the subsequent commissions. As we read the report of the Johnson Commission's Effects Panel it appears that the commission adopted a single model for the relationship between pornographic communication and behavior that can be regarded as socially harmful.

Figure 4.1 is our attempt to depict the principal model for behavior effect investigated by the Johnson Commission. In this model, pornographic communication either produces a state of sexual arousal in the subject or it does not. If the subject does not experience sexual arousal the inquiry about pornography causing harm to the subject has concluded. If the pornographic communication has caused sexual arousal, the next question is whether the state of arousal and other effects of that communication are followed by behavior. If the state of arousal is not followed by behavior, the inquiry about the relationship between pornography and harm from that individual has concluded. If the state of arousal is followed by behavior, than a further bifurcation is required in the analysis between those behaviors considered harmless and those behaviors judged to be harmful. If the behavior is regarded as harmless, the subjects who so behave are excluded from the social-harm analysis. Examples of such harmless behavior in the Johnson Commission report are masturbation (by those who already masturbate) and heterosexual intercourse (among those with an already established pattern of that activity). Examples of harmful behavior include sexual crimes such as child molestation and forcible rape. If these harmful behaviors follow pornographic stimulation, then the issue of whether the pornographic communication caused the behavior would need to be addressed.

Our suggestion that this model explains the pattern of analysis of pornographic communication followed by the Johnson Commission does not have obvious textual support in the commission's report. Figure 4.1 is our own invention, not that of the commission. But support for this interpretation may be found both in the nature of the questions that the commission staff regarded as necessary to research and in the sequence in which they are treated, as well as in those questions that were not regarded as significant research priorities. The sequence of questions in the Effects Panel analysis is: first, to study the existence and extent of sexual arousal; then, to study any behavior response to arousal; and finally, to classify the behavioral responses using both the respondents' and the commission's criteria for harmful and benign behavior.

Causal hypotheses outside that paradigm are not seen as important research questions by this commission. For example, individual subjects of pornographic communication who evince negative attitude changes with no immediate arousal or behavior response were not regarded as highly significant research interest to the Johnson Commission, as opposed to the high priority given this scenario by the Meese Commission. And variations in pornographic content that do not obviously affect the level of arousal seem to interest this commission less than those that obviously affect the level of arousal of particular subjects.

Adherence to this paradigm or pattern of investigation precluded study of the impact of pornographic communication on moral or cultural climate. For not only is the paradigm specific to the sequence of events hypothesized, it is also confined temporally and conceptually to a single proximate act or event.

One other aspect of this paradigm of the putative link between pornography and harm is significant. In investigating harm, the model emphasizes what is definitionally unique about pornography. The Williams Committee definition of pornography, which we approve, refers to explicit representation of sexual material designed to produce sexual arousal. By concentrating attention on the immediate behavioral impact of that arousal to the exclusion of other possibilities, the Johnson Commission restricted the search for harmful effects of those special features which set pornography apart from other forms of communication.

The Williams Committee

The Williams Committee uses its review of the social science research evidence en route to policy recommendations rather similar to those of the Johnson Commission, but in a way that renders it less vulnerable. Rather than rely on psychological and statistical evidence, the committee makes a point of underlining the methodological problems, ambiguities of interpretation, and the dangers of generalization we have been discussing. However, by merging a presumption against the regulation of consensual conduct in the absence of provable harm with a persistent verdict of "not proven" coming from its review of the social science research on harm, the Williams Committee finds existing research useful in support of its policy conclusions while keeping a comfortable distance from anything like asserting that the absence of harm from pornography has been established by evidence.

One explanation for this distinction relates to personnel. The Williams Committee was a group of lawyers and humanists availing themselves of social science evidence at their convenience rather than a group of social scientists committed in advance to the validity of their methods and the value of empirical studies. It was largely this commitment to social science that rendered the Johnson Commission less flexible in deciding how to reach its policy conclusions and therefore more vulnerable than Professor Williams and his colleagues.

The Williams Committee's discussion of the effects of pornography attempts to answer the question "whether pornography constitutes a class of publication to which, as such, there belongs a tendency to cause harms" (Home Office, 1971:60). The report deals first with the area where the harms alleged are of a definitely identifiable kind, in that the effects of the material are said to be kinds of behavior that are criminal. But it also deals with more impalpable social harms, which were not considered by the Johnson Commission, a neglect that occasioned considerable criticism (Clor, 1971; Packer, 1971; van den Haag, 1971; Wilson, 1971).

The Williams Committee based its approach on what it called "the harm condition," which is defined in its report as "that no conduct should be suppressed by law unless *it can be shown* to harm someone" (Home Office, 1979:50; emphasis added). As applied to its assigned task this meant that what, if anything, should be done about pornography should be determined by an investigation into the consequences of its existence or dissemination. It was for this reason that it reviewed the evidence supporting the view that

certain kinds of behavior, particularly in the form of criminal offenses of a
sexual nature, are either directly provoked by exposure to pornography or are
more likely to occur in an atmosphere created by it.

The committee's review considered three kinds of evidence relating to this
aspect of the harm alleged to be caused by the availability of pornography.
First, it dealt with anecdotal and clinical evidence drawn from particular
instances in which an association between crime and pornographic material
had been observed and a causal connection was claimed, including in this
category psychiatric evidence based on clinical experience. Second, it considered research studies involving experiments into, or observations of, human
responses to pornographic material. Finally, it reviewed evidence drawn from
statistical analysis of trends in known crime relative to the varying availability
of pornography.

The committee's conclusions in relation to the first type of evidence was
that "clinical opinion and our impression of the anecdotal evidence cohere:
the cases in which a link between pornography and crime has been suggested
are remarkably few." The report adds that stimuli which might have some
relation to sexual deviation or the commission of offenses may be found all
around us, including "even passages in the Bible," but "from our study of the
anecdotal and clinical evidence . . . there is very little indication that pornography figures very significantly among these stimuli" (ibid.:63–64).

In regard to research into the effects of exposure to pornographic or explicit
sexual material, the committee notes that "serious reservations inevitably
attach to research in this field." This is because there is considerable doubt
about the extent to which correlation experiments in artificial conditions can
be regarded as a reliable way of investigating complex behavior "even in many
other species, let alone in human beings." In addition, criminal and antisocial
behavior cannot for practical and ethical reasons be experimentally produced
or controlled and observations are therefore confined to "some surrogate or
related behavior" (ibid.:65).

Besides observations of behavior under experimental conditions, the committee also reviewed other evidence relating to sexual material, including
retrospective personal history studies of exposure to the material; self-
reports before and after experimental exposure; and physiological and
biochemical measures of change in response to experimental exposure. The
committee's report states that the reliability of studies that depend on retrospective surveys or self-reporting is highly suspect "and this is particularly
true where they touch on highly personal and value-laden subjects such as
sexual behavior." As to the studies of this nature carried out for the Johnson
Commission, the report notes "the difficulty of deriving any lessons from
them." The committee's general conclusion regarding the evidence from
research studies is that "no clear impression emerges from the results of this

work" and that "the only objective verdict must be one of 'not proven' " (ibid.:65–68).

Finally, in relation to this aspect of the harm said to be caused by pornography (that is, that people are more likely to be sexually assaulted as a result of its free availability), the committee examined in some detail the available statistical evidence regarding a possible link between pornography and sex crimes. The discussion deals principally with the available information, and the inferences that can be drawn from it, in respect of England and Wales and Denmark. Denmark was selected for attention in part because the Johnson Commission in reaching its conclusion on this question had relied on two technical reports dealing with the statistical relationship between the availability of erotic materials and the incidence of sex crimes in Copenhagen, Denmark, for the period 1958–69, which suggested that the legalization of pornography in 1967 had led to a reduction in sexual offenses.

The discussion is prefaced by a summary of the difficulties involved in "proving or even plausibly arguing for, causal relationships between general or diffuse social phenomena on a purely statistical basis." In this instance the imperfections of information about the incidence of sexual offenses and the absence of a reliable index of the availability of pornography, together with the fact that "the causes of crime are undoubtedly complex," are said to render any inference particularly hazardous (ibid.:69–71).

In regard to England and Wales, the committee's report deals with the case put to it that free availability of pornography could be linked to an increase in sexual offenses. After a detailed analysis of the available information the committee concluded:

First, there is no firm information about the availability of pornography over the years, and there is no foundation to suggestions that have been made about particular times at which pornography became increasingly available. Second, the rising trend in sexual offenses generally, including rape and sexual assault, starting long before it is alleged pornography began to be widely available. Third, the increase in sexual offenses generally, and in rape and sexual assaults, has been significantly slower (though in the case of rape alone the difference is less significant) in the last twenty years than that in crime generally. Fourth, the contrast between the upward trend in crime generally and the greater stability in the number of rapes and sexual assaults has been most marked in the years from 1973 to 1977 (except in the case of rapes alone reported to the police in London where the increase is consistent with that in other forms of crime), when this period appears to have been the one when pornography was most available. . . . It is not possible, in our view, to reach well-based conclusions about what in this country has been the influence of pornography on sexual crime. But we unhesitatingly reject the suggestion that the available statistical information for England and Wales lends any support at all to the argument that pornography acts as a stimulus to the commission of sexual violence. (ibid.:78, 80)

The committee dealt next with what it referred to as "something of a folk myth about the effect of the Danish liberalization [of the laws restricting pornography] on the incidence of sexual offenses" (ibid.:80). In this connection the committee paid particular attention to the work of Dr. Berl Kutchinsky, of the Institute of Criminal Science at the University of Copenhagen, who had carried out a preliminary study for the Johnson Commission in 1969.

Perhaps Dr. Kutchinsky's most striking data were that there had been a reduction of two-thirds in the number of sex offenses against children between 1967 and 1969, which was closely correlated with the increased availability of pornography. His explanation for this apparent relationship was that the literature concerning this type of offender indicates that those who interfere with children typically do so not because they are irresistibly attracted to children but as a substitute for a preferred relationship with a woman, which they found difficult to achieve; but if there was another substitute available in the form of pornography, then that served the purpose just as well. The fact that the reduction was most significant in offenses involving younger children and less so in relation to more "normal" offenses against older girls appeared to support the hypothesis.

On this the committee commented:

We recognize . . . that Dr. Kutchinsky has identified a very dramatic reduction in reported offenses against children which coincided with the sudden upsurge in the availability of pornography and which, in consequence of the careful studies undertaken by Dr. Kutchinsky, cannot readily be explained by any other likely factor. While Dr. Kutchinsky's explanation cannot be conclusive, we have to admit that it is plausible. (ibid.:84)

But it found that it was impossible to discern a significant trend in serious sex crimes, such as rape and attempted rape, that could be linked in any way with the free availability of pornography in Denmark since the late 1960s. The committee's general conclusion was:

While we were impressed by the thoroughness with which Dr. Kutchinsky had studied the situation and the restraint with which he sought to derive lessons from his findings, the fact remains that correlation studies are a weak research tool, partly because of the difficulties of measurement – which still exist in relation to both the availability of pornography and the incidence of offenses in Denmark, in spite of Dr. Kutchinsky's considerable efforts to overcome them – and partly because of the impossibility of translating a correlation into cause and effect. A common explanation of that correlation between two sets of social data is that each is affected by some third, possibly unknown, factor and no matter how strong a correlation, it can never, bearing in mind all the other factors and influences that are also present, "prove" anything. (ibid.:83–84)

Having dealt with the relationship between pornography and sex crimes, the committee next directed attention to "other kinds of consideration, including other concepts of harm which have been put to us" and which, it said, "are also important." In respect of many of these matters (for example, the effect of pornography on sexual behavior generally; the possibility that readers of pornography might be led into deviant sexual practices; the possibility that pornography could damage relationships and lead to marital breakdown) the committee found the evidence of detrimental effects too equivocal or too insubstantial to suggest that pornography was a significant cause of harm (ibid.:86–88).

On the question of the degradation of women, which is a feature of much pornography and is seen by some as demeaning in a way that could be regarded as socially harmful, the committee reported that "the consensus of those parts of the women's movement from which we heard tended to attach greater importance to freedom of expression than to the need to suppress pornography." With regard to the effects of pornography on children, "some of our expert witnesses" expressed "a certain caution about just how susceptible children were to such influences," although "most of our witnesses wished to see children and young persons protected." It was, however, "clear . . . that no very definite answer can be given about the age at which the special protection of children is no longer necessary" (ibid.:88–89).

The committee also considered the question of the harm done to those said to be exploited in the production of pornography, both adults and children. It concluded that in the case of children, "there are strong arguments that the prevention of this harm requires the power to suppress the pornographic product as well as the original act." But in respect to adult participants, "we were not able to conclude that participation in these activities was a cause of harm" (ibid.:90–91).

Finally, the committee considered those alleged harms of a less definite and more pervasive kind that, as we have noted, concerned many critics of the Johnson Commission, such as "cultural pollution, moral deterioration, and the undermining of human compassion, social values, and basic institutions." In this connection the committee noted that although "technical innovations have offered new scope to the producer of pornography," the output of pornography in earlier times was very considerable; indeed, in England during the nineteenth century it "was prodigious."

The committee warned that the arguments about long-term effects on civilization and culture involved the danger "of citing as a cause something that is itself only an effect or part of a cultural and historical process." It concluded that while cultural artifacts play a role not only in reflecting but also in influencing social development, "from everything we know of social attitudes and have learnt in the course of our inquiries, our belief can only be that the role of pornography in influencing the state of society is a minor one" (ibid.:92–95).

It is difficult for us to accept at face value the idea that indeterminate behavioral science findings and a presumption in favor of freedom of expression were all that lay behind the deregulation proposals made by the Williams Committee. Indeed, it is rather as though the committee played a game of peek-a-boo with the social science research on pornography and harm, in which attempts to demonstrate harm – for example, by Dr. John Court – are excoriated and the substantial number of studies reviewed and discussed are relied on at least to set an upper boundary to the amount of palpable harm that pornography might cause; but this is not acknowledged as a basis for action by the committee.

One feature that makes this interpretation seem plausible is the contrast between the Williams Committee's recommendations for adults and for children. The behavioral science evidence on the link between pornography and harm to young or adolescent consumers is nothing if not indeterminate, yet the Williams Committee endorses restrictions designed to provide "special protection" for "young people" (ibid.:125–126). It seems that something more is operative here than John Stuart Mill's distinction between "human beings in the maturity of their faculties" and "those who are still in a state to require being taken care of by others" (Mill, [1859] 1975:11). We suspect that the majority of the Williams Committee believed it was not likely that freely available pornography would significantly increase sex crime among adults. We further suspect that one important reason for this belief was the range of studies they scrutinized. So, to a limited extent this committee may have also indulged in the pleasures of behavioral science, but privately.

The Meese Commission

The Meese Commission was ambivalent toward social and behavioral science research on the harmful effects of pornography. Although it argued that statistical evidence was not required to make the case for governmental control, at the same time it relied on social science evidence much more explicitly than did the Williams Committee, and some of its statements about what research establishes are considerably less qualified than those of either the Williams or Johnson report.

We will show that in addition to this ambivalence, the Meese Commission was hampered by persistent and crucial problems arising from its handling of the question of definition. It had no clear conception of what constitutes pornography to discipline its survey of behavioral effects.

The report of the Meese Commission states that "a central part of our mission has been to examine the question whether pornography is harmful" and it contains a chapter entitled "The Question of Harm." It is a relatively brief chapter, taking up only 52 of the report's 1,960 pages. Later in the report, however, a longer chapter of 134 pages entitled "Social and Behavioral Science Research Analysis" concludes with a "Summary of Commission Findings of Harm from Pornography." This analysis is described as "a sensitive, balanced, comprehensive, accurate, and current report on the state of the research. We have relied on it extensively, and we are proud to include it here" (U.S. Department of Justice, 1986:323).

The chapter on the question of harm indicates that the commission's conclusions were based on several varieties of evidence: anecdotal evidence from "people claiming to be victims of pornography" or from offenders claiming that their crimes were committed as a result of exposure to pornography; evidence provided by "clinical professionals"; evidence from experimental behavioral and social scientists and from other forms of social science. The advantages and disadvantages of the different types of evidence are discussed and it is noted that in reaching conclusions, "each of us has relied on different evidence from among the different categories of evidence" (ibid.:322).

The commission's conclusions about harm are presented under four headings: Sexually Violent Material; Nonviolent Materials Depicting Degradation, Domination, Subordination, or Humiliation; Nonviolent and Non-Degrading Materials; and Nudity. It is stressed that the conclusions regarding the consequences of material within a given subdivision relate not necessarily to *all* the material but rather to "most but not all of what might be within a given category" (ibid.:321).

The first category (Sexually Violent Material) is defined as "material featuring actual or unmistakably simulated or unmistakably threatened violence presented in sexually explicit fashion with a predominant focus on the sexually explicit violence." It is stated that "the most prevalent forms of pornography, as well as an increasing body of less sexually explicit material, fit this description" (ibid.:323). No evidence is cited for the assertion about the degree of prevalence of this type of pornography; nor is it explained how "less sexually explicit material" can come within the category of material defined by its "predominant focus on the sexually explicit."

In relation to this category of material it is claimed that the experimental and other evidence show "a causal relationship between exposure to material of this type and aggressive behavior towards women." It is acknowledged that finding a link between exposure to pornography and sexual violence, whether lawful or unlawful, required assumptions not found exclusively in the experimental evidence. But the commission found that those assumptions were "supported by the clinical evidence, as well as by much of the less scientific evidence [self-reports of offenders themselves are cited in a footnote]. They are also to all of us assumptions that are plainly justified by our common sense" (ibid.:324–325).

In regard to the second category (Nonviolent Materials Depicting Degradation, Domination, Subordination, or Humiliation) the commission found that "effects similar although not as extensive as that involved with violent material can be identified . . . with respect to material of this variety, our conclusions are substantially similar to those with respect to violent material." It is noted that in this case "there is less evidence causally linking the material with sexual aggression but . . . the absence of evidence should by no means be taken to deny the existence of a causal link" (ibid.:330–331).

The commission's general conclusion about this type of material is:

On the basis of all the evidence we have considered, from all sources, and on the basis of our own insights and experiences, we believe we are justified in drawing the following conclusion: Over a large enough sample a population that believes that many women like to be raped, that believes that sexual violence or sexual coercion is often desired or appropriate, and that believes that sex offenders are less responsible for their acts will commit more acts of sexual violence or sexual coercion than would a population holding these beliefs to a lesser extent. (ibid.:333)

The third category (Nonviolent and Non-Degrading Materials), which comprises materials in which "the participants appear to be fully willing participants occupying substantially equal roles in a setting devoid of actual or apparent violence or pain," is said to be "quite small in terms of currently available materials." No evidence is cited in support of this statement; "but we are convinced that only a small amount of currently available highly sexually explicit material is neither violent nor degrading" (ibid.:335–336).

This is described as "our most controversial category" and members of the commission "disagree substantially about the effects of such materials." There were, however, areas of agreement: for example, "we are on the current state of the evidence persuaded that material of this type does not bear a causal relationship to rape and other acts of sexual violence." Again "we unanimously agree that the materials in this category in some settings and when used for some purposes can be harmful." Thus "we would unanimously take to be harmful to society a proliferation of billboards displaying [a] highly explicit photograph of a loving married couple engaged in mutually pleasurable and procreative vaginal intercourse" (ibid.:335–346). In this curious example, quite apart from the harm envisaged, it is not immediately obvious how the fact that the intercourse was, or was intended to be, "procreative" is relevant, or could be captured on film.

Finally, in regard to this type of material the commission refers to "perhaps the largest question, and for that reason the question we can hardly touch here . . . the question of harm as it relates to the moral environment of a society." On this question, unlike the Williams Committee, the commission found it impossible to reach agreement. "We have talked about these issues, but we have not even attempted to resolve our differences because these differences are reflective of differences that are both fundamental and widespread in all societies" (ibid.:345–346).

The fourth category (Nudity) was also "the subject of some difference of opinion." None of the commission members thought that the human body or its portrayal was harmful, but "with respect to . . . more explicit materials, we were unable to reach complete agreement." The only example of more explicit material given, runs as follows: "Consider a woman shown in a reclining position with genitals displayed, wearing only red feathers and high heeled shoes, holding a gun and accompanied by a caption offering a direct invitation to sexual activity." Not everyone would find this alarming apparition provocative; nor is it a very good example of the nude (that is, completely unclothed). However, the commission concluded that "by and large we do not find the nudity that does not fit within any of the previous categories to be much cause for concern" (ibid.:347–349).

The attorney general's commission had neither the funding nor the ability under its mandate to conduct or commission original research. But it did provide, in its chapter entitled "Social and Behavior Science Research Analysis," a review of research conducted in the fifteen years since the Johnson Commission published its report in 1970. The major question that framed the research review was: "What are the effects of exposure to pornography and under what conditions and in what kinds of individuals are these effects manifested?" (ibid.:901).

The use of the term "pornography" here is curious in the light of the commission's earlier resolution "to minimize the use of the word 'pornography' in this Report." But in the preliminary observations on terminology in this chapter it is said that "we will simply avoid the usual definitional morass by using the term 'pornography' to refer to the range of sexually explicit materials used in the various studies reviewed here" (ibid.:228, 902).

The review begins with an "overview" of the Johnson Commission and the Williams Committee research conclusions. It points out that since the Johnson Commission "the quantity and quality of research has been impressive [and] has provided a better insight into understanding the various conditions under which certain effects may or may not occur." It suggests that "the conclusion of the Williams Committee on the effects of viewing pornography" might be explicable and was not "surprising since much of the experimental work was published after 1978" (ibid.:905, 909).

It is pointed out that methodological and technological advances have enhanced the reliability of research findings. More sophisticated statistical techniques have allowed for better data analysis, control, and interpretation. Instruments such as the penile plethysmograph and the vaginal photo-plethysmograph now provide better measures of sexual arousal. In addition, "more recent studies have used, as stimulus materials: films, audio-tapes, videos, and material from various adult men's magazines, all easily available from outlets as diverse as the neighborhood video store, the corner news-stand, or the local adult bookstore" (ibid.:907).

The research review is set out under three headings: Public Attitudes Toward Pornography; Sex Offenders and Pornography; and Effects on the "Average Individual." It includes a brief note on "Other Effects of Sexually Explicit Materials," in which it is observed that looking at the entire potential range of effects that might occur as a result of exposure to sexually explicit materials, "if we take the commission of sex offenses to be one extreme of the continuum, then the other end might be represented by beneficial effects" (ibid.:1028). However, the amount of space devoted to possible beneficial effects (just over two pages) might not be an accurate measure of the importance the commission attached to this aspect. Although it was asked to "determine the nature, extent, and impact on society of pornography in the United States," the specific emphasis in its charter was on "the relationship between exposure to pornographic materials and *antisocial behavior*" (emphasis added).

The commission's review of the evidence regarding public attitudes toward pornography makes a comparison between survey and poll data findings for 1970 and 1985 in three areas: public exposure to sexually explicit materials; perception of the effects of pornography; and opinion on the regulation of pornography. In regard to public exposure the available data are highly unsatisfactory and comparable only in a limited way. This is in part because of variations in the questions asked and also because of changes in technology (widespread use of cable and home videos in 1985). Moreover, it is hard to know what to make of the responses of those who in 1970 said they had seen a pornographic movie in the previous year and mentioned such films as *Butch Cassidy and the Sundance Kid, The Graduate, Easy Rider,* and *Bonnie and Clyde.* The survey concludes that "the most frequent exposure to pornography is reported by adolescents between twelve to seventeen years" (ibid.:937).

With regard to perceptions of the effects of pornography, it is notable that "public opinion data both in 1970 and in 1985 show that a majority believe the use of sexually explicit materials provide entertainment, relieve people of the impulse to commit crimes, and improve marital relations" (ibid.:1028).

At the same time the "changes between 1970 and 1985 are most apparent in the increase in the numbers who perceive that exposure to these materials leads to loss of respect for, and the commission of sexual violence" against, women. It is notable that the 1985 questions referred to "sexually explicit magazines, movies, video cassettes, and books," whereas in 1970 they were framed in terms of "looking at or reading sexual materials" (ibid.:933, 937).

Opinions on the regulation of pornography in 1985 showed "a greater overall public tolerance for sexually explicit materials." Although a majority of both men and women were in favor of banning materials that depicted sexual violence, "there is also a greater willingness to impose restrictions on theater showing and magazine publication of sexual activities than on home videos (ibid.:937).

The section on sex offenders and pornography deals with the evidence relating to the "common contention . . . that exposure to pornography leads to the commission of sex offenses" by looking at the relationship between sexual-offense statistics and the availability of pornography; and also by examining interview data and experimental data derived from sex offenders.

In the summary of the commission's findings it is asserted that the social science evidence has "demonstrated" negative effects in respect of both the commission's first two categories of pornography: sexually violent material and nonviolent material depicting degradation, domination, subordination, or humiliation (ibid.:1034).

Unfortunately, if "to demonstrate" means what the dictionaries say (that is, "to prove" or "to establish as true"), then the social science evidence does *not* provide a demonstration of the commission's conclusions about harm. To take a specific example, it does not demonstrate the commission's conclusion "that substantial exposure to sexually violent materials as described here bears a causal relationship to antisocial acts of sexual violence and for some subgroups, possibly to unlawful acts of sexual violence" (ibid.:326).

The conclusions regarding this category of material are said to be based "primarily on evidence presented by professionals in the behavioral sciences," but the report adds that "we are each personally confident on the basis of our own knowledge and experiences that the conclusions are justified" (ibid.:329). In fact, the conclusion cited certainly cannot be derived from the behavioral science evidence, and at least two of the commissioners were not only well aware of that but also indicate this in the commission's report.

Thus, in one of the individual commissioner statements coauthored by Dr. Judith Becker and Ellen Levine, it is said that "the Commission sought to break down pornography into the various types of sexually explicit material available in our society. Unfortunately, social science research to date has not uniformly followed any such categorization . . . and the attempt to force the available social science data to fit the Commission's categories is fruitless. The statement continues: "It is essential to state that the social science research has not been designed to evaluate the relationship between exposure to pornography and the commission of sexual crimes; therefore efforts to tease the current data into proof of a causal link between these acts simply cannot be accepted" (ibid.:203–204).

The striking contrast between the confident conclusions of the main body of the report and this skeptical statement is not, however, merely an isolated example of dissent, for it reflects an extraordinary feature that pervades the whole of the report. Throughout the report there is evident an almost schizophrenic dissociation between the research findings and their interpretation by the commission.

On the one hand many passages in the report evince a clear recognition of the inadequacy of the data provided by social science research and awareness of the need for caution in drawing inferences. Thus, in the chapter on the question of harm, "In many respects research is still at a fairly rudimentary stage, with few attempts to standardize categories of analysis, self-reporting questionnaires, types of stimulus materials, description of stimulus materials, measurement of effects, and related problems" (ibid.:349). Again, in the chapter on social and behavioral science research: "We also are sensitive to the limitations and strengths of specific research approaches and we have taken special efforts to review these briefly in each major section of this Chapter, if only to underscore the fact that our evaluation of the research recognizes these limitations" (ibid.:902).

Unfortunately, this sensitivity to the limitations of research appears to dissolve when specific examples are under consideration. Nowhere is this extraordinary disjunction between principle and practice better demonstrated than in the discussion of sex offenders and pornography. It is evident in the treatment of both aspects of research related to that topic which the commission considered.

The first aspect the commission chose to examine was the relationship between sexual offense statistics and the availability of pornography. In this regard the commission drew the conclusion that examination of aggregate social indicators of pornography availability and sexual-offense statistics showed there was a significant relationship between pornography and sexual offenses, which was widely interpreted as "pornography causes rape."

The principal study on which the commission's review of social science research based this conclusion was one carried out by Baron and Straus (1985) which involved a fifty-state correlational analysis of rape rates and circulation rates of adult magazines using aggregate circulation rates for eight magazines (*Chic, Club, Gallery, Genesis, Hustler, Oui, Playboy,* and *Penthouse*). This study is cited as evidence for what is described as "the sex magazine/rape rate relationship" (U.S. Department of Justice, 1986:947).

One of the authors, Murray Straus, has since written to explain his research, stating, "I do not believe that this research demonstrates that pornography causes rape" (ibid.:206). Moreover, in the commission report itself, at the conclusion of a six-page discussion of "the relationship between these sexually explicit magazines' circulation rates and rape rates" (ibid.:947), there is a footnote stating that "Baron and Straus recently conducted additional analysis of their data" in which "the relationship between the sale of sex magazines and rape disappeared" (ibid.:950, 1112n). Yet this disappearing relationship is the crucial item in "the study on which the Commission has based its conclusion" (ibid.:206).

The other aspect of research related to sex offenders and pornography that the commission considered was that dealing with interview data from sex offenders and experimental laboratory studies. In regard to the former the report initially states that "the evidence from formal and informal studies of self-reports of offenders themselves supports the conclusion that the causal connection we identify relates to actual sexual offenses" (U.S. Department of Justice, 1986:325). Later in the report, however, it is acknowledged that "while self-reports of some offenders appear to implicate pornography in the commission of their sex offenses, the objective data of actual offenses committed . . . show no significant differences between those who use pornography and those who don't" (ibid.:976).

In fact, the conclusion of the section dealing with evidence from sexual offenders runs as follows:

While these figures are suggestive of the implication of pornography in the commission of sex crimes among *some* rapists and child molesters, the question still remains: is there a difference in the rates of offenses among those who use pornography versus those who don't? The only data available that directly address this issue suggest that these offenses occur regardless of the use of pornography by the offender. Those offenders who did not use pornography did not differ significantly from those who did in frequency of sex crimes committed, number of victims, ability to control deviant urges, and degree of violence used during commission of the sex crime. (ibid.:970)

In regard to experimental laboratory studies the commission claims that "clinical and experimental research . . . shows a causal relationship between exposure to sexually violent material of this type and aggressive behavior toward women." "Sexual violence," it states, "is reported in the research to result from substantial exposure to sexually violent materials" (ibid.:324, 326).

It hardly needs to be said that for both ethical and practical reasons laboratory experiments involving "exposure to sexually violent materials" followed by "sexual violence" on the part of experimental subjects have nowhere been carried out. Observations of behavior under experimental conditions can only be made on some proxy or substitute behavior. In other words, any relationship observed is one not between exposure to pornographic representations and behavior in the real world but between exposure to pornographic representation and another kind of artificial representation.

Moreover, the commission was well aware of, and explicitly acknowledged, both what the report refers to as "the problem of the ability to generalize the results [of experimental studies] outside the laboratory (what researchers call 'external validity')" and also "the problem of . . . the measures used to reflect 'antisocial behavior' " (ibid.:1007–1008). And at the conclusion of the survey of the evidence regarding effects on behaviors, in the final paragraph, in fact, there occur two sentences that have a ring of almost ingenuous honesty:

After all, the question which social scientists must ultimately address – with both theoretical and pragmatic or public policy implications – is what types of effects have been demonstrated for what classes of materials? Such investigations for some social scientists may have undesirable political or ideological implications but ignoring the issue also hampers our ability to explain the nature of effects more fully so as to provide for nonlegal policy strategies that are firmly anchored in social science findings. (ibid.:1021)

It is notable that there is no mention of the possibility that the results of such investigations might have some implications for the conclusions already arrived at, about which the commissioners were said to be "each personally confident on the basis of our own knowledge and experiences" (ibid.:329).

As we have seen, the major innovation of the Meese panel was a series of categories and a sustained critical analysis of the evidence relating to those categories.

The strongest conclusion of the commission was with respect to the category of what was called variously sexually violent material or violent sexually explicit material. The commission agreed unanimously that negative effects in both attitude and behavior have been consistently noted as resulting from this class of material. There was no finding of the Johnson Commission to compare with this class of material because violent pornography was not recognized by that commission as a separate category. However, since the Johnson Commission found no evidence that any pornography produced such behavioral effects, some clash is apparent. Part of the difference in conclusions may be explicable because this is one of two areas where the Meese Commission was relying on research conducted and published in the 1980s and unavailable to either of the two previous commissions.

At the outset it should be said that the behavioral effects attributed to stimuli that the Meese Commission classified as sexually violent material were laboratory simulations of, or substitutes for, aggressive behavior. Regarding evidence produced as to the negative effect of violent pornography, two special problems require sustained attention: one of definition and the other of attribution. The expression "violent pornography" contains two key terms, neither of which is clearly defined anywhere in the Meese Commission report.

We have previously discussed the problem in relation to the definition of pornography. We add here the point that there is also no definition of violence. The sequence of studies relied on in the section is described as involving "violent sexually explicit materials" (U.S. Department of Justice, 1986:977) without any claim that the material is pornographic. One such study used as stimuli two films, Lina Wertmuller's *Swept Away* and Sam Peckinpah's *The Getaway* (ibid.:983), neither of which was considered pornographic anywhere in the Western world. And with respect to *Swept Away*, the characterization of that film as violent is at minimum controversial.

The "definitional" problem is that the commission created a separate category for special public policy treatment and yet did not define it. It is difficult to assess whether the studies they cite deal with material meeting the commission's criteria of violent pornography, because those criteria are never stated. It is also difficult to understand how one could test the hypothesis about the differential effects of violent pornography without being able to describe clearly what sort of stimulus should be used as an independent variable.

This problem is compounded by a special problem of attribution that exists because of the nature of the studies. A typical set of studies is described by the commission as follows:

In a study designed to evaluate the effects of massive exposure to sexual violence and to further explore the components of the desensitization process, a series of four studies – all part of a Ph.D. dissertation – were conducted (Linz, 1985). College males were exposed to a series of "slasher films," all R-rated, using a formula of sexual explicitness juxtaposed with much blood and gore. A typical example is a scene from *Toolbox Murders* showing a naked woman taking a tub bath, masturbating, then being stalked and killed with a power drill by a masked male. Comparisons were also made among R-rated nonviolent films and X-rated nonviolent films, both of which included sexually explicit scenes (the former were of the teenage sex film variety).[1124]

Footnote 1124 tells us:

The following films were used: R-rated nonviolent "teen sex" films: *Porky's, Fast Times at Ridgemont High, Private Lessons, Last American Virgin,* and *Hots;* X-rated nonviolent films: *Debbie Does Dallas, Health Spa, The Other Side of Julie, Indecent Exposure,* and *Fantasy;* R-rated "slasher" films: *Texas Chainsaw Massacre, Maniac, Toolbox Murders, Vice Squad,* and *I Spit On Your Grave.* (ibid.:986–987)

For present purposes, we put to one side questions about whether either *Porky's* or *Texas Chainsaw Massacre* constitute pornography. Let us further assume that the *Toolbox Murders* audience experiences sharply different behavioral effects from those of audiences exposed to nonviolent sex films and nonviolent not-so-sexual films. Is this evidence of the harmful effect of violent pornography? In one important sense the answer must be no; because we do not know whether harmful differential effects can be attributed to the sexual content of the communication or not.

Figure 4.2 shows both the experimental conditions present in the studies cited by the commission and the crucial missing connection. The three conditions checked off were listed by the commission's staff survey. But if violent cues produce the same harmful effects without sexually arousing content, then what is harmful about the communication is not pornographic and what is pornographic about the communication is not harmful. In yet another demonstration of noncoordination, the negative effect of nonpornographic violence is mentioned in the Part II section of the commission's report (ibid.:328–329) but not discussed in the longer and more detailed survey of research.

Two illustrations of this problem will help point up its importance. The reader will recall the sequence from *Toolbox Murders* which showed a naked

VIOLENCE

	Yes	No
EXPLICIT SEX Yes	xx	xx
No		xx

Figure 4.2.   Sex and violence.

woman taking a tub bath, masturbating, and then being stalked and killed with a power drill by a masked male. Assuming that we find negative effects on attitudes to women and simulated aggressive behavior following exposure, the question arises: How would the same sequence influence behavior if the woman did not masturbate and was fully clothed when impaled on the power drill?

This is not an academic point if the sole basis for restricting the availability of a communication is not causally related to its propensity to cause harm. If violence alone or in the context of sexual suggestion produces negative effects, then the special focus on pornography is pointless. It would be as though a commission of inquiry studying the effect of multiple Bloody Mary cocktails on human behavior recommended a governmental ban on the production and sale of tomato juice.

We might ask why a problem of this size and salience is not addressed in the lengthy survey of research. Our own view is that this was facilitated by a lack of sustained attention to the definition of pornography and thus to the characteristic that sets off pornographic communication from other forms of communication. And this is, in fact, only one of the difficulties generated and exacerbated by inattention to definitional detail, as we shall see later in this section.

The Meese Commission also places special, separate emphasis on the category of "Nonviolent Materials Depicting Degradation, Domination, Subordination, or Humiliation" (U.S. Department of Justice, 1986:329–335). With respect to this category, the commission found evidence of a specific kind of effect: a change in attitude toward women, the use of force, and in the context of heterosexual encounters, "increased acceptance of the proposition that women like to be forced into sexual practices and that the woman who says 'no' really means 'yes' " (ibid.:332). The discussion of this category by the commission raises problems of definition and attribution that parallel the treatment of sexual violence. It also raises the perplexing issue of whether government action is justified when the harm produced by communications is an influence on attitudes or sentiments rather than a direct effect on conduct.

The problems of definition encountered in regard to this category are analogous to those discussed in relation to sexual violence. "Pornography" is still an undefined term. Because violence is also undefined the borderline between violence and nonviolence cannot be confidently delineated. And in this new category, a host of new terms are introduced and yet not defined: degradation, domination, subordination, and humiliation. The commission does state that "an enormous amount of the most sexually explicit material available, as well as much of the material that is somewhat less sexually explicit, is material that we would characterize as 'degrading' " (ibid.:331). But readers are not told what specific elements of currently available pornography render it degrading.

The problem of attribution is that depictions of relations between the sexes that would meet no one's definition of pornography might still produce negative effects in the form of attitude changes, changes as large as those produced by pornography. This cannot be known until pornographic and nonpornographic degradations of women are compared. Proposing special restrictions only on degrading communication that is also pornographic might again be like tolerating vodka while prohibiting tomato juice.

And there are special problems with arguments for the regulation of communication that see the social harm in changes in the attitude of audiences. Two elements of individual attitudes require special caution when considering issues of regulation: the distance of attitudes and sentiments from more palpable social harms and the closeness of toleration of differences in attitude and sentiment to the core value of free expression in a democratic society. Western legal thought in a diverse variety of areas distinguishes between prohibitable harms and what are usually called the attempt to influence mere attitudes or sentiments. This is seen throughout the criminal law and plays a central role in American constitutional law regarding the regulation of speech and written expression.

Problems with the regulation of wrongful thoughts and sentiments include the difficulty of making governmental judgments about the wrongfulness of sentiments in a plural society; the attenuated nexus between wrongful attitudes and wrongful conduct; and the difficulty of determining who among the population possesses an evil intent not yet manifest in overt behavior. But the difficulties involved in the regulation of attitudes and sentiments are not regarded as important in Western democracies because the attempt to alter attitudes and opinions is a central protected enterprise in those countries which place a high value on freedom of expression. We feel protected by the difficulty of a task that most of us believe should not be undertaken. Inefficiency is seen as a protector of civil liberty.

We shall return to these issues in the next chapter. For present purposes, it is important to note that the special status of attitudes and sentiments would seem to require particular scrutiny of the link between attitudes and conduct when considering the negative effects of communication. No such special scrutiny can be found in the Meese Commission's analysis.

The Meese Commission's next category is "sexually explicit materials that are not violent and are not degrading" (ibid.:335–347). This category has mystified two audiences: the commission's members and the report's readers. The problem the members of the commission had with it seems to center around the example of a "highly explicit photograph of a loving married couple engaged in mutually pleasurable and procreative vaginal intercourse" (ibid.:342). What seems to be special about the example is that it exemplifies this third category. Indeed, it is the only specific example of the category given anywhere in the report.

Two questions are to be asked about this example and thus about this category of material. Why should it be regarded as a subject for special treatment in a discussion of pornography? Why should there be a restriction of the availability of this kind of communication to a willing audience?

What distinguishes this from other sexually explicit materials the commission discussed is the absence of any intention on the part of the producers to inculcate bad attitudes in the audience to the communication. The situation is described in a way that assures us that the couple represents a model of positive, approved sexual behavior that every commission member could subscribe to. We take it that this is why the sexual intercourse has to be "procreative" as well as loving and pleasurable.

Why, then, should one consider the censorship of this type of model communication? Should not the intended behavioral message exempt this depiction from the restriction of sexually explicit material? The logical answer is that no distinction can be justified, for the behavioral model and the psychological and behavioral effects may be only distantly related one to another. The lady on the screen or in the photograph may be the wife of her sex partner but not of any man in the audience. Audience arousal therefore will occur in a whole separate set of contexts from that depicted on the screen. There is no reason to suppose that any person immediately aroused by observing the hypothesized scene would feel impelled to procreate. And there might be special problems if one of the depicted couple's children were to be sexually aroused by exposure to this particular depiction.

This category of material is invented in the Meese Commission analysis and distinguished by that commission's special emphasis on attitudes and values.

"We are dealing in this category with 'pure' sex . . . material . . . not perceived as harmful for the messages it carries or the symbols it represents" (ibid.:336, 340). Even so, there is confusion between intended effects and effects likely to be produced.

The conceptual problems of the Meese Commission are also implicated in the discussion of the subject of nudity (ibid.:347–349). On this topic the report states, "We pause only briefly to mention the problem of mere nudity." The pause is too brief for the commission to get around to stating expressly what the subject of nudity is doing in the commission's report. The problem, as the commission saw it in connection with "portrayals of nudity," was that "nudity without force, coercion, sexual activity, violence, or degradation" can have a "definite provocative element" (ibid.:348). What this suggests to us, above all else, is the need for a definition of pornography. Provocation to what, and the degree to which such provocation should be the subject of regulation, are topics that discussants are forced to regard as central if they pay attention to questions of definition.

What is there that is pornographic about pornography? Is any communication about sex pornographic? Or is it only communication about sex that creates harmful attitudes? What is the difference between harmful attitudes toward sex and harmful attitudes toward religious toleration and race relations? What is there about pornography that justifies separate analysis, and does this also justify special public policy?

Summary

It remains for us to summarize our view of the work of the three commissions and to suggest a short list of research questions that are worthy of consideration.

The Johnson Commission was rendered vulnerable to criticism by two kinds of biases and failed to explore a variety of possible pornographic effects, such as impact on attitudes, that might in turn condition aggressive behavior. Nor did it attempt to justify its relatively narrow focus. The bias of this commission in favor of unrestricted access to adults has been frequently noted. But it was the commitment of the commission to the utility and quality of behavioral science research that rendered it most vulnerable to criticism.

The Williams Committee, by contrast, used presumptions against regulation (the "harm" principle) to remain more skeptical of research than the Johnson Commission while endorsing the deregulatory thrust of that earlier commission. The Meese Commission raised the possibility of new subcategories of pornographic communication and focused attention on the attitudinal impact of the material. This was an effort pervaded by definitional and conceptual confusion, political agendas, and some result orientation in its view of research.

When the work of the more recent commission is reviewed together with that of the two earlier bodies, two specific lines of research seem promising. First, there is laboratory research designed to test the link between (a) sexual pornography and (b) apparently problematic attitudes and laboratory behavioral responses, and (c) postadministration observed behavioral effects. Second, we noted that the research relied on by the Meese Commission compared what were called violent stimuli with some sexual content with nonviolent stimuli with sexual content. At minimum, comparison should be made between the impact of sexual pornography with violent themes and a combination of violence and sexual themes well short of pornography.

We should here make a point about the public-policy context of research methodology. Unless the American law relating to freedom of expression is to be substantially altered, special regulation of pornography will be confined to communication (this is the realm of prurient interest) that seeks to provoke through sexual arousal. It is therefore the combination of this high level of sexual appeal with violent themes that should be tested for its special impact. If it is violence alone or violence in the context of less provocative sexual themes that produce troublesome consequences, existing standards of freedom of expression will preclude special regulatory consequences.

But it is possible that high levels of intentional sexual arousal combined with specific cues in relation to violence and coercion have differentially negative impacts on subject behavior. If highly sexually arousing violent materials have a more troublesome impact than soft-core sexuality with violence or nonviolent sexual provocation, then what is pornographic about violent pornography might be causally related to a palpable harm that would invite dialogue about regulation.

Currently we are light years away from any such conclusion. One reason for this is the lack of any evidence linking the kinds of attitudes studied in psychological experiments with behavioral harm such as criminal sexual aggression. The link between attitude and behavior should provoke much more research than it has to date.

5

Freedom of expression and the public law of pornography

This chapter examines the issues that emerge when a society that values free expression is also concerned about pornographic communication. In any country where freedom of expression is regarded as important, whether or not it is constitutionally guaranteed, it is recognized that some balance must be struck between the right to free expression and the right of government to prohibit or restrict the publication and distribution of material deemed harmful to individual citizens or to society. How that task is affected by the protections accorded to free expression by the First and Fourteenth Amendments to the U.S. Constitution is one of the issues to be explored here, as we examine how the three commission reports under review addressed these issues. Our intention in this chapter is to survey a great deal more than the constraints or restrictions imposed by the First Amendment on the regulation of pornography in the United States.

The first section of this chapter looks at the way in which pornography may implicate values of free expression and the potential harms pornography may cause. We attempt to construct an inventory of free-expression values and countervailing social harms from which a balancing of these interests may occur. The chapter's second section describes how the Williams Committee weighed the competing values in its report. The third section contrasts the two U.S. commissions' reports with each other and with the Williams Committee report.

An inventory of issues

Pornography as communication

There can be no doubt that pornography in whatever form belongs to the universe of spoken, written, or pictorial acts that contain and send information, signals, and messages. Even what the Williams Committee called "the most vacant and inexpressive pornographic material" (Home Office, 1979:54) has communicative content. As the Meese Commission acknowledged, "like

109

any other act, the act of making, distributing, and using pornographic items contains and sends messages" (U.S. Department of Justice, 1986:267). Messages are communications passed or sent between persons, and both the senders and recipients may have an interest in them, however distasteful or offensive they may be, or however limited for most people their emotive, intellectual, aesthetic, or informational appeal may be. We begin, therefore, by considering the interests of the senders and recipients of pornographic communication.

Free-expression interests in pornography

Senders' interests in self-expression and persuasion of others

John Stuart Mill, in his essay *On Liberty*, held it to be "imperative that human beings should be free to form opinions and to express their opinions without reserve" and wrote of "the baneful consequences to the intellectual, and, through that, to the moral nature of man, unless this liberty is either conceded or asserted in spite of prohibition" (Mill, [1859] 1975:53). Mill's justification of this proposition did not rely on any theory that individuals have a "right" to freedom of expression. Rather, he argued that freedom of expression was justified in terms of "the permanent interests of man" and "those interests . . . authorise the subjection of individual spontaneity to external control, only in respect to those actions of each, which concern the interest of other people" (Mill, [1859] 1975:12).

What exactly Mill meant by the term "interest" has produced considerable literature (e.g., Rees, 1960; Ten, 1968; and Wollheim, 1973). But few would deny that the development of the human personality depends to some extent on freedom for the expression of individual ideas, beliefs, sentiments, aspirations, and desires. Moreover, Mill's belief in the free development of individuality and individual self-expression is widely seen as "itself the condition of all that we understand by society, civilization, and culture" (Levi, 1959:41).

Pornographic material can be viewed as an expression of its creator's personal vision. As the Williams Committee noted, "there do exist some works which are indisputably pornographic in content and intention, but which are thought to succeed in realising other, artistic concerns. . . . It can reasonably be claimed, moreover, that they are not merely of artistic interest despite being pornographic but that their sexual intention is integrally bound up with their merits as expressive designs" (Home Office, 1979:106).

The interest in self-expression is, however, not confined to works that possess artistic merit. The self that is expressed may possess no artistic gifts and be in no way admirable or attractive. And not all self-expression is classified as speech because of its expressive content (U.S. Department of Justice, 1986:263).

The broad interest in self-expression is not merely a matter of soliloquy; what we put into words, represent in language, or symbolize in art is ordinarily addressed to others. When Mill spoke of "the necessity to the mental well-being of mankind (on which all their other well-being depends) of freedom of opinion, and freedom of the expression of opinion" (Mill, [1859] 1975:50), he was clearly not thinking of people talking to themselves. Nor was he thinking merely of the transmission of information.

For the expression of opinion is essentially the proposal to others for acceptance of an idea, impression, or evaluation that seems true, valid, or probable to one's own mind. Our interest in self-expression is very largely an interest in being able to influence others to an action or belief. Indeed, the primary reason for valuing, and for being apprehensive about, freedom of expression relates to the expression of thoughts and feelings (by means of vocal sounds, written symbols, or pictorial images), through an appeal to reason or emotion, as a means of persuasion.

Recipients' interests

Interests in new information and knowledge. The Williams Committee found it "a rather ironical comment on the survival power of good ideas that some submissions to us have put forward in defence of the *most vacant and inexpressive pornographic material* the formulations which Mill hoped would assist in furthering '. . . the permanent interests of a man as a progressive being' " (Home Office, 1979:54; emphasis added). The Meese Commission also took the view that "most of what we have seen that to us qualifies as hard core material" did not attain that "minimal threshold of cognitive or similar appeal," below which it could not be regarded as conveying arguments or information (U.S. Department of Justice, 1986:264–265).

By contrast, the Johnson Commission saw pornography, including "hard core material," as a significant "source of sex information." Indeed the Commission noted that "at least two medical schools and one religiously affiliated private training institute for professional workers have used what is generally termed 'hard-core pornography' in their sex education courses because no other materials are available explicitly depicting the wide range of sexual behavior with which professionals in human sexuality must be familiar" (U.S. Commission, 1970:31).

A technical report for the Johnson Commission considered pornography as one of the principal sources of information about sex. "Leakages from censorship produced a situation today in which there are two systems for the transmission of sexual information, the open and the behind-the-scenes. The latter includes pictorial and narrative erotic material, commonly judged illicit, which is nowadays rather widely available to preteens and teenagers" (U.S.

Commission, 1971–72, 5:351–352). The same report viewed "the materials designed to appeal to paraphilias" (U.S. Department of Justice, 1986:1364), which the Meese Commission deplored, as a useful tool for educational purposes: "Portrayal of the paraphilias in pornography can be put to good use in sex education as an indication of what can be avoided when one has a healthy exposure to, and healthy respect for, heterosexual eroticism" (U.S. Commission, 1971–72, 5:352).

Even "the most vacant and inexpressive pornographic material" may convey new information or knowledge to those who are unfamiliar with its content. Indeed, the informative nature of pornography constitutes one of the principal arguments advanced by the Feminist Anti-Censorship Task Force (FACT) for opposing censorship: "The chief result of closing down the porn industry would be to enhance sexual repression. People would have even less access to information about sex and erotic material than they do now" (Califia, 1986:23). Nor can there be any doubt that whatever the limitations of pornography as a medium for the communication of information about sex, its consumers have substantial interests in it.

Interests in sexual communication as point of view. The Williams Committee reported that "most of what is in our field of discussion contains no new perception and no idea at all, old or new, and that cannot seriously be disputed" (Home Office, 1979:57). The Meese Commission, however, noted that pornographic communication could be seen as "the process by which an alternative sexual vision is communicated, or . . . the process by which people use the traditional media of communication to experience and to understand a different sexual vision" in much the same way as they use those media for "communicating and experiencing different visions about, for example, politics or morals" (U.S. Department of Justice, 1986:263).

The commission also acknowledged that "a wide range of sexually explicit material" could be regarded as "conveying unpopular ideas about sex in a manner that is offensive to most people." On the other hand, it said that most hard-core pornography had no ideational or informational content. "Lines are of course not always easy to draw, but we find it difficult to understand how much of the material we have seen can be considered to be even remotely related to an exchange of views in the marketplace of ideas, to an attempt to articulate a point of view, to an attempt to persuade, or to an attempt seriously to convey through literary or artistic means a different vision of humanity or the world" (ibid.:265).

The difficulty involved in drawing lines is reflected in the case, referred to by the Williams Committee, of Pasolini's last film *Salò*, for which the British Board of Film Censors refused to issue a certificate. When it was shown in a

London club, police seized it, and those who had shown it were indicted. Because of a change in the law, the proceedings were withdrawn but the Director of Public Prosecutions announced that anyone who subsequently showed the film would be prosecuted. Because the film was the subject of legal action during its inquiries, the Williams Committee discussed it. On this subject, the committee report says:

The film displays scenes of extraordinary cruelty and repulsiveness. . . . It has the ritual form of a pornographic work – indeed it is specifically modelled on Sade's *120 Days of Sodom*. All of us agreed that it is obscene, in the sense that it is ruthlessly and almost unwatchably repellent. On its other qualities, and its merits, we found ourselves in great disagreement. Most of us felt that it was manifestly not designed to produce sexual excitement, and that it took great care not to do so, even incidentally; on this view of it, the work though obscene, is not pornographic, despite its form. Some of us, however, were more suspicious of its intentions. Those who were most impressed by it thought that it presented an extraordinary metaphor of political power and was a remarkable work, perhaps a masterpiece." (Home Office, 1979:108)

This example illustrates three interesting points. First, it is notable that the Williams Committee was unable to agree about whether the film was pornographic as the committee defined that term. Second, it demonstrates that even what may be "almost unwatchably repellent" cannot necessarily be dismissed as not "remotely related to the exchange of views in the marketplace of ideas." Third, it raises that "paradox of censorship" that Mortimer Adler said was made "so plain" by John Milton "that it has never been avoidable in all subsequent discussions of the problem" (Adler, 1937:106).

Milton's paradox, which has been found easily avoidable in much subsequent discussion, took the form of a rhetorical question: How can we find censors "unless we can confer upon them, or they assume to themselves, above all others in the land, the grace of infallibility . . . ?" (Milton, [1644] 1933:24). That is a political question, but it arises because we do not know the answers to other, quite different, questions about the ways in which ideas are mediated by language and symbolic forms.

Paul and Schwartz have argued that "some things which are quite obscene may also be important reflections of man's culture, thinking and ideas" and "that some things obscene, indeed some things very obscene, may still have value as expression for at least limited purposes" (Paul and Schwartz, 1961:201–202). The Williams Committee remarked that "work in some despised medium or style may subsequently turn out to have had more meaning than most experts would have originally supposed" (Home Office, 1979:110).

What may today seem wholly "vacant and inexpressive" or "unwatchably repellent" or totally unrelated to "the exchange of views in the marketplace of ideas" may well subsequently be recognized as reflecting some significant aspect of "man's culture, thinking, and ideas." We cannot anticipate the judgment of posterity, but we have an interest in being able to make our own judgment.

Interests in communication as a path to sexual arousal. According to the Johnson Commission, "experimental and survey studies show that exposure to erotic stimuli produces sexual arousal in substantial portions of both males and females" (U.S. Commission, 1970:24). The Williams Committee reported that "some of our witnesses were clearly concerned at the effects of pornography on sexual behaviour generally. But if sexual arousal results, this is hardly to be condemned in itself" (Home Office, 1979:86). The Meese Commission reported: "The manner of presentation and distribution of most standard pornography confirms the view that at bottom the predominant use of such materials is as a masturbatory aid" (U.S. Department of Justice, 1986:266).

Doubts have been expressed as to whether "the impact of pornography on the individual can in fact be shown to have any effect at all apart from the transitory state of excitement" (Gosling, 1961:58). But what the Williams Committee saw as "hardly to be condemned" has in fact been condemned on a number of grounds. Thus it seems likely that the definition of obscenity, derived from the Common Law as it has stood since *R. v. Hicklin* in 1968, found in the English Obscene Publications Acts of 1959 and 1964, reflects reprobation of sexual stimulation.

According to those Acts, an article legally is obscene if "its effects or (where the article comprises two or more distinct items) the effect of anyone of its items is, if taken as a whole, such as to tend to deprave and corrupt persons who are likely, having regard to all relevant circumstances, to read, see or hear the matter contained as embodied in it." On the way in which the English courts have interpreted those Acts, Professor Simpson comments that

they got themselves into a terrible muddle. After considerable dithering they came in time to say that an individual was "corrupted" if he indulged in sexual fantasies and no more; the purity of the mind was the principal object of the law, Lord Wilberforce assured us in the leading case of *D.P.P. v. Whyte* in 1972. Any old sexual fantasies, so Lord Pearson ruled, would do; they need not include any originality or abnormality. Lurking behind all this is no doubt the old horror of masturbation, though the case law has never openly said so, so strong is the taboo even today on mentioning the practice. (Simpson, 1983:8)

Moreover, pornographic material that seeks to produce sexual arousal has been condemned on aesthetic grounds. For example, one critic, Dr. Leonie Kramer, wrote in regard to John Cleland's *Memoirs of a Woman of Pleasure*, "it is without doubt in intention and design a pornographic book. I do not accept the view that pornography can be literature and vice versa. The impulse and intention of a pornographic work is, I believe, not only to shock by crudity, but actually to stimulate feelings of a prurient kind. When Cleland describes Fanny Hill's mounting sexual excitement as she watches the engagement of two 'lovers' he hopes to produce in his reader the effects that he is describing in his heroine. This kind of aim has nothing to do with literature" (Kramer, 1964:52).

Other critics have taken a different view of the literary merit of Cleland's book (for example, Quennell, 1963, and St. John-Stevas, 1964). But it can hardly be seriously maintained that none of the works, or passages in works, in which the author's intention was to produce in his readers the effects described in his characters can be regarded as literature. What Cleland calls "the old last act" (Cleland, 1963:32) is as suitable or proper as material for art as any other human activity and it is evident that in describing it, or portraying it, artists often seek to arouse their audience sexually.

Moreover, as Professor van den Haag has observed, "there is no doubt . . . that the artistically most perfect representation of sexual matters may quicken sexual appetites in the most perfect observer" (van den Haag, 1962:118). Indeed, it is precisely because it has that effect that some perhaps less than perfect observers have a special interest in it.

The harms of pornographic communication

The Johnson Commission's Effects Panel saw "the first task facing the Panel" as being "to identify presumed effects of erotic materials." In this connection, "two sources were consulted for guidance: (a) previous research in this area, and (b) the claims which had been made about the consequence of reading and viewing erotic material. Reviews of this literature generated several basic questions. If exposure to erotic materials does, in fact, have harmful effects what kinds of effects are these and who experiences them?"

The panel found that "existing empirical knowledge pertained generally to *sexual arousal* responses" but "found no research indicating the duration of arousal or how this situation might affect overt behavior, attitudes governing behavior, or mental health" (U.S. Commission, 1970:141–142). In regard to empirical knowledge the position is not a great deal better today, and legal judgments and social policy are, as they were in 1970, for the most part based on considerations other than evidence regarding effects. Nevertheless, the assumed nature of those effects clearly influences both legislative policy and judicial decision making in this area, and the topic cannot be ignored.

The list of potential harms we have gathered has been grouped under three headings: the causation of sexual conduct, the generation of negative sexual values and attitudes, and harmful impact on the general moral climate in society. Our discussion emphasizes the position of each commission on whether the supposed harms should weigh against a presumption of freedom to communicate. We list a wider variety of potential harms than those discussed in Chapter 3. Further, we are here interested in reporting the claims made about such harms rather than assessing the accuracy of the claims.

Inducement to sexual action

By the immature. More than two decades ago, Dr. Geoffrey Gorer, anthropoligist–sociologist, wrote:

> There does however remain the danger that through pornography the immature will be precociously excited into sexuality. . . . Social childhood is not necessarily defined by complete sexual abstinence, though it is noteworthy that in every society that is approaching or has achieved universal education the "age of consent" has been continuously and progressively raised. But sex should not (in the opinion of all complex societies) be a preoccupation of the young of either sex while they are still in the process of formal education. Nobody I think can say what effect exposure to pornography might have on the socially or physiologically immature; but it is feared lest its effects might be overstimulating. No one knows. . . . Since experiment is inadmissible, we have to fall back on hunch and preference; and both prudence and tradition suggest that it should be made (at the very least) extremely difficult for youngsters to acquire pornography. (Gorer, 1961:39–40)

The Johnson Commission reported that "exposure to explicit sexual materials in adolescence is widespread." It also said that the absence of empirical evidence supporting a causal relationship between exposure to and use of explicit sexual materials and social or individual harms "also applies to the exposure of children to erotic materials." It added, however, that "insufficient research is presently available on the effect of exposure of children to sexually explicit materials to enable us to reach conclusions with the same degree of confidence as for adult exposure" (U.S. Commission, 1970:21, 57).

The Williams Committee reported that it heard arguments about exposure to pornography involving "risk to the normal sexual development of the young." It heard "no evidence of actual harm being caused to children" and "children have not been used in experimental work on exposure to pornography." Nevertheless "the effects of pornography . . . were widely seen as particularly dangerous to the young, and most of our witnesses wished to see children and young persons protected" (Home Office, 1979:59, 88–89).

Two members of the Meese Commission, Becker and Levine, report:

> The most disturbing issue facing the panel this year was the concern about children and their exposure to child and adult pornography. Adolescents are acknowledged as an enormous market for pornographic materials, and despite legislative efforts to restrict access, this material remains easily available to youngsters.
>
> In fact, from an early age American children are bombarded by very stimulating sexual messages, most of which are not pornographic but certainly are frightening.

This year, for example, the AIDS epidemic has prompted health officials to broadcast urgent radio and television warnings against homosexual anal intercourse and group sex and pleas for the use of condoms.

Because children may have trouble with these very public messages and because too many young people get too much of their sex education from pornographic magazines and films, we strongly support relevant school sex education programs. Appropriate and accurate information about loving sexual experiences can help inoculate children against the potential damage from early exposure to negative images. Furthermore, we urge parents to monitor carefully their own children's exposure to these materials.

There cannot be enough done to protect our children – both from people who would abuse and seduce them into the abhorrent world of child pornography and from the unwelcome intrusion of too many sexual messages. (U.S. Department of Justice, 1986:209–210)

In criminal and deviant ways. The Johnson Commission reported, as noted earlier, that "extensive empirical investigations do not indicate any causal relationship between exposure to or use of explicit sexual materials . . . and crime, delinquency, [or] sexual or nonsexual deviancy" (U.S. Commission, 1970:57). Similarly, the Williams Committee concluded that "there does not appear to be any strong evidence that exposure to sexually explicit material triggers off anti-social sexual behaviour." With regard to "deviant sexual practices" it reported that "all the evidence points to the fact that material dealing with bizarre and perverted sexual activity appeals only to those with a pre-existing interest established by the experiences of early life . . . there is no evidence the exposure to such material inculcates a taste for it" (Home Office, 1979:86–87).

The Meese Commission, however, concluded "that the available evidence strongly supports the hypothesis that substantial exposure to sexually violent materials as described here bears a causal relationship to antisocial acts of sexual violence and, for some subgroups, possibly to unlawful acts of sexual violence" (U.S. Department of Justice, 1986:326). On the question of pornography and "sexual practices that differ from the norm" the commission reported that "there needs to be more research . . . about the effects of depictions of particular sexual practices on the sexual preferences of those who view them" (ibid.:344, 350).

By adults in immoral ways. The Johnson Commission stated that "in general, established patterns of sexual behavior were found to be very stable and not altered substantially by exposure to erotica. When sexual activity occurred following the viewing or reading of these materials, it constituted a temporary activation of individual's patterns of sexual behavior" (U.S. Commission, 1970:25). But it said that there was no "evidence that exposure to explicit sexual materials adversely affects character or moral attitudes regarding sex and sexual conduct" (ibid.:54).

The Williams Committee noted that to consider the possible effects of exposure to pornography on sexual behavior generally raised "problems of deciding what forms of legal behaviour are nevertheless undesirable, bringing to bear certain values." It reported that if, following exposure

more frequent sexual intercourse follows, there is no obvious need for concern, while if the result is masturbation still many will not be alarmed; if a greater repertoire of sexual activity is learned, many people would regard this as a benefit. The prospect of encouraging premarital or extra-marital sexual activity raises greater controversy, but the indications from research results are that sexual patterns of behaviour are fixed before reading pornography can exercise any influence. What people do is more affected by their existing habits and values than by exposure to pornography, and the sexual attitudes of groups who have been studied do not appear to have been much affected by seeing this kind of material. It is however true that attitudes towards pornography and its restriction are very much a function of other attitudes towards sex generally. (Home Office, 1979:86)

The Meese Commission noted, with regard to materials depicting "sexual practices frequently condemned in this and other societies," that

intuitively and not experimentally, we can hypothesize that materials portraying such 'an activity will either help to legitimize or will bear some causal relationship to that activity itself. . . . A larger issue is the very question of promiscuity. Even to the extent that the behavior depicted is not inherently condemned by some or any of us, the manner of presentation almost necessarily suggests that the activities are taking place outside of the context of marriage, love, commitment, or even affection. Again, it is far from implausible to hypothesize that materials depicting sexual activity without marriage, love, commitment, or affection bear some causal relationship to sexual activity without marriage, love, commitment, or affection. There are undoubtedly many causes for what used to be called the "sexual revolution," but it is absurd to suppose that depictions or descriptions of uncommitted sexuality were not among them. (U.S. Department of Justice, 1986:338–339)

An aid to seduction. A specific topic not mentioned in any of the commission reports (except with respect to minors) but raised in some discussion of pornography is the possibility of the use of pornographic material as an aid to seduction. The suggestion is that feelings of sexual arousal having been induced by such stimuli, seduction that might have been firmly resisted without such adventitious aids is facilitated. In this connection reference is often made to Casanova's claim to have used an illustrated edition of the Sonnets of Aretino as aid to seduction (Gorer, 1961:38; Kronhausen and Kronhausen, 1959:99).

Although the Kronhausens refer to Casanova's *Mémoires* as an example of "erotic realism" and to their author as a "champion of realistic romance" (Kronhausen and Kronhausen, 1959:93), other commentators have been more skeptical. Geoffrey Gorer says, in relation to Casanova's claim: "But he also successfully accomplished a great number of seductions without this adventitious aid. One would suspect that the impact of pornography was marginal, compared with the other techniques available to the seducer; but this would seem to be the only documented situation in which pornography has had an inciting effect" (Gorer, 1961:38). Yet although in some instances exposure to pornography might be likely to inhibit rather than to excite female erotic responses, it seems probable that Casanova's method will have been used with success in some, possibly "undocumented," situations. One witness before the Williams Committee spoke of "the danger . . . of pornography being used by an adult with a view, for example, to homosexual seduction" (Home Office, 1979:89).

In this connection Louis Proal, who was one of the presiding judges at a French court of appeal and a noted "authority on all questions connected with crime" at the turn of the century, thought that it was not pornography, which he dismissed in less than two pages, but romantic novels that were the real danger. "I have often noted in criminal proceedings," he wrote in his *Passion and Criminality*, "how seducers are in the habit of lending novels to girls they are trying to lead astray, and how they very soon attain their ends by this means" (Proal, 1900:423).

Promotion of moral decay

Pornography as a pollutant of the moral character of adult society. The Johnson Commission had little to say about the effect of the dissemination of pornographic material on "the commonly accepted, moral, social and ethical standards and ideals characteristic of American life." Indeed, it seemed more concerned with the way in which censorship "inhibits experimentation with new ideas, dampens response to social change, and limits the sources of cultural variety" (U.S. Commission, 1970:34, 35). The commission summed up its view on the alleged deleterious effect of the "distribution of explicit sexual materials to adults . . . upon the moral climate of America as whole" as follows:

The concern about the effect of obscenity upon morality is also expressed as a concern about the impact of sexual materials upon American values and standards. Such values and standards are currently in a process of complex change, in both sexual and nonsexual areas. The open availability of increasingly explicit sexual material is only one of these changes. The current flux in sexual values is related to a number of powerful influences, among which are the ready availability of effective methods of contraception, changes of the role of women in our society, and the increased education and mobility of our citizens. The availability of explicit sexual materials is, the Commission believes, not one of the important influences on sexual morality. (ibid.:54–55)

The Williams Committee, however, took this topic more seriously, noting that, among other alleged deleterious effects of pornography, "harms of a less definite and more pervasive kind have been alleged, which relate to general effects on society of pornography and violent publications and films, and which can best be summed up, perhaps, under the phrase, used by several witnesses, 'cultural pollution.' Such phrases certainly refer to something and we take seriously what they refer to." More specifically, the committee said:

The broadest arguments put to us concerned the social harms flowing from the widespread availability of pornography. In terms of cultural pollution, moral deterioration and the undermining of human compassion, social values and basic institutions. Arguments of this kind were less concerned with the possiblity of specific effects on individual behaviour than with the gradual infecting of society with a disregard for decency, a lack of respect for others, a taste for the base, a contempt for restraint and responsibility: in short, with the weakening of our civilisation and the demoralisation of society. (Home Office, 1979:59, 92)

A leading exponent of the view associating pornography with cultural sickness, Mr. David Holbrook, appeared as a witness before the committee and argued that as a result of pornography's having been allowed to increase in the culture in recent years,

debased sexuality has been thrust into our consciousness through powerful mass media. In consequence, in his view, there is now a widespread mental obsession with sexuality, a considerable degree of commercialisation of sex, a growing egotistical nihilism, a preoccupation with satiation and a corruption of culture. Culture has been debased to the extent that it is now difficult to write about sexual matters in an adult way because the expectation of the audience had been so corrupted. Writers wishing to appear trendy had committed intellectual treachery by praising the latest work of sex and violence, while those who attempted to raise a debate on the serious issues involved in the spread of pornography and its effect on culture were ignored and isolated. Mr. Holbrook complained that his books were no longer being reviewed because editors disagreed with the stand he had taken. (ibid.:92)

The Williams Committee said that arguments of this nature

should not be discounted or ignored simply because they are not based on direct tangible effects. Long-term effects on civilisation and culture are self-evidently important and should be considered as carefully as one can, even if they cannot be quantified and demonstrated. The arguments here do, however, involve the danger . . . of citing as a cause something that is itself only an effect or part of a cultural and historical process. There is also the danger that the cultural process is itself disliked because it is new, unfamiliar, and perhaps threatening, and things that are indeed extreme and ugly cultural phenomena, but perhaps not deeply significant ones, are seized on in order to attack social and moral developments which are indeed more significant, but less obviously to be rejected. (ibid.:93)

The committee concluded that the diagnosis of cultural sickness was not very closely connected with pornography. Sexual matters, it said, were now more openly discussed than before and the fact that pornography, which was "an age-old phenomenon," was less concealed than in the past was simply one aspect of that development. "We have no doubt that this new openness is among the things that have influenced the availability of pornography, rather than the reverse." It did not see "pornography as having a crucial or even a significant effect on essential social values" (ibid.:94–95).

The Meese Commission also took this matter seriously but was unable to reach an agreed conclusion about it. "Perhaps the largest question," the commission said, "and for that reason the question we can hardly touch here, is the question of harm as it related to the moral environment of a society. There is no doubt that numerous laws, taboos, and other social practices all serve to enforce some forms of shared moral assessment. The extent to which this enforcement should be enlarged, the extent to which sexual morality is a necessary component of a society's moral environment, and the appropriate balance between recognition of individual choice and the necessity of maintaining some sense of community in a society are questions that have been debated for generations." They were also questions about which there were "profound differences in opinion that can scarcely be the subject of a vote by this Commission."

"We all agree," the commission concluded,

that some degree of individual choice is necessary in any free society, and we all agree that a society with no shared values, including moral values, is no society at all. We have numerous different views about the way in which these undeniably competing values should best be accommodated in this society at this time, or in any society at any time. We also have numerous different views about the extent to which, if at all, sexual morality is an essential part of the social glue of this or any other society. We have talked about these issues, but we have not even attempted to resolve our differences, because these differences are reflective of differences that are both fundamental and widespread in all societies. That we have been able to talk about them has been important to us, and there is no doubt that our views on these issues bear heavily on the views we hold about many of the more specific issues that have been within the scope of our mission." (U.S. Department of Justice, 1986:345–346)

Availability of pornography as harming the moral values of youth. The Johnson Commission ordered a study designed to evaluate critically hypotheses about the impact of exposure to pornography and erotically realistic materials upon inter alia moral character. In the study the subjects were young men between the ages of eighteen and thirty. The aspects of character assessed were (1) moral blindness; (2) quality of moral reasoning; and (3) defective interpersonal character such as that exhibited in exploitative and shallow interpersonal relationships. It was found that there was "a modest relationship . . . between exposure to pornography and low scores on the moral character indices, but this relationship was due almost entirely to those subjects exposed late (after age 17), and it seemed most plausible to attribute the relationship to those with low character scores voluntarily exposing themselves to pornographic materials" (U.S. Commission, 1971–72, 7:173–243).

The commission did not directly address the question of the effect of the availability of pornography on the moral values of youth. It did, however, recommend that "a massive sex education effort be launched" and that "its purpose would be to contribute to healthy attitudes and orientations to sexual relationships so as to provide a sound foundation for our society's basic institutions of marriage and family." This was recommended as "a powerful positive approach to the problems of obscenity and pornography" that would provide "protection for the individual against distorted and warped ideas" (U.S. Commission, 1970:48). It was clearly implied that pornography did not encourage healthy attitudes and orientations toward sexual relationships and might be a source of warped ideas. But this was not explicitly stated.

The Williams Committee noted that most of its witnesses wished to see children and young persons protected from exposure to pornography. But the concern of witnesses appears, from the committee's report, to have focused not on harms to moral values, but rather on the possibility of "psychological damage" or deviant sexual development. There is nothing specific in the report about the moral values of youth (Home Office, 1979:88–89).

The Meese Commission in its discussion of the category of nonviolent and nondegrading materials disagreed about whether exposure to these materials was harmful to adults. But it reported:

We have little doubt that much of this material does find its way into the hands of children, and to the extent that it does we all agree that it is harmful. . . . We all agree about the questions of the desirability of exposing children to most of this material, and on that our unanimous agreement is that it is undesirable. For children to be taught by these materials that sex is public, that sex is commercial, and that sex can be divorced from any degree of affection, love, commitment, or marriage is for us the wrong message at the wrong time. (U.S. Department of Justice, 1986:344)

Offensiveness

The presence of pornography offends large groups in the population. Dr. Weldon T. Johnson, who was the senior author of "The Impact of Erotica: Report of the Effects Panel to the Commission on Obscenity and Pornography" in the Johnson Commission's report, has said that the "Commission found that although substantial proportions of people are worried about the effects of erotic materials, there is also considerable annoyance that such materials merely exist" (Johnson, 1971:190).

It is not always easy to decide whether opposition to pornography derives from disapproval of its presence in a community, or disgust occasioned by exposure to it, or both. Two studies of citizen action groups organized against pornography, carried out for the Johnson Commission, found that "their goals tend to be amorphous and ill-defined" (U.S. Commission, 1970:33).

One study, which dealt with "selected individual characteristics of [anti-pornography groups'] central participants" found that "generally [they] themselves had not been exposed to pornography when young." Moreover, some "had never seen what they would define as pornographic movies and had never read what they would define as pornographic books or magazines. Yet nearly all of them had opinions expressed in terms of type and content, about the nature of such movies, books, and magazines. Apparently, much of the knowledge concerning pornographic materials was hearsay from 'opinion leaders' " (U.S. Commission, 1971–72, 5:144, 210, 211).

In the commission's Effects Panel report it is stated that one of the "especially prominent" assertions made about "erotica" is that it "is an offense against community standards of good taste." "Many public statements about erotica," it is said, "reveal that some persons . . . simply disapprove of its existence." But the panel also remarked that "there is a tendency to move from this argument [i.e., about offensiveness] to the 'harmful effects' assertion without recognizing the shift in concern" (U.S. Commission, 1970:142).

Professor A. W. B. Simpson has noted a similar "shift in concern" reflected in commentaries on the Williams Committee's report. "Since the report's publication," he says, "I have been struck by the number of critics who both assert that pornography is *intrinsically* evil (and imagine that this provides a reason why it should be banned by criminal law) and who go on to allege that it is intrinsically evil *because of its consequences,* as if they could not escape from the language of utilitarianism however hard they try" (Simpson, 1983:80).

The Williams Committee did refer to the question "whether the fact that many people in society think something morally wrong is good enough reason for there being a law against it." But it said that if the harm condition for legislation ["no conduct should be suppressed by law unless it can be shown to harm someone"] is accepted, then the answer to this question will be "no." And the committee had declared, "We accept the harm condition," so that the question of the offensiveness of the existence or presence of pornography in society as opposed to the offensiveness of exposure to pornographic material was not considered (Home Office, 1979:50).

The Meese Commission, although it regarded examination of the question of whether pornography was harmful as "a central part of our mission," reported:

To a number of us, the most important harms must be seen in moral terms, and the act of moral condemnation of that which is immoral is not merely important but essential. From this perspective there are acts that need be seen not only as causes of immorality but *as manifestations of it.* Issues of human dignity and human decency, no less real for their lack of scientific measurability, are for many of us central to thinking about the question of harm. And when we think about harm in this way, there are acts that must be condemned not because the evils of the world will thereby be eliminated, but because conscience demands it. (emphasis added)

The commission also said: "We believe it useful in thinking about harms to note the distinction between harm and offense. Although the line between the two is hardly clear, most people can nevertheless imagine things that offend them, or offend others, that still would be hard to describe as harms" (U.S. Department of Justice, 1986:303–304). None of this is entirely clear, but it seems to express, or at least to imply recognition of, the idea that the mere existence of pornography may be offensive.

Exposure to pornography offends large groups in the population. The Johnson Commission found that "there is very little consensus among people regarding . . . the 'offensiveness' of a given sexual depiction." It did, however, find "that certain explicit sexual materials are capable of causing considerable offense to numerous Americans when thrust upon them without their consent."

In this connection it referred to the "unwanted intrusion on individual sensibilities" involved in the display of potentially offensive sexually explicit pictorial materials in places easily visible from public thoroughfares or the property of others; and also to unsolicited advertisements containing potentially offensive sexual material communicated through the mails. The commission took the view that the offensiveness caused by undesired exposure to sexual depictions was sufficiently serious in scope or degree to warrant legislative action (U.S. Commission, 1970:41, 60).

The Williams Committee had no doubt that "for many people, pornography is not only offensive, but deeply offensive." In particular, "publicly displayed pornography . . . is straightforwardly offensive to those who do not want to take it in." Moreover, it said, "the reactions that many people experience to publicly displayed pornography are not just a matter of arbitrary taste, but are deep reactions . . . the offensiveness it displays to them is, in both a psychological and an ethical sense, a deep offensiveness" (Home Office, 1979:96–102). Like the Johnson Commission, the Williams Committee thought that legislation to deal with "offensiveness" was justified.

The Meese Commission noted that for many people the harm caused by pornography related to the way in which it may "intrude on the lives and sensibilities of the majority of the population who wish to have nothing to do with it." The commission said that "there may be many materials that regardless of their alleged harmlessness, and regardless of the fact that they are not legally obscene, ought not to be displayed in a manner that offends unwilling viewers" (U.S. Department of Justice, 1986:389–390).

Like the Johnson Commission and the Williams Committee, the Meese Commission favored restrictions on the public display of sexually explicit material. "We believe," the commission said, "that public display regulations, including but not limited to the control of advertising materials displayed on the exterior of adult establishments, and including but not limited to the display ordinances requiring shielding of the cover of sexually explicit magazines, are fully justifiable measures in a society that has long restricted indecent exposure" (ibid.:390–391).

The calculus of balance in the Williams Committee

Competing interests

As we have noted, the Williams Committee accepted "the harm condition": the principle that no conduct should be suppressed by law unless it could be shown to harm someone. Moreover, it found that almost without exception the evidence received by the committee, insofar as it touched on matters of principle, either stated something like this condition or took it for granted. "Virtually everyone . . . whatever their suggestions, used the language of 'harm' and accepted, so it seemed, the harm condition" (Home Office, 1979:50).

"The shortest argument for the harm condition," the committee said, "is simply that there is a presumption in favour of individual freedom: that the incursions of government into that freedom have to be justified; that the proper sphere of government is the protection of the interests of citizens; and so what is justifiably curbed by government is only what harms the interests of some citizens" (ibid.:51).

The basis for the value of free expression was stated by the committee as follows:

That we do not know in advance what social, moral or intellectual developments will turn out to be possible, necessary or desirable for human beings and for their future, and free expression, intellectual and artistic – something which may need to be fostered and protected as well as merely permitted – is essential to human development, as a process which does not merely happen (in some form or another, it will happen anyway), but so far as possible is rationally understood. It is essential to it, moreover, not just as a means to it, but as part of it. Since human beings are not just subject to their history but aspire to be conscious of it, the development of human individuals, of society and of humanity in general, is a process itself properly constituted in part by free expression and the exchange of human communication. (ibid.:55)

The presumption in favor of freedom of expression, however, had to be weighed against, and could be overruled by, considerations relating to harms the communication in question might cause. But the committee went further than asserting merely a presumption in favor of freedom of expression. "It is rather that there is a right to free expression . . . and weighty considerations in terms of harm have to be advanced by those who seek to curtail it" (ibid.:56). It is necessary, therefore, to consider the nature of those harms which might be considered sufficiently substantial to outweigh the right to free expression and justify the suppression of publications.

Harms to be balanced

In considering the harms supposedly caused by pornographic publications the Williams Committee made a detailed study of a variety of allegations or claims about various harms and their association with pornography. The kinds of harm cited are summarized in the committee's report as follows:

In evidence put to us it was claimed that crimes, particularly sexual crimes, are caused by exposure to pornographic or violent films or publications. There are other arguments about individual behaviour being modified or conditioned by what was read or seen in ways that were less specifically anti-social but which conflicted with perceived standards of morality or with the expectations of society. Some emphasised the aspects of pornography which degrade women in that much material is not only offensive, but encourages a view of women as subservient and as properly the object of, or even desirous of, sexual subjugation or assault. Others emphasised the exploitation of those who participate in the production of pornography and the damaging effects this was believed to have. At a rather more general level, some people saw certain kinds of material, in presenting a distorted view of human experience, as damaging to human relationships by hindering the full development of the human personality or corrupting the imagination. So we heard arguments about pornography leading to sex crimes, and violence in the media engendering crimes of violence, about pornography leading to marital breakdown by encouraging unusual and sometimes abhorrent sexual demands (usually by husbands of their wives) and arousing false expectations of sexual fulfillment, about the encouragement of promiscuity and sexual deviation, about the promotion of self-gratification and a contempt for discipline, about the engendering of hate and aggression, about the risk to the normal sexual development of the young, about people becoming desensitized or callous through a diet of violence. (Home Office, 1979:58–59)

Although the committee in its review of the harms possibly caused by pornography emphasized "the area where the harms are of the most definitely identifiable kind," it did not confine itself to that area. Besides those types of harm, the committee also considered, as noted earlier, "harms of a less definite and more pervasive kind . . . which relate to general effects on society of pornography and violent publications and films" (ibid.:59, 61).

The criteria for choice

Having stressed the weight of proof that should rest on anyone who proposed the curtailment of free expression, in order to protect the consumers of pornographic material or society from those consumers, the committee nominated "two general principles" to govern the evaluation of claims about harms due to pornography. The principles are that the alleged harms should be shown to exist beyond reasonable doubt and that they should be traceable specifically to the kind of material in question.

The first principle, the requirement for legal purposes, that the alleged causation of harm should lie "beyond reasonable doubt" was not, of course, novel. It reflected the causal concept of obscenity in terms of doing harm embodied in the celebrated "deprave and corrupt" test that was supposed to be applied in English law in deciding what was obscene. The committee noted that this concept had in practice "proved very resistant to being given the precise application, and submitting to the canons of proof, required by the law." But it does not appear to have regarded that as a disadvantage.

The second principle was the requirement that if a certain class of publications, in this case pornographic publications, was to be legally banned, then harms had to be ascribable to that class of publications. The question was not whether pornographic communication had ever harmed anyone but "whether pornography constitutes a class of publication to which, as such, there belongs a tendency to cause harms" (Home Office, 1979:59–60).

The Committee also drew a distinction between two different kinds of objectives that can be served by legal action on pornography. The first objective would be the prevention of harms such as crime or antisocial behavior caused by, or involved in, the production of pornography, which would call for the suppression or prohibition of certain publications. The second objective would be the prevention of the offensiveness of the public display of pornographic material, which could be met by a system of restriction. In relation to this second objective the committee nominated a third principle.

The third principle was designed to govern the imposition of restrictions on the public display of pornography on grounds of offensiveness. The principle in question is "the requirement that matter to be restricted should be 'offensive to reasonable people.' " This employed the concept of a reasonable person "already known to the law in connection with judgements of responsibility, negligence, and reasonable foresight." It was felt to be necessary because people differ in the extent to which they find things offensive: "Some people will be offended by almost anything, and others by nothing at all" (ibid.:102, 122).

Striking the balance

At first sight, the Williams Committee's "requirement . . . that the causation of harm should lie 'beyond reasonable doubt' " (Home Office, 1979:59) seems to have enabled the committee to make short work of any proposal that would censor sexual communication to consenting adults. The harm principle, as construed by the committee, eliminated all of the negative influences noted other than sex crimes and other antisocial conduct. The burden of proof removed the prospect of sex crime or violence as a support for censorship. Indeed, the burden of demonstration is so high in the Williams Committee calculus that there is some question about how the ban on public display or the prohibition of the use of children in pornographic productions is upheld. It appears to be achieved at the cost of some inconsistency.

In regard to public display, the committee referred to the prohibition of public sexual activity. "Laws against public sex," it reported, "would be generally thought to be consistent with the harm condition, in the sense that if members of the public are upset, distressed, disgusted, outraged or put out by witnessing some class of acts, then that constitutes a respect in which the public performance of those acts harms their interests and gives them a reason to object."

"The offensiveness of publicly displayed pornography," the report continued, "seems to us . . . to be in line with traditionally accepted rules protecting the interest in public decency. Restrictions on the open sale of these publications, and analogous arrangements for films, thus seem to us to be justified" (ibid.:99). It should be noted, however, that being "in line with traditionally accepted rules" is very different from being in line with the committee's requirement that the causation of harm should like beyond reasonable doubt if there was to be legislation against pornography.

Similar considerations apply to the committee's recommendation "that films, even those shown to adults only, should continue to be censored" (ibid.:146), which was made, despite representations from such bodies as the Fabian Society, the Defence of Literature and the Arts Society, the Films Committee of Writers Guild, and the British Federation of Film Societies, that the barriers to free communication of both facts and ideas should be removed. In fact, the committee formulated a "proposed prohibition test" according to which a film could be totally banned as "unfit for public exhibition, being one that . . . is unacceptable because of the manner in which it depicts violence, sexual activity or crime" (ibid.:156).

In this connection, the committee refers to films that "seemed to have no purpose or justification other than to reinforce or sell the idea that it can be highly pleasurable to inflict injury, pain or humiliation (often in a sexual context) on others." In regard to this type of material, the committee reported that "it *may* be that this very graphically presented sadistic material serves only as a vivid object of fantasy, and does not harm at all. There is certainly no conclusive evidence to the contrary. But there is no conclusive evidence, in favour of that belief, either, and in this connection it seems entirely sensible to be cautious" (ibid.:145). It hardly seems necessary to point out that this "entirely sensible" policy is hard to reconcile with the "beyond reasonable doubt" formula.

Finally, there is the question of children as consumers, or participants in the production, of pornography. With regard to children as consumers of pornographic material, the committee reported that although "the effects of pornography were widely seen as particularly dangerous to the young . . . we heard no evidence of actual harm being caused to children" by exposure to pornography (ibid.:88–89). Nevertheless, it asserted that "paternalistic protection in the literal sense, the protection of children and young people, is a proper and very important aim of the law in this area. . . . There may well be material which . . . responsible parents would not want to be available to children and young people, and this is properly something to be restricted" (ibid.:12).

The committee noted that the minimum age for admission to "X" films was eighteen, the age customarily adopted by the owners of existing pornography shops as the minimum for entry to such shops. Some witnesses, including representatives of the British Youth Council, made the point that it was very odd that married couples free to engage in sexual activity (sixteen being the age at which young people can, with parental consent, marry) should be considered too young to view the portrayal of sexual activity by others. But the committee concluded "that it would be wrong for us to recommend that the age be lowered" either for the showing of films or the sale of pornography. The argument in support of that conclusion runs as follows:

We thought that the argument that those who could lawfully engage in sexual activity should be allowed free access to pornography took an over-simple view of pornography. Much of what we have seen does not merely portray straightforward sexual activity of the kind that those who propose such arguments seem to have in mind. Those responsible for the censorship of films firmly believe that there is much film material that is totally unsuitable for adolescents. . . . Arguably, many publications fall into the same category. . . . There was no consensus among our expert witnesses about the age at which young people cease to need special protection, given the varying ages at which a certain level of maturity is reached. But the evidence we received gave some grounds for thinking that many young people of sixteen might still be vulnerable. Moreover, we felt bound to take into account, as the films censors sometimes do, that there is often a "slippage" problem in applying age restrictions, and that, for example, the adoption of eighteen as the age below which protection is given will in practice mean that far fewer fifteen-year-olds will be put at risk than if the prescribed age were sixteen. (ibid.:125–126)

Here, too, the "beyond reasonable doubt" requirement is dealt with by ignoring it.

In regard to the question of harmful effects on children as participants in the production of pornography, the Williams Committee stated that "although the evidence we received did not all point in the same direction . . . few people would be prepared to take the risk where children are concerned and just as the law recognizes that children should be protected against sexual behavior which they are too young to properly consent to, it is almost universally agreed that this should apply to participation in pornography . . . children are the most obvious examples of a group who are capable of exploitation because they do not enjoy a fully developed right to choose" (ibid.:40).

Later in its report, the Williams Committee speaks of "one class of potential harms which seems to us very clear and definite and to call for prohibition of certain publications . . . that of harms to those involved in the production of pornography"; and of its "conclusion that there were such harms involved in the exploitation of children." It recommends that "the law should prohibit both the acts concerned and the circulation of material depicting them" (ibid.:131). Nevertheless, although the harms seemed to the committee "very clear and definite," it is evident once again that in striking the balance between freedom of expression and harm, the committee's general principle, that proof of harm beyond reasonable doubt was required if freedom were to be restricted, was forgotten.

The First Amendment and the American pornography commissions

Pornography and First Amendment values

Any prohibition or restriction upon the dissemination of pornographic materials involves the regulation of the books or pictures that citizens may read or see. The First Amendment to the Constitution provides that government "shall make no law . . . abridging the freedom of speech, or of the press" (U.S. Constitution, Amendment I). The United States Supreme Court has for a long time held that the First Amendment does not protect hard-core pornography that rises to the court's definition of obscenity.

In brief, the traditional approach of the Supreme Court has been to distinguish between those communications that could be judged obscene – which were not protected by the First Amendment from government efforts to prohibit them – and writings, photographs, and motion pictures not judged obscene that were protected by the First Amendment and could not be prohibited.

The current legal status of pornography is defined in what is called the *Miller* test, which has now been in existence for more than fifteen years. To be without First Amendment protection, material must meet the tripartite test enunciated in *Miller v. California* (413 U.S. 15 [1973]). According to the *Miller* test, material is obscene if all three of the following conditions are met:

1. The average person, applying contemporary community standards, would find that the work, taken as a whole, appeals to the prurient interest (in sex); and
2. the work depicts or describes, in a patently offensive way, sexual conduct specifically defined by the applicable state (or federal) law; and
3. the work, taken as a whole, lacks serious literary, artistic, political, or scientific value.

The Supreme Court has ruled that "average person" as used here "means what it usually means" and is no less clear than "reasonable person" long used in other contexts (*Rinkus v. United States*, 436 U.S. 293, 300 [1978]). As to the other elements of this definition: "Virtually every word and phrase in the *Miller* test has been the subject of extensive litigation and substantial commentary in the legal literature. The result of this is that there is now a large body of explanation and clarification of concepts such as 'taken as a whole,' 'prurient interest,' 'patently offensive,' 'serious value,' and 'contemporary community standards' " (U.S. Department of Justice, 1986:257).

Other constitutionally mandated aspects of obscenity law, apart from this definition, include the prohibition of prosecution for an obscenity offense unless it can be shown that a person had knowledge of the general contents, character, and nature of the materials involved (*Smith v. California*, 361 U.S. 147 [1954]) and limitations on the procedures surrounding the initiation of a prosecution, to prevent suppression prior to a judicial determination of obscenity (*Heller v. New York*, 413 U.S. 483 [1973]). In addition, child pornography has been determined by the Supreme Court to be "without the protection of the First Amendment" (*New York v. Ferber*, 458 U.S. 747 [1982]).

The Meese Commission summed up the current position as follows:

In the final analysis, the effect of *Miller, Jenkins*, and a large number of other Supreme Court and lower court cases is to limit obscenity prosecutions to "hard core" material devoid of anything except the most explicit and offensive representations of sex . . . it should be plain both from the law, and from inspection of the kinds of material that the law has allowed to be prosecuted, that only the most thoroughly explicit materials, overwhelmingly devoted to patently offensive and explicit representations, and unmitigated by any significant amount of anything else, can be and are in fact determined to be legally obscene. (U.S. Department of Justice, 1986:259, 260)

Three things should be said about this legal framework in relation to our discussion of pornography. First, the Supreme Court's definition of obscenity is not coterminus with the definition of pornography adopted in Chapter 2. A writing or picture could be both sexually explicit and likely to cause sexual arousal and still be nonobscene and thus not subject to prohibition under First Amendment standards.

Second, the test for what constitutes obscenity has changed over the years and is neither clear nor widely popular. The de facto range of sexually explicit communications protected by constitutional courts widened in the United States after the *Roth* decision in 1957 (*Roth v. United States*, 354 U.S. 476 [1957]), expanded more rapidly in the 1960s, and contracted (by allowing community standards in particular localities a role in permissible definitions) in the mid-1970s.

Related to the uncertainty of judicial standards is the fact that case-by-case determination must be made by courts when government efforts to suppress particular examples of hard-core pornography are the basis for criminal-law enforcement. To some extent, it has been acknowledged to be an ad hoc and unpredictable process under current tests.

Against this background, the contrasting approaches of the two U.S. commissions are worthy of attention. Further, it is interesting to contrast the approach of the U.S. commissions with that of the Williams Committee, which dealt with the free-expression issues without the First Amendment test.

The Johnson Commission, referring to "its mandate from Congress to recommend definitions of obscenity which are consistent with constitutional rights," concluded that "the construction of such a definition would be extremely difficult." Moreover, it said that "the spirit and letter of our Constitution tell us that government should not seek to interfere with . . . the free communication of ideas among Americans – one of the most important foundations of our liberties." It concluded that there was "no warrant for continued governmental interference with the full freedom of adults to read, obtain or view whatever such [i.e., obscene] material they wish" and recommended "that federal, state, and local legislation prohibiting the sale, exhibition, or distribution of sexual materials to consenting adults should be repealed" (U.S. Commission, 1970:41, 51, 52).

The Meese Commission, by contrast, took the view that "the standard pornographic item . . . is so far removed from any of the central purposes of the First Amendment . . . that including such material within the coverage of the First Amendment seems highly attenutated." It concluded "not that obscenity regulation creates no First Amendment concerns, nor even that the Supreme Court's approach is necessarily correct. But we do believe the Supreme Court's approach is most likely correct" (U.S. Department of Justice, 1986:267–268). As we shall see, contrasting general sentiments lead to diametrically opposed First Amendment conclusions.

Senders and recipients in the Johnson Commission

Pornographic communication, whether it takes the form of spoken, written, printed, photographed, painted, sculpted, or drawn material, involves both senders and recipients of whatever is communicated. The Johnson Commission gave positive value to the communication interests of those who intend to send and receive sexually arousing communication as well as those who might accidentally offend against governmental prohibitions of obscenity. The commission argued that "Americans deeply value the right of each individual to determine for himself what books he wishes to read and what pictures or films he wishes to see. Our traditions of free speech and press also value and protect the right of writers, publishers, and booksellers to serve the diverse interests of the public" (U.S. Commission, 1970:53–54).

When the commission recommended the repeal of legislation prohibiting the sale, exhibition, or distribution of explicit sexual materials to consenting adults, it defined the term "explicit sexual material" as being used "to refer to the entire range of explicit sexual depictions or descriptions in books, magazines, photographs, films, statuary and other media. It includes the most explicit descriptions, or what is often referred to as 'hard-core pornography' " (ibid.:51). It took the view that the laws prohibiting the consensual sale or distribution of such materials were extremely unsatisfactory in their practical application.

The legal definition of obscenity in terms of "appeals to the 'prurient' interest of the average person, is 'patently offensive' in the light of 'community standards,' and lacks 'redeeming social value,' " the commission said, represented "vague and highly subjective aesthetic, psychological and moral tests" that provided no meaningful guidance and resulted in erroneous, inconsistent, and indefensible decisions by the courts. Furthermore, errors in the application of the law and uncertainty about its scope did not merely trouble pornographers and purveyors of pornography but also caused "interference with the communication of constitutionally protected materials" (ibid.:53).

Concerning the recipients of pornographic communications, the commission reported that "a majority of the American people presently are of the view that adults should be legally able to read or see explicit sexual materials if they wish to do so" and that such materials were "sought as a source of entertainment and information by substantial numbers of American adults." Moreover, not only was there no evidence that exposure to pornography adversely affects moral character or attitudes, it was "exceedingly unwise of government to attempt to legislate individual moral values and standards independent of behavior, especially by restrictions on consensual communication." To do so would "tend to establish an official moral orthodoxy, contrary to our most fundamental constitutional traditions." As noted earlier, however, the commission did favor restriction on the public display of "explicit sexual pictorial material . . . capable of causing offense of a substantial number of persons" (ibid.:53, 55, 61). But this was protecting those who might otherwise become the involuntary audience of pornography.

The Meese Commission report takes no stand on whether pornography without further literary or artistic merit has positive social value. The commission instead argued that any positive value associated with pornographic communications was adequately protected by the current constitutional standard. In discussing the threat of criminal prosecution, the commission gave serious consideration only to the liberty interests of legitimate artists that might be swept into the net of overly broad state regulation or pornography. It reported that it had "heard in one form or another from numerous organizations of publishers, booksellers, actors and librarians, as well as from a number of individual book and magazine publishers." Most of them, the commission said, had "urged general anti-censorship sentiments upon us" and expressed "fears of excess censorship." The commission reported, however, that "when we do our own researches, we discover that, with few exceptions, the period from 1974 to the present is marked by strikingly few actual or threatened prosecutions of material that is plainly not legally obscene."

The Meese Commission also discussed what is commonly referred to as the "chilling effect": the possibility that, even absent actual restriction or successful or threatened prosecution, the prospect of such action deters filmmakers, photographers, writers, and other creative artists from exercising their abilities to the fullest or from doing anything that is not "safe." The commission took the view that "the likelihood of actual or seriously threatened prosecutions is almost completely illusory . . . in almost every case those fears are unfounded . . . the fears seem to be fears of phantom dangers . . . at least for the past ten years no even remotely serious author, photographer, or filmmaker has had anything real to fear from the obscenity laws." The commission concluded that it was not the case "that the law is mistaken. It is those who are afraid who are mistaken" (U.S. Department of Justice, 1986:269–272).

The commission's lack of interest in the recipients of pornographic communication – the consumers of pornography – noted earlier in Chapter 3, is also apparent in relation to its discussion of the "presumptive relevance of the First Amendment." The commission argued in this connection that, as the predominant use of "most standard pornography" was "as a masturbatory aid," the whole matter was "far removed from any of the central purposes of the First Amendment." The argument runs as follows: "But once the predominant use, and the appeal to that predominant use, becomes apparent, what emerges is that much of what this material involves is not so much a portrayal of sex, or discussion of sex, but simply sex itself. As sex itself, the arguments for or against restriction are serious, but they are arguments properly removed from the First Amendment questions that surround primarily materials whose overwhelming use is not as a short-term masturbatory aid."

The commission did "not say that there is anything necessarily wrong with" the use of pornographic material as a masturbatory aid but apparently felt that its use for that purpose by consumers did not deserve separate First Amendment protection (ibid.:266–267).

Attitudes toward judicial intervention in pornography

Current legal tests for obscenity, with the need for case-by-case determination of whether sexually explicit materials are pornographic, render this area a hotbed of judicial activism. It is the Johnson Commission's proposition rather than the stance of the Meese Commission that would lessen case-by-case judicial involvement. But this factor is not considered important in either report. Both are in striking contrast to usual complaints about government by the judiciary.

The Legal Panel report for the Johnson Commission noted that legislation had "in recent years been introduced in Congress which would withdraw the jurisdiction of all federal courts to review findings made by federal juries or by state juries or courts that particular material is obscene" (U.S. Commission, 1970:369). The commission itself recommended against adopting any legislation to limit or abolish the jurisdiction in obscenity cases of the Supreme Court of the United States or of other federal judges and courts.

The commission took the view that it would be "exceedingly unwise to adopt the suggested proposal from the point of view of protection of constitutional rights." Juries and lower courts, it said, "on occasion find guilt in cases involving books and films which are entitled to constitutional protection, and state appeals courts often uphold such findings. These violations of First Amendment rights would go uncorrected if such decisions could not be reversed at a higher court level."

The commission went on to say in more general terms that it recommended

against the creation of a precedent in the obscenity area for the elimination by Congress of federal judicial jurisdiction in other areas whenever a vocal majority or minority of citizens disagrees strongly with the results of the exercise of that jurisdiction. Freedom in many vital areas frequently depends upon the ability of the judiciary to follow the Constitution rather than strong popular sentiment. The problem of obscenity, in the absence of any indication that sexual materials cause societal harm, is not an appropriate social phenomenon upon which to base a precedent for removing federal judicial jurisdiction to protect fundamental rights guaranteed by the Bill of Rights." (U.S. Commission, 1970:64)

The Meese Commission in its brief historical overview noted that active Supreme Court scrutiny of obscenity regulation began in the early 1960s following the case of *Roth v. United States* (354 U.S. 476 [1957]), in which the First Amendment was first taken to limit the particular works that could be found obscene. It further reported that by the late 1960s, as a result of the Supreme Court's practice of reversing obscenity convictions with respect to a wide range of materials, many of which were quite explicit, "obscenity regulation became essentially dormant." The Supreme Court decisions of 1973, however, most notably *Paris Adult Theaters I v. Slaton* (413 U.S. 49 [1973]) and *Miller v. California* (413 U.S. 15 [1973]), made it "clear once again that the First Amendment did not protect anything and everything that might be sold to or viewed by a consenting adult" (U.S. Department of Justice, 1986:246–248).

The commission did not question the need for judicial scrutiny. Indeed it said quite explicitly:

To the extent, therefore, that regulation of pornography constitutes an abridgment of the freedom of speech, or an abridgment of the freedom of the press, it is at least presumptively unconstitutional. And even if some or all forms of regulation of pornography are seen ultimately not to constitute abridgments of the freedom of speech or the freedom of the press, the fact remains that the Constitution treats speaking and printing as special, and thus the regulation of anything spoken or printed must be examined with extraordinary care. For even when some forms of regulation of what is spoken or printed are not abridgments of the freedom of speech, or abridgments of the freedom of the press, such regulations are closer to constituting abridgment than other forms of governmental action. If nothing else, the barriers between permissible restrictions on what is said or printed and unconstitutional abridgments must be scrupulously guarded. (U.S. Department of Justice, 1986:249–250)

The calculus of balance under the First Amendment

The Johnson Commission seems to have had no great difficulty in deciding which factors to consider in reaching a conclusion about the relevance of the First Amendment to pornographic communication. "The spirit and the letter of our Constitution," it said, "tell us that government should not seek to interfere with the fundamental rights or freedoms guaranteed by the First Amendment unless a clear threat of harm makes that course imperative" (U.S. Commission, 1970:54).

As to what was guaranteed by the First Amendment, the commission took it to be "the full freedom of adults to read, obtain or view whatever such [sexual] material they wish" (ibid.:52). At the same time, it "concluded that consensual exposure of adults to explicit sexual materials causes no demonstrable damaging individual or social effects" (ibid.:44). The practical consequence of this simple syllogism was the recommendation that all legislation prohibiting the sale, exhibition, or distribution of sexual materials to consenting adults should be repealed (ibid.:51).

The Meese Commission differed in two significant respects. First, it did not agree that the First Amendment offered general protection for freedom of expression. "The special power of the First Amendment," it said, "ought, in our opinion, to be reserved for the conveying of arguments and information in a way that surpasses some admittedly low threshold of cognitive appeal." Moreover, it was in no doubt that "most of what we have seen that to us qualified as hard-core material falls below this minimal threshold of cognitive or similar appeal" (U.S. Department of Justice, 1986:264–265).

Nevertheless, the commission took it as "a central part of our mission . . . to examine the question whether pornography is harmful." In this connection it took "a conscious decision not to allow our examination of the harm question to be constricted by the existing legal/constitutional definition of the legally obscene [but] to look at the potential for harm in a range of material substantially broader than the legally obscene." We have already considered the commission's findings in relation to harm that were contrary to those of the Johnson Commission, but this aspect of the report was not advanced as relevant to the constitutional definition of obscenity or to any calculus of balance under the First Amendment.

The political uses of First Amendment doctrine to argue particular regulatory results

The Johnson Commission was assigned "to recommend such legislative, administrative, or other advisable and appropriate action as the commission deems necessary to regulate effectively the flow of such traffic [i.e., in "obscene and pornographic materials"], without in any way interfering with constitutional rights" (U.S. Commission, 1970:1). The Meese Commission was asked "to make specific recommendations to the Attorney General concerning more effective ways in which the spread of pornography could be contained, consistent with constitutional guarantees" (U.S. Department of Justice, 1986:1957).

In neither case was their attention focused primarily on determining the meaning or scope of the First Admendment. They were asked to make what were essentially political recommendations that did not interfere with, or were consistent with, constitutional rights or guarantees. They were not asked to determine what the First Amendment was designed to promote, or what Chief Justice Burger in *Miller* called "the grand conception of the First Amendment and its high purposes in the historic struggle for freedom" (*Miller v. California*, 413 U.S. 15, 34 [1973]).

It was therefore almost inevitable that both commissions sought to interpret the First Amendment guarantees in terms consistent with their recommendations rather than to make recommendations that gave effect to the "high purposes" of the First Amendment. Thus, the Legal Panel to the Johnson Commission was asked to take on the task of "exploring constitutional limitations" (U.S. Commission, 1970:295), and the Meese Commission spoke of its "obligations not to recommend what we believe to be unconstitutional" (U.S. Department of Justice, 1986:260).

The Johnson Commission's interpretation of definitional and constitutional considerations was informed by its own view of the wisdom and appropriateness of obscenity prohibitions. Similarly, in regard to the Meese Commission's interpretation of the First Amendment, although the commission acknowledged "dissent existing even within the Supreme Court and . . . disagreement with the Supreme Court majority's approach, predominant among legal scholars," it nevertheless took a quite different view of the purpose of the First Amendment. The Johnson Commission was convinced there was "a constitutional right in adults to obtain obscene materials for private use" (U.S. Commission, 1970:363). The Meese Commission did "not believe that a total expansive approach is reasonable for society or conducive to preserving the particular values embodied in the First Amendment" (U.S. Department of Justice, 1986:264).

But what were "the particular values embodied in the First Amendment"? The Johnson Commission seems to have accepted the theory of broad First Amendment protection later expounded by Supreme Court Justice William O. Douglas in *Miller v. California:*

> To give the power to the censor, as we do today, is to make a sharp and radical break with the traditions of a free society. The First Amendment was not fashioned as a vehicle for dispensing tranquilizers to the people. Its prime function was to keep debate open to "offensive" as well as to "staid" people. The tendency throughout history has been to subdue the individual and to exalt the power of government. The use of the standard "offensive" gives authority to government that cuts the very vitals out of the First Amendment. As is intimated by the Court's opinion, the material before us may be garbage. But so is much of what is said in political campaigns, in the daily press, on TV, or over the radio. By reason of the First Amendment – and solely because of it – speakers and publishers have not been threatened or subdued because their thoughts and ideas may be "offensive" to some. (*Miller v. California*, 413 U.S. 15, 45 [1973])

The Meese Commission, by contrast, referred to the citation by the Supreme Court of "legitimated state interests at stake in stemming the tide of commercialized obscenity" in *Paris Adult Theater I v. Slaton,* including "the interest of the public in the quality of life and the total community environment, the tone of commerce in the great city centers, and possibly the public safety itself." And the commission noted that in this case the Court had also quoted former Chief Justice Earl Warren's opinion in *Jacobellis v. Ohio,* where he declared there is a "right of the nation and of the states to maintain a decent society" (U.S. Department of Justice, 1986:1273–1274; *Paris Adult Theater I v. Slaton,* 413 U.S. 49, 58 [1973]; *Jacobellis v. Ohio,* 378 U.S. 184, 199 [1964]).

The First Amendment and the limits of public law

One other method of comparing the two U.S. commissions' views on free expression is to examine the forms of regulation each would allow with respect to two headings: the usual tools of censorship such as prior restraint and criminal penalties, and new restrictions such as civil damages and regulations, which we call "semicensorship."

Censorship and criminal prosecution

Prior restraint

"One of the most well-established propositions of constitutional law relating to the guarantees given to free expression," the Johnson Commission reported, "is that government may not prevent the dissemination of a particular book or work until after a judicial determination is made that the prohibition of that work is consistent with applicable law and with the Constitution" (U.S. Commission, 1970:326). In fact, however, the commission found that "police . . . frequently issue a warning to the distributor [of obscene materials] that he will be arrested unless distribution of the objectionable material is stopped. This warning process may often result in withdrawal of material from circulation in a jurisdiction without the institution of a formal proceeding on a determination of whether the material is, in fact, obscene." It also found that the police had been "accustomed in many places to instituting prosecution through . . . large scale seizures of all copies of an allegedly obscene work" (ibid.:326, 333, 334).

The Meese Commission noted "the possibility that in some areas prosecutions might be attempted of works of undoubted merit in the name of obscenity law, or that obscenity prosecution might be threatened as a way of exercising permissible control over works that are not even close to being legally obscene." But it declared that although "we are sensitive to the risks of censorship beyond the bounds of what the First Amendment or good sense should allow . . . we have found many of these claims to be little more than hyperbole – providing little in the way of real evidence" (U.S. Department of Justice, 1986:381–382).

Criminal penalties

The Johnson Commission, as noted, recommended the repeal of all federal, state, and local legislation prohibiting the consensual distribution of obscene or sexual material (including "hard-core pornography") to adults. It did, however, recommend that the states adopt legislation prohibiting the commercial distribution or display for sale of certain sexual materials to young persons. It also recommended the enactment of state and local legislation prohibiting open public displays of sexually explicit pictorial materials; and it approved," in principle, of the federal legislation, enacted as part of the 1970 Postal Reorganization Act, regarding the mailing of unsolicited advertisements of a sexually explicit nature" (U.S. Commission, 1970:56, 60).

The Johnson Commission also formulated "Drafts of Proposed Statutes" in respect of both the sale and display of explicit sexual materials to young persons and the public display of sexually explicit pictorial materials. In neither case, however, did the commission specify penalties for violation of the statutes. In both cases, under the heading "Penalty," the draft statutes read: "Whoever violates the provisions of this section shall be liable to [left to state option]" (ibid.:66, 67). Nor is there any discussion of penalties for violation of the 1970 Postal Reorganization Act.

With regard to "The Sufficiency of Existing Criminal Laws," the Meese Commission declared, "we do not find the existing state of the law unsatisfactory." The commission did, however, report that "the conclusion is unmistakable that with respect to the criminal laws relating to obscenity, there is a striking underenforcement, and that this underenforcement consists of undercomplaining, underinvestigation, underprosecution, and undersentencing" (U.S. Department of Justice, 1986:367, 368).

With regard to sentencing specifically, the commission said that "the evidence was almost unanimous that small fines and unsupervised probation are the norm, with large fines or sentences of incarceration quite rare throughout the country." It said that "there seems to be a substantial interposition of judgment of seriousness between legislative determination and the actual sentence" with the result that "people who have control over the sale of illegally obscene materials do not go to jail . . . and if they do it is still less often and for less time than do people committing other crimes that allow equivalent statutory sentences" (ibid.:367, 368).

Because sentencing usually involved only a fine and unsupervised probation, the commission said that penalties were "often treated by the defendant as little more than a cost of doing business." In this connection the commission recommended the use of the Racketeer Influenced and Corrupt Organization (RICO) Act as a method of requiring many of those convicted of multiple and substantial obscenity violations "to disgorge the profits from their enterprises." It also recommended mandatory minimum sentences for second and further offenses while noting that "in many areas mandatory sentencing may result in plea bargains for lesser charges, or prosecutorial reluctance to proceed against someone the prosecutor is unwilling to see go to jail" (ibid.:368–370).

The Meese Commission also discussed briefly the question of decriminalization, recognizing that "this is an area marked by serious debate involving plausible arguments both for and against." It reported that "there are vast real and symbolic differences between not doing what has not been done before and undoing what is currently in place. To undo makes a statement much stronger than that made by not doing." And it concluded that "with reference to criminal sanctions against the legally obscene . . . the burden must be on those who would have us or society make the specially strong statement implicit in the act of repeal" (U.S. Department of Justice, 1986:356–358). It is clear from the tone of the report, although not explicitly stated, that the commission felt that that burden had not been discharged.

Semicensorship

Civil liabilities

In recent years considerable controversy has surrounded a proposed antipornography ordinance drafted by Andrea Dworkin and Catharine MacKinnon, some aspects of which are discussed in Chapter 6. The ordinance was proposed in different versions in Minneapolis, Minnesota; Los Angeles, California; Cambridge, Massachusetts; and Indianapolis, Indiana. It was adopted only in Indianapolis in June 1984 but was subsequently held unconstitutional by the U.S. District Court for the Southern District of Indiana (*American Booksellers Association v. Hudnut*, 598 F. Supp. 1316 [S.D. Ind. 1984]), a decision affirmed by the U.S. Court of Appeals for the Seventh Circuit (*American Booksellers Association v. Hudnut*, 771 F.2d 323 [7th Cir. 1985]) and the Supreme Court of the United States (*Hudnut v. American Booksellers Association*, 54 U.S.L.W. 3560 [Feb. 24, 1986]).

The basis for the finding of unconstitutionality was that the definition of pornography adopted in the ordinance was substantially broader than that in *Miller*. We here discuss briefly only the fact that the ordinance provided for a civil remedy rather than a criminal one, by way of suits for damages against the makers, distributors, sellers, and exhibitors of pornography for violation of the civil rights of women by discrimination on the basis of sex. This has been defended on the ground that it is not censorship because the state is not authorized to initiate criminal prosecutions.

In defense of the use of civil rather than criminal sanctions, one proponent of the ordinance has written: "I have no particular interest in increasing the power of the *state* over sexuality or speech. I do not have that kind of faith in the government. . . . Suppressing obscenity criminally has enhanced its value, made it more attractive. . . . Censoring pornography has not delegitimized it" (MacKinnon, 1987:140). The Meese Commission reported in this connection that "we endorse the concept of a civil remedy" and that "civil remedies available to a wide range of people ought seriously to be contemplated" (U.S. Department of Justice, 1986:595).

The Meese Commission, however, thought that because of the possibility of publishers "being forced to defend a wide range of suits that might raise claims that are totally without merit," some procedure was required to provide "for some preliminary determination by a judge or magistrate that the suit was plausible before the complaint was allowed to be filed" (ibid.). The ordinances, however, contain no such provisions and critics of them have argued that "the prospect of having to defend a potentially infinite number of privately filed complaints creates at least as much of a chilling effect against sexual speech as does a criminal law" (Duggan, Hunter, and Vance, 1986:80). Moreover, if the suggestion that this would not constitute censorship is not disingenuous, it is certainly ingenuous.

Restrictive regulation

A variety of proposals for, or measures of, regulation place important burdens on producers of pornography and tend to discourage production. One such stratagem is embodied in the Meese Commission's Recommendation 37: "Congress should enact a statute requiring the producers, retailers or distributors of sexually explicit visual depictions to maintain records containing consent forms and proof of performers' ages." The proposed legislation imposes the record-keeping obligation on wholesalers, retailers, distributors, producers, and anyone engaged in the sale or trade of sexually explicit material. All producers would have to obtain release froms from each performer with proof of age, to be filed at a specified location listed in the opening or closing footage of a film, the inside cover of a magazine, or standard locations in or on other material containing visual depictions. In addition:

The name, official title and location of the responsible person or corporate agent supervising such records would also be listed to avoid use of corporate shields. The release forms should be available for inspection by any duly authorized law enforcement officer upon demand as a regulatory function for the limited purpose of determining consent and proof of age. . . . A producer should be required to maintain these records for a minimum period of five years. Failure to comply with any of these requirements would be punishable as a felony. (U.S. Department of Justice, 1986:618–621)

The need for this legislation is said to arise because the existence of pseudo-child pornography (in which models over eighteen are presented in such a way as to make them appear to be children) has made it increasingly difficult for law enforcement officers to ascertain whether an individual in a film or other depiction is a minor. The concern said "to be addressed through this legislation is the safety and well being of children," including such things as damage to self-esteem, career prospects, personal and professional life.

The proposed legislation would not apply merely to the production of child pornography or pseudo-child pornography but to all sexually explicit material that features *actual* or *simulated:* sexual intercourse, including genital–genital, oral–genital, anal–genital, or oral–anal, whether between persons of the same or opposite sex; bestiality, masturbation; sadistic or masochistic abuse; or lascivious exhibition of the genitals or pubic area of any person (ibid.:618, 619).

It seems unlikely that all this recording and preserving of records would do anything to aid either the career prospects or professional lives of those whose data are filed at specified locations, or to affect the domestic commercial production of child pornography, which the commission acknowledged had already been substantially curtailed and of which there was "comparatively little" anyway (ibid.:409). What it is clearly intended to do is to hamper and obstruct the production of all kinds of pornographic material.

Regulation by zoning is another method that can be employed to achieve prior restraint of pornographic communication. The use of municipal zoning ordinances to regulate establishments that specialize in sexually explicit material usually involves a definition of sexually explicit material that is more expansive than *Miller* and includes more than could be criminally prosecuted under *Miller*. The Supreme Court has approved this sort of zoning regulation in *Young v. American Mini Theaters Inc.* (427 U.S. 50 [1976]) and in *City of Renton v. Playtime Theaters Inc.* (106 S. Ct. 925 [1986]).

The Supreme Court held that the Renton ordinance was a "content neutral" time, place, and manner regulation of speech because it was not aimed at the content of the speech but was directed at such secondary effects as the protection of the city's retail trade, the maintenance of property values, and the preservation of the quality of urban life; and that reasonable alternative avenues of communication were available (*City of Renton v. Playtime Theaters Inc.*, 106 S. Ct. 925 [1986]). But it is clear that such zoning regulation could achieve the effects of virtual prohibition, even though the Supreme Court has held that a zoning regulation must not have the effects of a total prohibition (*Schad v. Mt. Ephraim*, 452 U.S. 61 [1981]).

Time, place, and manner regulations, however, need not necessarily represent attempts to restrict expression because of its messages, its ideas, its subject matter, or its content. It is true that zoning regulations for "adult" entertainment businesses can be used to discourage them by restricting them to the most unattractive, inaccessible, and inconvenient areas of the city or by limiting them to locations so inaccessible as to be no locations at all. But there is no reason why regulation of "adult" businesses either by dispersal or by effective concentration should amount to censorship. If such regulation allows for reasonable alternative avenues of communication and is not designed simply to restrict the exercise of First Amendment rights, it may be inconvenient but it will not necessary be censorial. All three commissions would approve some such regulation as consistent with free expression values.

Conclusion

We have set out to study not the proper relationship of First Amendment doctrine to pornography but rather the way in which government commissions deal with the issues of free expression. The existence of the Williams Committee report allows some contrast between the U.S. commissions and the discussion of free expression in a nonconstitutional context.

The Williams Committee considered the same harms and benefits as its American cousins did, and dealt with the issues at the same level of generality. The presence of a First Amendment context was important to the American commissions in two respects: First, lawyers played a more important role in the commissions' processes because legal issues played a more conspicuous role in the discussion of permissible regulation. Second, there was a need for detailed argument about constitutional precedent and its meaning.

But this was ultimately the legal argument of advocates rather than judges, and it was advocacy after the fact of each commission's reaching basic conclusions about the regulation of pornography. The First Amendment context in the United States seems to have affected the style of commission inquiries on the subject of pornography more than their substance.

In one respect the discussion of free-expression issues as First Amendment issues risks confusion. Any definition of First Amendment rights that excludes certain categories of the "offensive" or the "sexually explicit" may generate the impression that people have no free-expression interest in sending offensive or sexually explicit messages, or that potential audiences have no interest in receiving them. That is *not* the law. The use of a balancing process to justify government restriction on some forms of communication is not the same as finding that such communications have no value or that the desire of potential audiences to receive them is utterly unworthy of respect.

There are four distinct free-expression interests implicated in decisions about the regulation of pornographic communication. First, there is the claim of individuals to publish material they believe to be of interest or value, which, although not intended to be pornographic, might be regarded by others as pornographic. Second, there is the right of an audience to see or hear such material even if in the eyes of some persons it might be regarded as obscene. The prevailing obscenity standards in American court cases are, in fact, designed to prevent communications about sex being accidentally classified as pornographic and therefore subject to state regulation. Both these interests are recognized by the two American commissions as well as the Williams Committee. Third, there is the interest in sending explicitly pornographic communications or messages. Here it is claimed that the interest in free expression includes the free expression of ideas or images intended to arouse sexually. Fourth, it is claimed that the interest in freedom of choice includes the right to choose to be exposed to intentionally pornographic communication.

The Johnson Commission and the Williams Committee appear to have endorsed an adult right to choose to be exposed to pornographic material. It is, however, seen as an interest that may be qualified by the requirements that offense should not be given to other nonconsenting adults and that minors should not be harmed. The Meese Commission seems to have attached no importance at all to the pornographer's interest in pornographic communications that can be classified as obscene. Moreover, it evidently saw no significant value in citizens' right to choose their level of exposure to pornographic communication.

The reason why this interest is ignored, if not categorically rejected, was never explicitly addressed by the Meese Commission. Yet it would seem obvious that the question of the value to be attached to an individual's right to see or her sexually explicit communication, including pornographic communication that meets the current legal test of obscenity, must be an important, if not crucial, consideration in the determination of appropriate regulation of the dissemination of pornographic communication.

II

Public policy after liberalization

Introduction

Throughout Part I, the written record of three governmental commissions was the focus of discussion. In this section, we address four topics of significance to understanding pornography as a social issue that were not considered in detail by the commissions.

In Chapter 6, we examine the question of pornography and the status of women through a narrow but interesting lens, concentrating on the radical feminist critique of Catherine MacKinnon and Andrea Dworkin. Chapter 7 describes the many issues involving pornography and child welfare. Chapter 8 discusses the prospects of influencing the content and distribution of pornography with strategies other than censorship. Chapter 9 deals with the steps likely to be taken in public policy toward pornography in the last decade of the century.

These issues have one important common element – they all acquire special significance when general policies of censoring pornography are withdrawn and the open availability of pornography becomes a social fact.

As long as pornography could be suppressed because of its sexual content, the question of pornography as gender discrimination was not an important part of the case for prohibition. It is when the erotic content of pornography no longer justifies restriction that the issue of the other aspects of pornography's effects becomes important. The issue of pornography as sex discrimination is crucial in policy terms because it would now be an independent basis for its legal restriction.

The special problems of pornography and child welfare are also obscured by a general policy of prohibition. If all who act in pornographic movies are outside the law, the special dangers of child participants and the related question of who should be considered a child are not of crucial policy importance. And if pornography cannot be distributed to adults, no special analysis is necessary to justify banning its distribution to children. It is when children become a potential exception to a general policy of availability that the special status of childhood becomes a significant policy issue. So the peculiar nature of child welfare interests is of particular concern in a postliberalization era.

As long as censorship is used by government as a first resort, more limited strategies of coping with the harms that pornography might cause are of little interest. Censorship occupies the field. To speak of more modest measures is as hard as getting people to pay attention to the role that small arms might play in a general nuclear war. It is only when censorship is not an acceptable general strategy that other, less drastic government policies can receive attention. And the role of nongovernment groups also seems more important when governmental suppression is no longer a general official policy.

In the immediate aftermath of liberalization, the future course of government policy seems difficult to predict in a way that does not happen during less dynamic periods. Will the pendulum swing back? Now that noncensorship has been a social fact for more than a decade, what are we learning about some of its midrange social impacts? These issues, too, are the special concern of a postliberalization era.

It is our view that these last years of the twentieth century are a period of adjustment, a transitional time when the issues generated by the availability of pornography seem more important than they will in later years. Many of the phenomena that puzzle observers, including the missionary zeal of antipornography groups and the sharp contrast between the two American commissions, can be best understood as the expected friction of a transition period.

The most likely sequel to the stresses and conflicts that follow a sharp shift in policy is not so much a counterreformation as a settling down. Perhaps then the path toward equilibrium will produce a time when public policy toward smut is not only less contentious but also less important as a political and social issue.

6

Pornography and the subjugation of women: the radical feminist challenge

In this chapter we review the lively recent debate on pornography and women's rights from what has been called the "radical feminist perspective." After a brief historical introduction, we review the critique by two radical feminist writers, Andrea Dworkin and Catharine MacKinnon, as well as critical reactions to this theoretical perspective. We then consider the issue of the impact of pornography on the status of women from outside of the framework of the Dworkin–MacKinnon point of view.

The relationship between pornography and the status of women is a broad and multifaceted topic, one that deserves book-length treatment on its own. Even the ostensibly narrow topic of pornography and feminist thinking quickly broadens when the reader confronts the wide variety of feminist perspectives and the very different policies toward pornographic communication they imply.

Such broader concerns with feminist theory are beyond our present scope and our scholarly capacities. But the focus on the Dworkin–MacKinnon analysis as a particular subject for a chapter requires a specific justification.

The particular feminist critique we consider here is both conceptually novel and historically important. The label "radical feminist" is the self description of the two authors of this approach, whose writings have played a major role in establishing pornography as an agenda item in feminist studies as well as justifying legislative initiatives in Minneapolis and Indianapolis. This new critique has assumed historical importance in much the same way as have some of the commission reports discussed in Part I.

We consider the writings of Dworkin and MacKinnon for many of the same reasons we examined the Meese Commission in detail: to gain understanding and perspective. Our treatment of the Dworkin–MacKinnon analysis parallels that of the commission reports, focusing first on issues of definition and then on the effects of pornography and the question of free expression. This parallel treatment is intended to show how and why the radical feminist approach differs from the analysis of the governmental commissions.

151

The issue of pornography as an instrument of the degradation or subordination of women was not dealt with as a central theme by any of the three bodies whose work we have examined. Indeed, the issue seems almost to have escaped altogether the attention of the Johnson Commission, apart from its noting that the available evidence suggested that fears about explicit sexual materials leading people to lose respect for women were "probably unwarranted" (U.S. Commission, 1970:201).

When the Williams Committee reported in 1979, it devoted only one paragraph to "the degradation of women in pornography," against which, the report said, "many of our women correspondents wanted the law to be invoked." The committee had received evidence with "a specifically feminist viewpoint" that tended to see pornography as a "form of sexism" and as "one of the instruments of women's repression." But it took the view "that pornography (at least on these grounds) should not be singled out for special treatment under the law" (Home Office, 1979:88).

Nearly a decade later the Williams Committee's summary treatment of this topic may appear analogous to a discussion of the American Indian wars without any mention of the Indians' perspective. But there is no doubt that the committee was influenced by the fact, noted at the end of that paragraph, that "the consensus of those parts of the women's movement from which we heard tended to attach greater importance to freedom of expression than to the need to suppress pornography" (Home Office, 1979:88). Moreover, as one of the committee's members, Professor A. W. B. Simpson, has since pointed out, "the radical feminist attack on pornography has . . . been developed since the Report was written" (Simpson, 1983:67).

The Meese Commission found that

an enormous amount of the most sexually explicit material available, as well as much of the material that is somewhat less sexually explicit, is material that we would characterize as "degrading," the term we use to encompass the undeniably linked characteristics of degradation, domination, subordination, and humiliation. The degradation we refer to is degradation of people, most often women, and here we are referring to material that . . . depicts people, usually women, as existing solely for the sexual satisfaction of others, usually men, or that depicts people, usually women, in decidedly subordinate roles in their sexual relations with others, or that depicts people engaged in sexual practices that would to most people be considered humiliating. Indeed, forms of degradation represent the largely predominant proportion of commercially available pornography. (U.S. Department of Justice, 1986:331)

But the Meese Commission, like the Williams Committee, did not focus on the role of pornography in reinforcing women's subservient role in society. In a footnote to the report, it says explicitly:

We restrict our analysis in large part to degradation that is in fact depicted in the material. It may very well be that degradation led to a woman being willing to pose for a picture of a certain variety, or to engage in what appears to be a non-degrading sexual act. It may be that coercion caused the picture to exist. And it may very well be that the existing disparity in the economic status of men and women is such that any sexually explicit depiction of a woman is at least suspect on account of the possibility that the economic disparity is what caused the woman to pose for a picture that most people in this society would find embarrassing. We do not deny any of these possibilities, and we do not deny the importance of considering as pervasively as possible the status of women in contemporary America, including the effects of their current status and what might be done to change some of the detrimental consequences of that status. But without engaging in an inquiry of that breadth, we must generally, absent more specific evidence to the contrary, assume that a picture represents what it depicts. (U.S. Department of Justice, 1986:331 n. 47)

It is relevant to mention here that the Canadian Special Committee on Pornography and Prostitution, four out of the seven members of which were women, viewed with sympathy the feminist argument that pornography was "an evil which limits the full human rights and dignity of women." It also made some proposals for legislation reflecting that view. The committee acknowledged that the theoretical basis for this approach derived "in great measure . . . from the work of two American thinkers, Catharine MacKinnon and Andrea Dworkin" (Canada, 1985:201, 305), which we discuss in some detail in this chapter.

The Dworkin–MacKinnon critique

Professor Simpson noted that "virtually everything which has been produced by the radical feminist movement on the subject [i.e., pornography] is American" (Simpson, 1983:67). It remains true that the most forceful statement of the radical feminist critique of pornography may be found in two books by American authors: Andrea Dworkin's *Pornography: Men Possessing Women* (1981) and Catharine A. MacKinnon's *Feminism Unmodified: Discourses on Life and Law* (1987). It is on these two works that our analysis of that critique is focused.

It is, of course, true that not all that can be said about pornography and the subordination of women is to be found in the works cited. Moreover, there are, as we shall see, other radical feminists who take a very different view, rejecting the Dworkin–MacKinnon analysis as "a dangerous oversimplification that is ultimately harmful to women" (Ellis, O'Dair, and Talmer, 1986:6). Nevertheless, that analysis represents a novel approach to the problem of pornography as well as a categorical and uncompromising challenge to more conventional views that is widely regarded as of historic significance.

We here consider their critique under three headings: the definition of pornography, the effects of pornography, and the implications for freedom of expression. After looking at what others have said, we will offer our own views on the subject of this specific debate and the larger issue of pornogra-phy and status of women.

Definition

As noted in Chapter 2, an essential preliminary to any discussion of pornogra-phy must be some attempt at the definition of pornography. It is therefore fortunate that, as Catharine MacKinnon reports, the ideas on this subject held by the two authors "were developed and refined in close collaboration." "What Andrea Dworkin and I mean by pornography," she says,

is rather well captured in our legal definition: Pornography is the graphic sexually explicit subordination of women, whether in pictures or in words, that also includes one or more of the following: (i) women are presented dehumanized as sexual objects, things, or commodities; or (ii) women are presented as sexual objects who enjoy pain or mutilation; or (iii) women are presented as sexual objects who experience sexual pleasure in being raped; or (iv) women are presented as sexual objects tied up or cut up or mutilated or bruised or physically hurt; or (v) women are presented in postures of sexual submission, servility, or display; or (vi) women's body parts – including but not limited to vaginas, breasts, and buttocks – are exhibited, such that women are reduced to those parts; or (vii) women are presented as whores by nature; or (viii) women are presented being penetrated by objects or animals; or (ix) women are presented in scenarios of degradation, injury, torture, shown as filthy or inferior, bleeding, bruised, or hurt in a context that makes these conditions sexual. (MacKin-non, 1987:262)

Pornography is further defined as including "the use of men, children, and transsexuals in the place of women." It is also said somewhat cryptically that "the definition does not include all sexually explicit depictions *of* the subordi-nation of women. This is not what it says. It says, this which *does* that: the sexually explicit that subordinates women." By way of contrast it is said that "erotica, defined by distinction as not this, might be sexually explicit materi-als premised on equality" (ibid.:176).

Because the problem of pornography is itself essentially a matter of deter-mining limits, we should examine this definition closely. It is immediately evident that it is not in the usual sense a definition (i.e., a statement indi-cating the meaning or use of a word) at all. "What Andrea Dworkin and I mean by pornography" may be "rather well captured" but what the term means in ordinary usage, as reflected in dictionaries, for example, is ignored.

This does not render irrelevant their discussion of the problem of pornogra-phy. For it is clear that in choosing this strategy of definition, as opposed to what is ordinarily understood by the term, they are doing so deliberately in order to focus attention on aspects of that problem that they regard as impor-tant and neglected.

"*What Andrea Dworkin and I mean by pornography*"

What they provide, in fact, is not a statement of the ordinary meaning or use of the word "pornography" but rather what has been called a stipulative definition of it. Stipulative definition, as noted in Chapter 2, involves "establishing or announcing or choosing one's own meaning for a word." It has been illustrated as follows: "Humpty Dumpty insisted that words were to mean what he chose that they should mean. He did not concern himself with any lexical inquiries, that is, with finding out what some set of people actually had meant by some word. He laid down what the word was to mean when he used it. That was stipulative definition" (Robinson, 1950:19, 59; see also Morris, 1960:30–31).

A stipulative definition is not an attempt to report actual usage. "It is more like a *request* to the reader that he will understand the word in a certain way, or a *command;* and these, though significant utterances, have no truth value. It is a proposal rather than a proposition" (Robinson, 1950:63). And although Dworkin and MacKinnon nowhere explicitly state that they are offering a stipulative definition, it is clear from their use of the term "pornography" and their specification of its denotation that that is what they are doing.

A. W. B. Simpson in a critique of the kind of definition offered by Dworkin has said that it is not "presented against the background of any attempt to analyse pornography into different forms, some catering for more peculiar perversions and some not, some concerned with women, some wholly directed towards homosexual men. Pornography is treated as simply one indivisible phenomenon; it is hard to believe that some feminists writers have ever seen any" (Simpson, 1983:71). In fact, however, in MacKinnon's more recent work (1987), the Dworkin–MacKinnon discussion of pornography does seem to take cognizance of many aspects of the greater variety of pornographic material available. Moreover, as it is rarely possible to recite the whole of the denotation of a word, it is usual to do what they have done and only list some of the things to which the word is applied. The fact is that "no collection of cases . . . is ever sufficient to determine uniquely the denotation of a term" (Lewis, 1929:78).

Joel Feinberg, however, makes a more pertinent point that is relevant to the Dworkin–MacKinnon definition when he says: "It will not do then to isolate the most objectionable kinds of pornography, the kinds that are most offensive and even dangerous to women, and reserve the label 'pornographic' for them alone. This conscious redefinition is what numerous feminist writers have done, however, much to the confusion of the whole discussion" (Feinberg, 1985:145). For it does seem that in their selection of the items to which the term "pornography" is applied in their definition, Dworkin and MacKinnon have done just that.

Indeed, in focusing on material that involves "graphic sexually explicit subordination of women . . . enjoying pain or humiliation or rape; being tied up, cut up, mutilated, bruised, or physically hurt . . . presented in scenarios of degradation, injury, torture; shown as filthy or inferior, bleeding, bruised, or hurt in a context that makes these conditions sexual" (MacKinnon, 1987:176), they select those kinds of pornography which are not only "most objectionable" and "most offensive . . . to women" but also to many men.

The highly selective characterization of pornography that is emphasized in the Dworkin–MacKinnon definition refers principally to a type of material that a majority of males as well as females would regard as offensive. The Williams Committee was not expressing an idiosyncratic view when it declared that much pornography is "trash, ugly, shallow, and obvious" and that "many people" find it "upsetting and disagreeable . . . not only offensive but deeply offensive" (Home Office, 1979:96).

Even the boldest champions of freedom in art and literature usually hasten to add that they personally dislike or disapprove some types of pornography and find it repugnant. No doubt some of these professions of distaste are disingenuous and represent what has been called "nose-holding orthodoxy (I personally hate this stuff but defend its right to exist)" (McGrath, 1985: 67). But distaste for most of the material that is nominated as representative of pornography by Dworkin and MacKinnon is not a minority matter.

The inadequate and tendentious nature of their definition can be seen not only in the nature of what is included in it but also in what is excluded. For example, it takes no account of what the Meese Commission called "our most controversial category . . . of sexually explicit materials . . . materials in which the participants appear to be fully willing participants occupying substantially equal roles in a setting devoid of actual or apparent violence or pain" (U.S. Department of Justice, 1986:335). This may be what MacKinnon calls "erotica . . . sexually explicit materials premised on equality" (MacKinnon, 1987:176), but for a great many consumers this would be the most popular form of what they regard as pornography. "The most commonly available form of pornography is non-violent representations of nudity or sexual activity aimed at heterosexual men" (Ellis et al., 1986:4). Indeed, if one compares the Dworkin–MacKinnon critique of pornography with the late Kenneth Tynan's celebrated defense of hard-core pornography (Tynan, 1970:111), it is difficult to believe that they are talking about the same subject.

It is notable, too, that they seem to exclude from their definition not only "pornography . . . wholly directed towards homosexual men" (Simpson, 1983:71) but also those "pornographic materials intended for men, that appeal to their masochistic side exclusively, in which they are 'ravished' and humiliated by some grim-faced amazon of fearsome dimensions" (Feinberg,

1985:145). Perhaps these types of material are excluded because they cannot be regarded as "a practice of sex discrimination, a violation of women's civil rights," which is also said to be a definition of pornography (MacKinnon, 1987:175).

Thus, a legitimate criticism of this approach to the definition of pornography would be not simply that it does not provide a true account of the materials to which the word is ordinarily applied, but rather that it constitutes a radical redefinition of the term. And a large proportion of the items included in the core concept of pornography as defined by Dworkin and MacKinnon would be regarded by many as a reflection of pathological perversity rather than material that would sexually arouse the normal heterosexual male.

"A medium–message combination"

To criticize the Dworkin–MacKinnon definition simply because it does not conform with ordinary usage is, however, to miss the point of their critique. For, as Robert Post has pointed out, "they use the term 'pornography' to signify their concern with the sexually explicit subordination of women" (Post, 1988; see also Dworkin, 1985:15–17). Pornography for them is "an institution of gender inequality" and "a practice of sex discrimination, a violation of women's civil rights" (MacKinnon, 1987:148, 175). In this sense, what they provide is more in the nature of what C. L. Stevenson called "persuasive definition" (Stevenson, 1944:210–226, 277–290), a device designed to "get other people to share our own valuations . . . to change people's opinions" (Robinson, 1950:169). This may be what Catharine MacKinnon means by saying that their definition is "a medium–message combination" (MacKinnon, 1987:77).

In short, when they say in the opening words of their definition that "pornography is the graphic sexually explicit subordination of women, whether in pictures or in words that also includes one or more of the following: (i) women are presented dehumanized as sexual objects, things, or commodities" (MacKinnon, 1987:262), they are quite deliberately advancing a particular point of view about the function of pornography. And it is a point of view considerably more radical than was recognized in the Williams Committee's acknowledgment that there is a sense in which pornography "*uses* women as simply the objects of men's sexual needs" (Home Office, 1979:88).

Something of the nature of that point of view is expressed by Andrea Dworkin: "The major theme of pornography as a genre is male power, its nature, its magnitude, its use, its meaning. Male power, as expressed in and through pornography, is discernible in discrete but interwoven, reinforcing

strains: the power of self, physical power over and against others, the power
of terror, the power of naming, the power of owning, the power of money,
and the power of sex" (Dworkin, 1981:24). A passage from Catharine
MacKinnon is a little more explicit:

> In Andrea's work, expression is not just talk. Pornography not only teaches the reality
> of male dominance. It is one way its reality is imposed as well as experienced. It is a
> way of seeing and using women. Male power makes authoritative a way of seeing and
> treating women, so that when a man looks at a pornographic picture – pornographic
> meaning that the woman is defined as to be acted upon, a sexual object, a sexual
> thing – the *viewing* is an *act*, an act of male supremacy. (MacKinnon, 1987:130)

A crucial element in the Dworkin–MacKinnon conception of pornography
is that "woman is defined as to be acted upon, a sexual object, a sexual thing."
This clearly means more than that women are presented simply as the objects
of male sexual desire.

What is meant seems to be explained at some length in the chapter on the
objectification of women in Andrea Dworkin's *Pornography: Men Possessing
Women* (Dworkin, 1981:101–128). Objectification is there defined as "an
internalized, nearly invariable response by the male to a form that is, in his
estimation and experience, sufficiently whatever he needs to provoke
arousal." Male supremacy is said to depend "on the ability of the men to
view women as sexual objects. . . . The primary target of objectification is
the woman" (ibid.:113).

Without a woman "as fetish – the charmed object," Dworkin says "the
male . . . would be unable to experience his own selfhood, his own power, his
own penile presence and sexual superiority." From the male viewpoint, the
woman's purpose is "to be that thing that enables him to experience raw
phallic power. In pornography, his sense of purpose is fully realized. She is
the pinup, the centerfold, the poster, the postcard, the dirty picture, naked,
half-dressed, laid out, legs spread, breasts or ass protuding. She is the thing
she is supposed to be: the thing that makes him erect." Thus,

> in literary and cinematic pornography, she is taught to be that thing: raped, beaten,
> bound, used, until she recognizes her true nature and purpose and complies –
> happily, greedily, begging for more. She is used until she knows only that she is a
> thing to be used. This knowledge is her authentic erotic sensibility: her erotic destiny.
> The more she is a thing, the more she provokes erection; the more she is a thing, the
> more she fulfills her purpose; her purpose is to be the thing that provokes erection.
> She starts out searching for love or in love with love. She finds love as men understand
> it in being the thing men use. (ibid.:128)

Unfortunately, the concept of objectification does not really help to eluci-
date any precise definition of pornography, nor does it explain why pornography should be selected as the subject of special attention by those concerned
with "gender inequality" (MacKinnon, 1987:148). For it seems impossible,

in terms of this concept, to draw any distinction between the pinup–centerfold and portrayals of women being "raped, beaten, bound, used" until they comply "happily, greedily, begging for more." Indeed, it is difficult within this frame of reference to draw any meaningful distinction between pornography and the most idealized representations of women in art and literature.

That this does not misinterpret Andrea Dworkin's meaning is clear from her analysis of the male idealization of female beauty in the same chapter. "Men," she says, "perpetually searching to justify their perpetual search for objects that move them to experience their own desire transmuted to power, claim especially to love beauty as such; and under the formidable guise of aesthetic devotion, objectification is defended or presented as the recognition of the beautiful. Women ideally embody beauty: so the theory goes, even though men in practice seem to hate the female body per se."

She goes on to say that the

notion that female beauty inspires male love is pervasive. One can hardly argue (so it seems) with the aesthetic values of the sublime artists of male culture who freeze the female form in time and render it exquisite, as in, for instance, the Venus de Milo, ancient Aphrodite, the women of Rubens, and so forth. It is nearly unconscionable to challenge, for instance, the aesthetic sensibility in Keats's exquisite "Ode on a Grecian Urn," where the object is first the urn itself, then the figures on it:

> Bold Lover, never, never canst thou kiss;
> Though winning near the goal – yet, do not grieve;
> She cannot fade, though thou hast not thy bliss,
> For ever wilt thou love, and she be fair!

In this instance, according to Dworkin, the

meaning of the male idealization of beauty is hidden by the very beauty of the art that proclaims women, at her highest, a beautiful object. Keats has found the ideal crystallization of objectifying love: the bold lover perpetually desires the unchanging beauty of the unchanging female frozen in time; she will always love and she will always be fair; he will always love because she will always be fair. This same model of love is found in every soap and cosmetic commercial. In Keats, objectification is raised to its highest aesthetic level. With pinups too the bold lover will forever love and she be fair. (ibid.:115)

It is in fact extremely difficult to derive from either Dworkin or MacKinnon a precise account of what they mean by pornography or how it can be meaningfully distinguished from any other material in which women are "objectified." At one point Dworkin appears to draw a distinction between "silly and commonplace" objectification "as when Ernest Hemingway had his fourth wife, Mary Welsh, dye her reddish hair blond" and objectification that "is clearly sinister."

But she then goes on to say:

The relationship between the supposedly silly and commonplace objectification of blonds as beautiful and the sinister objectification of those considered in some way filth is, of course, a direct one: the same value system is embodied in this range of sexual obsession, sexual response. With this value system in mind, it becomes clear that the love of blonds is in fact as socially significant as, and inseparable from, the hatred of those who are seen to embody opposite qualities or characteristics. Objectification, in fact and in consequence, is never trivial. (ibid.:114–115)

It is true there is one passage in *Pornography: Men Possessing Women* that appears to offer a solution to the problem of differentiating between pornography and other types of sexually explicit material: "The word *pornography* does not mean 'writing about sex' or 'depictions of the erotic' or 'depictions of sexual acts' or 'depictions of nude bodies' or 'sexual representations' or any other such euphemism. It means the graphic depiction of women as vile whores" (ibid.:200).

But it is also said that "male renderings of women in art, literature, psychology, religious discourses, philosophy, and in the common wisdom of the day, whatever the day, are bizarre, distorted, fragmented at best, demented in the main . . . all women are viewed to some degree as monstrous, sluts, depraved, with appetites that, if unleashed, would swallow up the male, destroy him" (ibid.:64–65).

And again: "In the male system, women are sex; sex is the whore. The whore is *pornē*, the lowest whore, the whore belongs to *all* male citizens: the slut, the cunt" (ibid.:202). Viewed in this perspective, pornography is seen not as a singular literary or artistic genre at all but rather as simply a documentary reflection of reality: "that reality the pornography imposes on women's real lives, those lives that are so seamlessly *consistent* with the pornography that pornography can be credibly defended by saying it is only a mirror of reality" (MacKinnon, 1987:149).

In expounding "the feminist analysis of Andrea Dworkin," Catharine MacKinnon says that "pornography is not imagery in some relation to a reality elsewhere constructed. It is not a distortion, reflection, projection, expression, fantasy, representation, or symbol either. It is sexual reality" (ibid.:149). It is difficult to interpret this kind of figurative language; presumably if pornography *is* sexual reality, some other kinds of "graphic depiction of women" are not. But it is unclear what the implications of this analysis may be for distinguishing between pornographic and nonpornographic depictions.

One reason Dworkin and MacKinnon fail to draw any clear distinction is that apparently they do not recognize any significant distinctions in this area. Commenting on the difficulties courts have in framing workable standards to separate "prurient" from other sexual interest, commercial exploitation from art, and obscenity from great literature, MacKinnon says: "These lines have proven elusive in law because they do not exist in life. Commercial sex resembles art because both exploit women's sexuality . . . pornography converges with more conventionally acceptable depictions and descriptions just as rape converges with intercourse because both express the same power relation . . . legal standards will be practically unenforceable, will reproduce this problem rather than solve it, until they address its fundamental issue – gender inequality – directly" (ibid.:154).

Yet if "gender inequality" is the problem, why does its presentation in sexually explicit or pornographic forms present a special problem? Here, the difficulty is that of distinguishing between types of sexually explicit objectification and nonsexually explicit communications that also present women as objects. Here must lie the central justification for paying special attention to, and proposing a special regulatory regime for, pornography. The MacKinnon–Dworkin definition of pornography requires that the depiction so classified must be "graphic, sexually explicit subordination of women" but does not clarify why the classified material should require sexual explicitness. If there are two communications in which "women are presented as whores by nature," and one involves graphic sexual explicitness and the other does not, only the former will be classified as pornographic.

The problem with this is that we are never told why the depiction of women as whores is either more objectionable or more harmful if presented graphically. The same can be said of presenting women as dehumanized sexual objects, things, or commodities, or in scenarios of degradation. Beyond the assertion that "pornography makes sexism sexy" (MacKinnon, 1987:200), the special harm of those portrayals involving explicit sex, what must be the essence of this definition of pornography, is not explained and not discussed.

Perhaps the special harm of the sexually graphic representation of gender inequality is that it makes the continuation of an unjust regime attractive to males because of its sexual benefits. Sexually graphic exploitation of women is a danger because it has the capacity to perpetuate male domination. Yet even if the appeal of sex sells gender inequality, it is the concept or message rather than the sexually arousing character of the particular communication that is a problem in this view. It is the message that subjugation of women has sensual benefits, rather than the sexually arousing medium for that message, that seems to be the problem. If there is a particular danger in presenting that obnoxious message in a sexually arousing way, this is not established in the radical feminist critique. Yet it is the special danger of a sexually arousing form of sexism that is critical if the radical critique has any special force for what the rest of the community regards as pornography.

"Male culture," according to Andrea Dworkin, "thrives on argument and prides itself on distinctions" (Dworkin, 1981:127). In some contexts, this may be a feature of male culture, but it is hardly the case in relation to pornography. In that connection the most striking feature of male culture seems to be its inability to draw clear distinctions and extricate itself from what Walter Allen calls "the morass of the subjective," in which he says, "we find ourselves floundering" whenever we try to define or discuss pornography (Allen, 1962:143). Unfortunately, the radical feminist critique does little to help extricate us from the morass.

Comparison of definitions

If we compare the Dworkin–MacKinnon definition of pornography with those considered in Chapter 2, what strikes us is that the reasons given for rejecting the use of the term by the Johnson Commission and the Meese Commission are precisely what seems to render it attractive to Dworkin and MacKinnon. The Johnson Commission, it will be recalled, rejected it "because it most often denotes subjective disapproval of certain materials" (U.S. Commission, 1970:3 n. 4). The Meese Commission rejected it because "the appellation pornography is undoubtedly pejorative. To call something 'pornographic' is plainly, in modern usage, to condemn it" (U.S. Department of Justice, 1986:228).

This is hardly a matter that could cause Dworkin and MacKinnon any concern. Their extended definition of pornography is one which might itself be regarded as offensive. Moreover, it contains a variety of value-laden terms, such as "filthy," "inferior," and "degradation," that do not identify the nature of the material to which they are intended to refer but rather connote an attitude to it. In fact, the definition they provide is one that, as A. W. B. Simpson said of Lord Longford's characterization of pornography, "embodies a ground for objecting to it" (Simpson, 1983:62).

A comparison of the Dworkin–MacKinnon definition of pornography with that of the Williams Committee brings out another crucial contrast. A pornographic representation, both in ordinary usage and according to the Williams Committee's definition, has not only a certain content "explicit representations of sexual material (organs, postures, activity, etc.)" but also a certain function or intention "to arouse its audience sexually" (Home Office, 1979:103). But it is easy to conceive of material coming within the Dworkin–MacKinnon definition that in function or intention would not be in the least sexually arousing.

Indeed, by their definition of pornographic material it is impossible to distinguish it from purely misogynic material designed not to arouse sexual feelings at all but simply to induce hatred of, or contempt for, women. A good example of a misogynic but not pornographic work is Otto Weininger's *Sex and Character* (1903), which Dworkin cites as providing an example of the objectification of women (Dworkin, 1981:110). One of the passages she quotes from that book is: "To put it bluntly, man possesses sexual organs, her sexual organs possess woman" (Weininger, [1903] 1975:92), which she translates as "To put it more bluntly, she is cunt, formed by men, used by men, her sexual organs constituting her whole being and her whole value" (Dworkin, 1981:110). Another passage cited by Dworkin is: "There are certainly no women absolutely devoid of the prostitute instinct to covet being sexually excited by any stranger" (Weininger, [1903] 1975:219; Dworkin, 1981:207).

In fact, Weininger's book could not be described as pornographic in any usual sense of that term. Weininger was a homosexual, a man who, according to Dworkin, "holds his own as a misogynist." As she correctly stated, his book, which is pervaded by a profoundly misogynous spirit, portrays women as "worthless, lying, cheating, deceiving" (Dworkin, 1981:110) and anything but sexually desirable. If there was ever a man to whom Max Beerbohm's joke about "the confirmed misogyn" being "a ladies' man" (Beerbohm, 1920:181) did not apply, it was Weininger.

His work, although it contains explicit references to sexual activity, so far from being sexually arousing in intention or function is chillingly anaphrodisiac. Yet it provides an excellent example of the "sexually explicit subordination of women, whether in pictures or in words, that also includes one or more of the following: (i) women are presented dehumanized as sexual objects, things, or commodities" (MacKinnon, 1987:262). Indeed, that is precisely what Dworkin's citation of his work is intended to illustrate. Is it then to be regarded as pornography?

The inability to distinguish between the pornographic and the misogynic in terms of their definition reflects the fact that Dworkin and MacKinnon do not in their writing draw any distinction between these two genres. They attempt in their definition to combine what is ordinarily regarded as pornographic with what would ordinarily be regarded as misogynic. But it is what is misogynic that is central to their definition. Their definition not only fails to differentiate these particular kinds of material but also fails to demarcate any cognizable boundary between pornographic and nonpornographic material. As we have seen, it almost seems to be designed to blur or obscure any conceivable line of demarcation.

Moreover, because their concern is with the subordination of women it is difficult to understand the selection of pornography as their principal target. Pornography is described as "a major social force in institutionalizing . . . second class status for women" (ibid.:200–201). Yet a far more powerful and pervasive influence in securing and maintaining the subservient status of women in American society has been the Christian Bible. For there could be no more explicit license extended to misogyny and the subordination of women than can be found in the Epistles of Saint Paul.

Effects

On the question of the harmful effects of pornography the radical feminist critique is not a great deal more specific than it is in relation to the definition of pornography. Thus, Catharine MacKinnon says:

> If pornography is an act of male supremacy, its harm is the harm of male supremacy made difficult to see because of its pervasiveness, potency, and success in making the world a pornographic place. Specifically, the harm cannot be discerned from the objective standpoint because it *is* so much of "what is." Women live in the world pornography creates. . . . So the issue is not whether pornography is harmful, but how the harm of pornography is to become visible. As compared with what? To the extent pornography succeeds in constructing social reality, it becomes *invisible as harm*. (MacKinnon, 1987:154–155; see also 166 and 174)

It is difficult to interpret statements of this nature about harms that cannot be observed from an objective standpoint; that are so pervasive, they cannot be sufficiently isolated to be perceived; that are, in fact, invisible. This country has never experienced a shortage of pervasive, potent, insidious threats to the American Way of Life, as Richard Hofstadter demonstrated in his celebrated essay *The Paranoid Style in American Politics* (Hofstadter, 1965:3–40), but there have usually been some discernible harms that could be attributed to them.

At other points, however, Catharine MacKinnon does appear to claim that pornography has at least some observable effects with something "unfudge-ably substantive" about them, to use her own expression (MacKinnon, 1987:164). For although she maintains at one point that comprehension of "the relation between pornography and life . . . will require an entirely new theory of social causality" (ibid.:161), at other times she is quite specific about a causal relationship between pornography and harm.

Thus she says: "Specific pornography does directly cause some assaults. Some rapes *are* performed by men with paperback books in their pockets" (ibid.:184); "although police have known it for years, reported cases are increasingly noting the causal role of pornography in some sexual abuse" (ibid:185); "the pornography doesn't just drop out of the sky, go into his head, and stop there. Specifically, men rape, batter, prostitute, molest, and sexually harass women" (ibid:186).

These assertions are supported by anecdotal evidence that points to no more than the banal conclusion that some rapists are consumers of pornography. It establishes no causal connection between pornography and rape whatsoever. MacKinnon acknowledges that none of the available research has found any significant difference between convicted rapists and the rest of the male population "in levels and patterns of exposure, response to, and consumption of pornography." Her response to this is that "it does not make sense to assume that pornography has no role in rape simply because little about its use or effects distinguishes rapists from other men, when we know that a lot of those other men *do* rape women; they just never get caught" (ibid.:184–185).

But even if it were true that all unconvicted rapists were avid consumers of pornography, this would establish no more than that there was a negative relationship between the consumption of pornography by rapists and the likelihood of their being apprehended and convicted of rape. If there were such a relationship, it would suggest not that pornography caused rape, but that pornography conferred on rapists immunity from arrest and conviction for rape.

If that were the case, it would certainly indicate that pornography was harmful. But it would be harmful in a very different way from that suggested by MacKinnon. Moreover, it would be difficult to reconcile with her anecdotal evidence about rapes being performed by men with paperback books in their pockets or with works with titles like *Violent Stories of Kinky Humiliation, Bizarre Sex Crimes*, and *Shamed Victims* back at home (ibid.:184–186).

MacKinnon supplements her anecdotal evidence for the existence of a causal role for pornography in rape with some observations about "causality in its narrowest sense," referring in this connection to "recent experimental research on pornography." This, she claims, "shows that the materials covered by our definition cause measurable harm to women through increasing men's attitudes and behaviors of discrimination in both violent and nonviolent forms."

"Exposure to some of the pornography in our definition," she says,

increases the immediately subsequent willingness of normal men to aggress against women under laboratory conditions. It makes normal men more closely resemble convicted rapists attitudinally. . . . Exposure to pornography also significantly increases attitudinal measures known to correlate with rape and self-reports of aggressive acts, measures such as hostility toward women, propensity to rape, condoning rape and predicting that one would rape or force sex on a woman if one knew one would not get caught. On this latter measure, by the way, about a third of all men predict that they would rape, and half would force sex on a woman. (ibid.:187)

Three things should be said about the assertions made about, and the inferences drawn from, the findings of experimental research by MacKinnon. In the first place, no research has been done showing that "the materials covered by our definition cause measurable harm to women." Indeed, research in which subjects were induced to cause measurable harm to women have not been carried out and would not be permitted. In the second place, no reliable research has been done showing that subjects' attitudes toward women, or modes of behavior toward women, outside the conditions of the psychological laboratory, have been changed in any way at all.

In the third place, the most recent and thorough review of research findings in this area carried out under the aegis of Edward Donnerstein (to whose
work MacKinnon makes frequent reference) reaches much more cautious
conclusions:

In the light of the scientific literature reviewed in the previous chapters, we can
conclude that some forms of pornography, under some conditions, promote certain
antisocial attitudes and behavior. Specifically we should be most concerned about the
detrimental effects of exposure to violent images in pornography and elsewhere,
particularly material that portrays the myth that women enjoy or in some way benefit
from rape, torture, or other forms of sexual violence. To date, the evidence supporting
the contention that so-called degrading pornographic materials, as long as they are not
violent, are harmful is sparse and inconsistent. The few studies that have been done on
these materials, including our own, have yielded contradictory findings. (Donnerstein
et al., 1987:171)

In fact, the most that is claimed in relation to violent pornography is that it
"may have negative effects on attitudes about women, and *appears to* increase
aggressive behavior against women – *at least in the laboratory"* (Donnerstein et
al., 1987:107; emphasis added). On the crucial question as to whether these
"negative effects" in the laboratory have any relation to real-world behaviors,
two studies are cited (Malamuth, 1983, 1986). They are both laboratory studies
involving notoriously unreliable data from self-reports. Moreover, the author
of those studies himself concluded that "the fact that a man finds depictions of
women being raped sexually arousing *does not imply* that he will behave aggressively against women in the real world" (ibid.:106; emphasis added).

MacKinnon quotes Donnerstein as saying "we just quantify the obvious"
(MacKinnon, 1987:188). Yet the thesis advanced by the radical feminists is not
self-evident. The idea that intellectually and psychologically normal men will
as a result of exposure to violent pornographic images become convinced that
women enjoy torture, rape, and other forms of sexual violence is not obvious.
Nor is the further hypothesis that this will lead to the elimination of inhibition
or restraint in regard to causing pain and injury to other human beings.

There is a final issue with respect to the effects of pornography that parallels problems of definition discussed earlier in this chapter. If the harm of
pornography is in its status as "an act of male supremacy," it is not obvious
why sexually graphic portrayals produce this harm more frequently than less
sexually explicit male chauvinist appeals.

The debate on feminism and pornography

"The most dismaying aspect of the feminist antipornography campaign," says
Walter Kendrick in *The Secret Museum* (1987), "is its exact resemblance to
every such effort that preceded it, from Lord Campbell's and Justice Cock-

burn's, through that of Comstock and all the Societies for the Suppression of Vice, to the modern vigilantism of Leagues and Legions of Decency" (Kendrick, 1987:239).

Two things in Kendrick's statement are misleading. In the first place, the antipornography campaign in question is not supported, but actively opposed, by many feminists. In the second place, the resemblance to campaigns that preceded it is far from exact; there are differences and they are significant differences.

The other feminists

As to the first point, there has been in recent years considerable debate among feminists about the issue of pornography. It has been rightly said that on this issue "the women's movement has been divided with a degree of bitterness that shocks both sides" (Ellis, 1986:38). What Catharine MacKinnon calls "the feminist critique of pornography" (MacKinnon, 1987:147) is repudiated by some feminists who believe that that critique and the campaign based on it are "more likely to impede, rather than advance, feminist goals" (Duggan et al., 1986:81).

In 1984 the Feminist Anti-Censorship Task Force (FACT) was formed by a group of feminist activists and scholars in New York who opposed the antipornography ordinances written by Andrea Dworkin and Catharine MacKinnon. Subsequently FACT chapters came into being in a number of cities when the ordinance was proposed, including Madison, San Francisco, Los Angeles, and Cambridge. Such groups as Women Against Violence in Pornography and the Media (WAVPM) and Women Against Pornography (WAP) have been criticized by feminists opposed to censorship as "being used by much more powerful segments of our society to create a sex-negative social climate that will facilitate the suppression of all forms of sexual dissent" (Califia, 1986:24).

Feminists have argued in defense of pornography. For example: "I am convinced that pornography, even in its present form, contains important messages for women . . . it does not tie women's sexuality to reproduction or to a domesticated couple or exclusively to men . . . specifically what we might take *from* pornography is a vision of the mutability of sexual experience and a variety of directions for sexual experimentation. Whatever its limitations pornography does demystify a number of sexual practices that have been taboo for women" (Webster, 1986:34–35).

They have asserted also that

the existence of pornography has served to flout conventional sexual mores, to ridicule sexual hypocrisy and to underscore the importance of sexual needs. Pornography carries many messages other than woman-hating: it advocates sexual adventure, sex outside of marriage, sex for no reason other than pleasure, casual sex, anonymous sex, group sex, voyeuristic sex, illegal sex, public sex. Some of these ideas appeal to women reading or seeing pornography, who may interpret some images as legitimating their own sense of sexual urgency or desire to be sexually aggressive. (Duggan et al., 1986:82)

Feminists have also argued that pornography "in rejecting sexual repression and hypocrisy – which have inflicted even more damage on women than on men – expresses a radical impulse." And "if feminists define pornography, per se, as the enemy, the result will be to make a lot of women ashamed of their sexual feelings and afraid to be honest about them. And the last thing women need is more sexual shame, guilt, and hypocrisy – this time served up as feminism" (Willis, 1986:55–56).

One feminist writer has gone so far as to suggest that insofar as pornography involves exploitation it is men who are most exploited. "Actually, since there are so few women (but hundreds of thousands of pictures of them), the overwhelming feeling is one of the commercial exploitation of male sexual desire. There it is, embarrassingly desperate, tormented, demeaning itself, begging for relief, taking any substitute, and *paying* for it. Men who live for this are suckers, and their uncomfortable demeanor shows they know it. If, as a woman, you can detach yourself . . . you see how totally tragic they appear" (English, 1985:53).

Pornography and power

The second respect in which Kendrick's statement is misleading is that it ignores the fact that the feminist campaign to which he refers, unlike all the earlier campaigns, is based on the view that pornography is a political problem. Andrea Dworkin in her preface to *Pornography: Men Possessing Women* says: "This is not a book about the First Amendment. By definition the First Amendment protects only those who can exercise the rights it protects. Pornography by definition – 'the graphic depiction of whores' – is trade in a class of persons who have been systematically denied the rights protected by the First Amendment and the rest of the Bill of Rights." The question she was raising, she said, was "not whether pornography keeps women from exercising the rights protected by the First Amendment" (Dworkin, 1981:9).

Since that time, however, what Catharine MacKinnon calls "the larger implications of a feminist critique of pornography" have been developed, principally by Ms. Mackinnon herself. What those implications are can best be illustrated initially by quotation. "The feminist critique of pornography," says MacKinnon, is "a political argument for a redistribution and transformation in the terms of power." Pornography is a question "of power and powerlessness. It is first a political question, a question of sexual politics . . . it is part of the violation and exploitation of women as a class" (MacKinnon, 1987:225). And again, "The social preconditions, the presumptions, that underlie the First Amendment do not apply to women. The First Amendment essentially presumes some level of social equality among people and hence essentially equal social access to the means of expression. In a context of inequality between the sexes, we cannot presume that that is accurate" (ibid.:129).

From this perspective, when pornography is said to be degrading to women what is meant is not merely that it is offensive to women but that it is actually a means of degradation. When Catharine MacKinnon says "pornography makes all women into cunts" (ibid.:224), she is not saying that pornography is objectionable because women are portrayed in pornographic material as merely female genital organs; she is saying that pornography is "sex discrimination . . . it is part of the violation and exploitation of women as a class" (ibid.:225).

Maze-bright rats: variations on a theme

On this view, those feminists who do not accept the Dworkin–MacKinnon analysis are collaborators who "speak for the pornographers" (MacKinnon, 1987:199) and fail to recognize that "pornography is a major social force for institutionalizing a subhuman, victimized, and second-class status for women in this country" (ibid.:200–201). The possibility that there might be rational grounds for disagreement is ignored. The only question to be answered is: "Why are women lawyers, feminists, siding with the pornographers?" (ibid.:205).

The answer to that question can only be ad hominem, and a number of variations on that theme are deployed. As for women lawyers: They are taught at law school "to forget your feelings, forget your community, most of all, if you are a woman, forget your experience. Become a maze-bright rat." Subsequently, when they defend pornographers they are "defending a source of their relatively high position among women under male supremacy, keeping all women, including them, an inferior class on the basis of sex, enforced by sexual force" (ibid.:205).

In "the established abstract refuges of academia" also, women do not question "the structure of power that has put [them] where they are" and seem unaware "that their failure to question it helps to keep most women out and down. Some of the women who are the most successful in existing terms [are] the most likely to defend those abuses of women, such as prostitution and pornography, which keep their own value high, high at least among women" (ibid.:216).

Then there are those who are "simply conservative," for whom "acknowledging civil rights for women in pornography suggests that they are victims of restricted options on the basis of their sex and that some are directly coerced. . . . These women sense a judgment on their lives: that they have gone along with and sometimes even enjoyed inequality in the sexual sphere. They would rather live that way forever, and make sure other women do too, than face what it means, in order to change it. They recommend appeasement" (ibid.:226).

These women, blinded by self-interest or self-delusion, cheerfully accept and even defend the status quo, and tacitly approve a distribution of power in society that "keeps the value of the most exceptional women high to keep other women out and down on their backs with their legs spread" (ibid.:205). They are simply engaged in a "denial of reality" (ibid.:219).

Freedom of expression and "reality" in the Dworkin–MacKinnon critique

The "reality" they are denying is the reality of male supremacy and of women's subservient role in society, and also the reality of pornography as a practice of sex discrimination and a violation of women's civil rights. It was in accordance with that view of reality that Andrea Dworkin and Catharine MacKinnon at the request of the city of Minneapolis conceived and drafted an ordinance incorporating the definition of pornography that, in a slightly modified version, is reproduced at the beginning of this chapter.

The ordinance was passed by the Minneapolis City Council on December 30, 1983. It was vetoed by the mayor, reintroduced, passed again, and vetoed again in 1984. A revised version of the ordinance was passed in Indianapolis and signed into law in 1984. A group of publishers and booksellers challenged the law in federal district court, where they won. This decision was then upheld by the federal appeals court (*American Booksellers v. Hudnut*, 771, F.2d 323, 7th Cir. 1985), where the ordinance was declared a violation of First Amendment rights. The city appealed to the U.S. Supreme Court, and on February 24, 1986, the Court affirmed the ruling that the Indianapolis antipornography ordinance was unconstitutional (106 S. Ct. 1172, 1986).

Catharine MacKinnon comments on this, that with its "repudiation of a law guaranteeing women's rights against pornography" the U.S. Supreme Court has "officially sanctioned" the status of women alluded to in her assertion that "pornography makes all women into cunts" (MacKinnon 1987:224). The point at issue is not seen as relating to freedom of expression. Rather, the point is

that the assumptions the law of the First Amendment makes about adults – that adults are autonomous, self-defining, freely acting, *equal* individuals – are exactly those qualities that pornography systematically denies and undermines for women. Some of the same reasons children are granted some specific legal avenues for redress – relative lack of power, inability to command respect for their consent and self-determination, in some cases less physical strength or lowered legitimacy in using it, specific credibility problems, and lack of access to resources for meaningful self-expression – also hold true for the social position of women compared to men. (ibid.:181)

In fact, on the question of freedom of expression the Dworkin–MacKinnon position is not at all clear and seems at times to be equivocal. A. W. B. Simpson says of Dworkin, "insofar as I can understand her preface [to *Pornography: Men Possessing Women*], she reserves her position on any of the questions which might arise over a supposed clash between liberty of expression and condemnation of pornography" (Simpson, 1983:72). MacKinnon is perhaps somewhat more explicit. She acknowledges that "in the philosophical terms of classical liberalism" there is a "dilemma." But she says, "if women's freedom is as incompatible with pornography's construction of our freedom as our equality is incompatible with pornography's construction of our equality, we get neither freedom nor equality under the liberal calculus" (MacKinnon, 1987:166).

As to what should be done about this, Ms. MacKinnon is "unclear," as she candidly acknowledges in a comment on *"Playboy*'s principled civil libertarianism [which] comes from the bedrock of their material self-interest."

I have no particular interest in increasing the power of the *state* over sexuality or speech. I do not have that kind of faith in the government. It has largely operated from the same perspective that *Playboy* does – that is, the male point of view. At least, no one has yet convinced me that extending the obscenity prohibition, liberalizing its application, would do anything but further eroticize pornography. Suppressing obscenity criminally has enhanced its value, made it more attractive and more expensive and a violation to get, therefore more valuable and more sexually exciting. Censoring pornography has not delegitimized it; I want to delegitimize it. What would do that is unclear to me at this time. Maybe there is a way. There needs to be. It is not that I think the state can't do anything for women in this area. I think making sexual harassment sex discrimination has helped delegitimize sexual harassment. That is as far as I have gotten with the problem at this time. (ibid.:139–140)

Dworkin and MacKinnon claim that their antipornography ordinances are not censorship laws because the state is not authorized to initiate criminal prosecutions, but are rather a "women's attempt to gain civil rights against pornographers" (ibid.:4). They are civil laws that allow individuals to sue the makers, sellers, distributors, or exhibitors of pornography, not criminal laws. As some of their feminist critics have argued, however, "their censoring impact would be substantially as severe as criminal obscenity laws. Materials could be removed from public availability by court injunction, and publishers and book sellers could be subject to potentially endless legal harassment." Moreover, "the prospect of having to defend a potentially infinite number of privately filed complaints creates at least as much of a chilling effect against sexual speech as does a criminal law. And as long as representatives of the state – in this case, judges – have ultimate say over the interpretation, the distinction between this ordinance and 'real' censorship will not hold" (Duggan et al., 1986:72, 80).

Nevertheless, it is very difficult in the end to say precisely what the implications of their critique of pornography are for freedom of expression. Their inability to define pornography satisfactorily results in what MacKinnon acknowledges as an "inability to draw a line between pornography and everything else." As to that, she says, "to me that exposes the pervasiveness of the value system Andrea analyzes, its presence in literature, in advertising, in daily life. If I have any difficulty distinguishing those areas from pornography, it is not because I don't think some things are worse than others, because they are, but because the same values pervade them all" (MacKinnon, 1987:131).

The attack on pornography as a purveyor of sexist values, values that pervade literature, advertising, entertainment, and, on this view, almost all aspects of social existence, seems to be justified simply on the ground that "some things are worse than others." But although that proposition is incontrovertible, in this view pornography is really no more than a symptom, something that accompanies and indicates the existence of an underlying pathological condition. And although it may be judged more disfiguring or blatant or distasteful than some of the other symptoms, there is no reason to believe that suppressing it will cure the disease. Moreover, the medicine prescribed seems likely to have secondary effects that will prove undesirable, indeed unacceptable, not merely to male consumers of pornography but to all citizens.

The subordination–degradation hypothesis revisited

We have not tried to conceal our skepticism regarding both the diagnosis and the prescription offered by Dworkin and MacKinnon. Rejection of the Dworkin–MacKinnon analysis, however, does not entail dismissal of the question of the subordination and degradation of women in pornographic material as being of no significance. There is no doubt that many of the images of women in currently available pornography are "degrading" as that term is generally understood. Moreover, attention to the nature of those images can teach us a good deal about both pornographic communication and the social order in which it circulates.

Yet if much contemporary pornography degrades women, is it correct to describe that aspect of it as sex discrimination? Is that the essential nature of the social harm involved? Is our understanding of the phenomenon increased by thinking of it in those terms? Was not the Williams Committee correct when it said that "if pornography degrades then it degrades also the men it portrays as well as those who consume it" (Home Office, 1979:88)?

The uncouth, insensitive, brutish performances of which most current pornography consists depreciate the human dignity of all the participants. But that which degrades everyone involved discriminates against no one. If "pornography makes all women into cunts" (MacKinnon, 1987:224), that is not the only transformation accomplished. At the same time, it makes all men into penises. Members of both sexes are reduced to genitalia. Much of what is detrimental about such portrayals seems different from the asymmetrical treatment of the sexes.

To some extent it is to be expected that communication specifically designed to arouse sexually will concentrate attention on sexual organs and functions. Yet there is nothing inherent in the nature of pornography that dooms the genre to be composed solely of genital or anatomical images. Nor does it have to be either misogynous or male-oriented. As one feminist writer has put it, "if we could imagine operating without all the internal and external constraints society has imposed on us, feminists might create a truly radical pornography that spoke of female desire as we are beginning to know it and as we would like to see it acted out" (Webster, 1986:35). Another feminist has argued that "what we need more than women against pornography are women pornographers" (English, 1985:58).

Yet it is undeniable that a great deal of contemporary pornography does reduce human beings to the genital level and is designed principally for male consumption. The sex differential in the use of pornography has frequently been exaggerated, but men are undoubtedly still the primary consumers of all forms of pornographic communication. Catharine MacKinnon's assertion that "most women tend to avoid pornography as much as possible," for which the only evidence cited is "personal observation" (MacKinnon, 1987:266), may or may not be true. But it is certainly true that more males are exposed, and more frequently exposed, to pornography than females.

Thus, in a sense it is true to say that pornography has a more negative impact on the status of women than on the status of men. For insofar as in the major part of that material women are depicted in a dehumanized form, as present simply to satisfy men's sexual appetites, they are reduced to the level of objects, in the quite specific sense that they represent the person or thing to which action is directed. So it is not altogether misleading to assert that women are differentially at risk from any degradation involved in pornography.

There is a related hypothesis that might be investigated by experimental psychologists. Whereas male authority figures have long been accepted in modern Western societies, the assumption by women of high-status roles that are independent of their sex is much less firmly rooted. The hypothesis to be tested is that an extended portrayal of women as "voracious cunts," to use

Andrea Dworkin's phrase (Dworkin, 1981:224), would have more impact on men's comfortably accepting a woman as physician or tax accountant than an equally extended portrayal of men as aggressive penises would have on women's acceptance of the authority of a male doctor or tax accountant. The reason would be the greater difficulty men have segregating the sexual meanings of women in their midst from social roles where female sexuality is not relevant to performance.

To test this hypothesis would require considerable ingenuity and could not be confidently resolved by the administration of questionnaires twenty minutes after exposure. But if the hypothesis proved correct, if the negative spillover from pornographic reductionism to the social reality of gender roles hurts women more than men, it seems likely that the explanation of the differential impact would not be related to the roles performed by the men and women in the pornographic movies but rather to the relative vulnerability of the roles of the two sexes in society.

In fact, the linkage between sex and status in society long predated the mass production of pornography in our time. Nor does its reflection in the nature of much pornography require explanation. A sexist society produces a pornography – and not only pornography – that reflects the relative position of men and women in that society. But what is degrading to women in such material is not inherent in the nature of pornography. There seems to be no necessary connection between who is in a literal sense on top in pornography and the roles played by men and women in the social order. In this analysis, it is the traditional missionary attitude rather than the missionary position that is the problem.

Viewed in this light, as sexism diminishes in our society and the relative position of women improves, the kind of pornography that consumers demand may change. It seems utterly improbable that the demand for material designed to arouse its audience sexually will cease to exist. And it may be, as A. W. B. Simpson has suggested, that "lewd male fantasy . . . remains a permanent feature of the male character" (Simpson, 1983:75). It seems likely, however, that a society in which males were less dominant would produce a pornography that was less debased and less dehumanized. Currently, as Betty Friedan has said, "some pornography certainly does degrade women. It also degrades men and it degrades sex" (Friedan, 1986:43). The attempted suppression of material of that character would not produce a more just or civil society; but a more just and civil society would undoubtedly produce less of that kind of material.

7

Pornography and child protection

On one question commissions on pornography are simultaneously unanimous and unhelpful. It is generally agreed that children constitute a special case in relation to governmental policy on pornography. Yet, until the Meese Commission, little time or space was devoted to exploring the special character and requirements of policy toward children.

There is very little in the Johnson Commission's report, which notes that "a large majority of sex educators and counselors are of the opinion that most adolescents are interested in explicit sexual materials, and that this interest is a product of natural curiosity about sex" (U.S. Commission, 1970:29). The commission took "the view that parents should be free to make their own conclusions regarding the suitability of explicit sexual materials for their children" (U.S. Commission, 1970:57); and, as we shall see, it appears to have regarded the use of children as the subjects of pornography as not a serious problem. Only about 4 out of 270 pages in the Williams Committee's report (Home Office, 1979:88–90, 123–124, 125–126, 131–132) deal with the topic of children as consumers of, or participants in, pornography.

The Meese Commission has two contributions on child pornography. A 14-page treatment of the problem in Part II of the report is followed in Part III by a 140-page listing of recommended law enforcement and victim aid responses (U.S. Department of Justice, 1986:405–418, 595–735). This long chapter will be discussed in the next section.

The Canadian Special Committee on Pornography and Prostitution proved to be no exception to the rule. Its report includes only 4 pages (out of a total of 753) devoted to discussion of "the issue of children or young people and pornography in Canada" (Canada, 1985:569–572). A further 45 pages detail the present state of the relevant laws in Canada and elsewhere and include proposals for changes in the law (Canada, 195:579–591, 601–603, 609–618, 627–650).

There is no doubt that the formulation of social policy regarding both exposure to, and involvement in the production of, pornographic material on the part of children evokes questions and raises issues that do not arise in connection with adults. Moreover, the tendency in recent years for Western democratic governments to deregulate the treatment of explicit sexual materials for adults does not diminish but rather increases the significance of issues involving children and pornography.

We begin our treatment of the topic with an analysis of the Meese Commission recommendations for legislative action on child pornography. We then consider, separately, the jurisprudential problems raised when children become the subjects in pornographic communications and when they are the target audience of pornography.

Paved with good intentions

The 16-page review of the problem of child pornography in Part II of the Meese Commission's report is, as noted, followed in Part III by a 140-page chapter on proposed law enforcement responses. It is as though a one-page diagnosis were followed by ten pages of prescription. And the prescription in this case consists mainly of penal folk remedies.

The commission proposes no fewer than forty-eight initiatives in this chapter, a majority of all the report's recommendations on all matters. Yet the chapter is a case study in the hazards of nonspecificity.

In one sense, the commission's agenda was a narrow one: They were only considering the problems of children participating in the production of pornography. While the terms "child" and "minor" are frequently used in the discussion of these forty-eight recommendations, it is only in the discussion of federal law that the appropriate age limit or age limits for the protection of children are discussed. The commission asserts that the expansion of the child pornography age standard from under age sixteen to under age eighteen in 1984 federal law was inadequate and suggests in its Recommendation 38 that Congress should enact legislation prohibiting producers of certain sexually explicit visual depictions from using performers under the age of twenty-one"(U.S. Department of Justice, 1986:623). In fact, the "certain sexually explicit visual depictions" include all of the acts prohibited under current federal law except simulations. The commission never discusses how simulated sexual acts will be differentiated.

Presumably the twenty-one-year-old age boundary recommended for federal legislation is the commission's notion of the appropriate single age boundary for both federal and state criminal law. Certainly nothing in the discussion of Recommendation 38 is specifically federal about the justifications for the twenty-first birthday. The rationales provided for age twenty-one include the high levels of poverty associated with youths aged eighteen to twenty-one, higher rates of infant and maternal mortality associated with the pregnancies of women aged fifteen to nineteen, the greater risks that accompany abortions in late adolescence for white women, and the permanent stigma associated with adolescent participation in pornography: "The adolescent 'porn star' must always live in fear that the film or photograph will surface, once again wreaking havoc in his or her personal and professional life" (ibid.:627). The double standard of age eighteen for simulated sex and twenty-one for real sex is never justified in any detail. The economic issues and pregnancy risk just discussed might extend to some distinctions between real and simulated sex for vaginal intercourse, but certainly not for masturbation or oral–genital sex and some of the others specifically listed by the commission as to be prohibited.

Notwithstanding the lack of justification, this single age of the twenty-first birthday for actual sex seems to hold for the whole topic of child pornography in these recommendations.

There are several problems involved with taking the series of forty-eight recommendations by the Meese Commission seriously as policy analysis. We will here provide only some samples. First, the spirit of youth protection that informs Recommendation 38 does not extend evenly throughout the commission's recommendations, something that can be seen in Recommendation 37, the first of the child pornography proposals. The commission proposes that "Congress should enact a statute requiring the producers, retailers, or distributors of sexually explicit visual depictions to maintain records containing consent forms and proof of performers' ages" (ibid.:618). Under this provision, producers of pornography fulfill the proof requirement by obtaining a driver's license, birth certificate, or other verifiable or acceptable form of age documentation from each performer (ibid.:620, 464n). Forms will be filed at specific location listed in the opening or closing footage of the film and maintained for five years. Failure to comply with any of these requirements would be punishable *as a felony*. And producers would have the burden of verifying the actual age of the performer. These forms would be available for police inspection for up to five years after the release of the pornographic depiction. What will happen under the Freedom of Information Act to public requests for access to this data is not discussed.

Why this provision? The reason provided is: "The decision by [a] young performer to appear in pornographic materials has serious implications for his or her future personal life and career prospects. The existence of the material and its intermittent resurfacing may destroy employment prospects and threaten family stability" (ibid.:623). The only authority for this, other than the story in *Playgirl* of Sylvester Stallone's financial need and subsequent embarrassment at having appeared in a skin flick, are references to the Los Angeles Hearings testimony of Miki Garcia and the Washington, D.C., Hearings testimony of Tom (ibid.:623, 627).

Immaturity does not end at the twenty-first birthday, and the permanent record and impossibility of denial that are generated by this statutory proposal will place young performers over the age of twenty-one in increased risk of stigma all in the name of protecting starving eighteen-, nineteen-, and twenty-year-olds from employment in the production of pornography.

Further, by the commission's own admission, late adolescents who are denied employment in the pornographic representation of actual sex acts will seek employment either in the pornographic representation of simulated sex (if they are over eighteen) or through acts of prostitution, regarded, at least in the discussion of Recommendation 37, as a species of lesser harm.

The point we seek to make here is not that the commission was wrong in its judgment that larger stigma for twenty-one-year-old victims of pornography was outweighed by the protection it felt those under twenty-one would receive from its proposal. Nor do we think we are second-guessing a considered judgment by the commissioners that increasing the pressure for acts of prostitution by young offenders aged eighteen to twenty is preferable to allowing them to appear in pornographic films. We do not think these matters were ever seriously considered.

And the problems with these proposed changes pale in comparison to some of the consequences associated with the commission's use of a unified age standard of twenty-one for all child pornography other than simulation and thus presumably in all its state law recommendations. Perhaps the most stunning recommendation in the whole Meese Commission Report is Number 45: "State legislatures should amend laws, where necessary, to make the knowing possession of child pornography a felony" (ibid.:648).

Why should the knowing possession of a photograph involving a person under twenty-one engaged in sexual intercourse or masturbation become a felony under state law? No justification broad enough to cover all acts of what it defines as child pornography is given by the commission. The broadest justification offered is "the . . . use of [pornography by] pedophiles . . . for sexual arousal and gratification" (ibid.:648–649).

There are two problems with this as a justification for the commission's recommendations. First, it is unclear that the use of photographs by pedophiles while they masturbate should be considered harmful enough to generate eligibility for more than a year in the state penitentiary, the traditional criterion for felony status. Second, it is not clear that the only people to be sexually aroused by pornographic representations of persons under the age of twenty-one are pedophiles.

The age boundaries for child pornography were set by the commission at eighteen and twenty-one, not in relation to pedophilia but because of the economic circumstances, immaturity, and permanent stigma of late adolescents engaging in pornographic performances. Yet the jurisprudence of the commission's definition of child pornography, contained in its Recommendation 38, seems to have been forgotten eleven pages later when it seeks to educate states about the proper definition and penal treatment of possession of child pornography.

And that is just the beginning. In its Recommendation 53, the commission suggests that "state legislatures should amend or enact legislation, if necessary, to permit judges to impose a sentence of lifetime probation for convicted child pornographers and related offenders" (ibid.:670). If the felony of possession of child pornography is one of the "related offenses," and there is no indication that it is not, lifetime probation would be available for felons convicted of possession of pictures of persons under the age of twenty-one engaged in sexual intercourse or masturbation.

Are these people pedophiles? Does the commission mean to make all individuals in possession of such photographs eligible for lifetime probation? Were the commission members thinking of the age boundaries they recommended in Recommendation 38 when they made the lifetime probation recommendation? Indeed, is there any self-conscious coordination between the various proposals spread so widely and so thinly throughout this chapter? The problem of the right foot not knowing what the left foot is doing is particularly problematic when the organism being examined is a centipede.

What the Meese Commission calls "the horror of child pornography" calls for detail and rigor in the analysis of penal policy. This chapter is intended as a foundation for the more rigorous consideration of child welfare issues in the construction of government policy toward pornography.

The special nature of the problem posed for public policy regarding children and pornography does not lie on a single dimension. Children differ from adults in many respects, and we must distinguish the several issues that give this problem its unique and inconvenient character. Accordingly, this chapter is organized under five headings:

Children as subjects
Children as objects
Child pornography and social values
The criminal enforcement of child protection
The boundaries of childhood

Children as subjects

No mainstream commentary we have seen takes exception to prohibiting the use of children in the production of commercial, or for that matter private, pornography; or to the use of the criminal law to enforce that prohibition. About what the Meese Commission referred to as "The Special Horror of Child Pornography" (U.S. Department of Justice, 1986:405), there is probably less dispute than in regard to any other issue in the pornography debate. There is disagreement about the nature and extent of the child pornography industry; but about its undesirability there appears to be, apart from the pedophile lobby, virtual unanimity.

The distinguishing characteristic of this particular pornographic genre has been described as being "that actual children are photographed while engaged in some form of sexual activity, either with adults or other children" (ibid.:405). The principal concern felt about this type of material relates not to the harmful effect it might have on consumers of the material, but to the possible harmful effects on the children participating in its production.

In this connection the Meese Commission reported that "none of us doubt that child pornography is extraordinarily harmful both to the children involved and to society, that dealing with child pornography in all its forms ought to be treated as a governmental priority of the greatest urgency, and that an aggressive law enforcement effort is an essential part of this urgent governmental priority" (ibid.:418). Professor Trevor Gibbens, who told the Williams Committee that "long-term damage to those involved was more doubtful than is widely assumed," did not, however, argue that "the use of children in pornography was anything but undesirable" (Home Office, 1979:90).

It may be that in regard to this type of material the Johnson Commission's finding in respect of erotic material in general, "that although substantial proportions of people are worried about the effects . . . there is also considerable annoyance that such materials *merely exist*" (Johnson, 1971:219 n. 96), applies with peculiar force. Certainly there appears to be, as the Williams Committee noted, almost universal agreement that the protection for children provided by law, against sexual behavior which they are too young to properly consent to, should apply to participation in pornography (Home Office, 1979:90).

About the extent of the problem of child pornography, one of the Johnson Commission's technical reports, entitled "Commercial Traffic in Sexually Oriented Material in the United States (1969–1970)," stated that the producers of American stag films or blue movies "have avoided using pre-pubescent or pubescent children in their films"; and that although young males were used as models in "homosexual magazines," magazines "wholly composed of [nude] photos of young girls were unknown" (U.S. Commission, 1971–72, 3:100 n. 79, 188).

In 1978, however, it was claimed that child pornography was "one of the fastest growing industries in the United States." There were, it was said, "264 'kiddie porn mags' of the Lolita type produced each month . . . 300,000 children under sixteen being involved in the commercial sex industry" (Eysenck and Nias, 1978:20–21). And in 1977 the Senate Judiciary Committee found that child pornography was "a large industry – representing millions of dollars in annual revenue – that operates on a nationwide scale" (U.S. Congress, Senate, 1977:6).

In 1986 child pornography was described in *Harvard Women's Law Journal* as one of the "major industries in this country" (Loken, 1986:133). Moreover, in 1986 the Meese Commission found that in addition to the "domestic commercial child pornography industry" there was "a commercial network for child pornography, consisting to a significant extent of foreign magazines"; and that "although the publication of these magazines is largely foreign, there is substantial evidence that the predominant portion of the recipients of and contributors to these magazines [is] American" (U.S. Department of Justice, 1986:408–409).

In no case was any real evidence cited in support of these assertions, and other observers have been skeptical. Berl Kutchinsky argues that "the numbers of children exploited by pornographers have probably been greatly exaggerated" and that "the market for child pornography is quite limited." Kutchinsky does not deny that child pornography, which "long existed as an obscure, rare, and expensive commodity," did after 1970 become more readily available. "In the mid-1970s," he says, "Danish, West German, and Dutch child pornography magazines featured *Playboy*-like centerfolds, contact advertisements, short stories in several languages, and articles advocating the legalization of 'child sexuality.' "

But he reports that concern about the child models involved led to widespread restrictive legislation so that by 1980 "there was hardly a single country in which child pornography could legally be reproduced and sold." The demand for it, he asserts, came from "a small, very much outcast sexual minority" (Kutchinsky, 1983:1080–1081). The Williams Committee reported in relation to child pornography that there was only a small area not covered by the law on sexual offenses and that "on the evidence we received, this area is even smaller in practice than it may appear on paper" (Home Office, 1979:88).

About the extent of this "Special Horror," the Meese Commission report provides no precise information. It states that "prior to the late 1970s, when awareness and concern about child pornography escalated dramatically, commercially produced and distributed child pornography was more prevalent than it is now." But about how "it is now" the report is indecisive. "We have little doubt that there is some distribution in the United States of commercially produced material, although the extremely clandestine nature of the distribution networks makes it difficult to assess the size of this trade" (U.S. Department of Justice, 1986:408–410).

According to the Meese Commission, "the greatest bulk of child pornography is produced by child abusers themselves in largely 'cottage industry' fashion." This "noncommercial use of and trade in noncommercially produced sexually explicit pictures of children" is said to be substantially larger than domestic commercial production. Efforts to deal with the problem will fail, it says, if the noncommercial side of the practice is underestimated (ibid.:409–410). But what would constitute either an underestimate or an overestimate is not indicated.

It should be remembered, however, that vagueness and imprecision characterize the commission's references to the extent not merely of child pornography but of all types of pornography. The commission was able to report that a particular category of pornographic materials was "the most prevalent" or "increasingly prevalent"; that "an enormous amount" of the material available had a certain character; and that a certain class of material was "as it stands a small class" (ibid.:323, 331, 347). But what these references might be intended to denote in more specific quantitative terms is never made clear.

Perhaps because the problem of child pornography is uncontroversial it has not been the subject of serious empirical study, logical analysis, or strategic planning. Possibly unanimity in condemnation led to the assumption that no detailed examination was necessary, and thus a considerable number of general statements float on top of an abundance of unexamined issues relating to the possible harms involved in children's participation in the production of pornographic material.

To begin with, two definitional issues of some importance require attention. Both the character of child pornography and the meaning of the term "child" in this context need to be defined. As to "child pornography" we here refer to the use of children in explicit sexual depictions designed to excite sexually at least some members of the adult population. This definition, which derives from the Williams Committee's discussion of pornography (Home Office, 1979:103–104), is in accordance with ordinary usage, but it raises the question of who should be considered a child for the purpose of public policy toward child pornography. The discussion of the Meese Commission proposals shows that this is not a matter of small importance and may explain some of the apparently conflicting statements made about the amount of child pornography in debate on the matter.

There are, in fact, three different definitions of childhood that may apply in the discussion of child pornography. In the first place the reference may be to the sexually immature, thus giving the concept an explicitly biological connotation. Second, the term "child" may be used to refer to preadolescents of those in the very early years of adolescence (e.g., fourteen or fifteen years of age), thus being defined in social rather than biological terms. Third, childhood may be defined in legal terms as referring to all those below the legal age of majority.

We distinguish these three different uses of the term "child" not in order to nominate one of them as especially appropriate. More important to us is that the implications in terms of the population involved in child pornography vary considerably depending upon which definition is adopted.

Thus, the character and size of the audience attracted by child pornography involving the participation of eleven-year-olds are likely to be quite different from those of the audience attracted by pornography involving seventeen-year-olds; midadolescent subjects are likely to attract much larger audiences than more immature subjects. Such differences may explain some differences of opinion about the nature and extent of the child pornography problem.

The Meese Commission did advert to this matter parenthetically in a footnote where it states that "a significant amount of sexually explicit material involves children over the applicable age of majority who look somewhat younger" and that "in general this variety of material does not cater to the pedophile, but instead to those who prefer material with young-looking models." Because those who are used are not actually minors the commission reported that this type of publication "would not qualify as child pornography" (U.S. Department of Justice, 1986:405 n. 70).

But differences in definition also bear on the different kinds of harm that may be specific to the participation of children in the production of pornography. In the first place, we may be concerned about children, however defined, participating in the production of pornography because it is reasonable to expect any harm experienced to be greater and qualitatively different from that which might be anticipated in the case of adults. Children may not be as resilient as adults and not as familiar with varieties of sexual behavior. They may suffer pains and experience special fears that would be less likely to affect more mature subjects. Obviously, the likelihood of these kinds of harm occurring will depend to a large extent on the category of children involved. Thus, Professor Trevor Gibbens told the Williams Committee "that young girls often had the ability to exploit what they saw as a 'good racket' and were quite capable of still growing up into well-adjusted women" (Home Office, 1979:90). But his statement is more likely to refer to sixteen-year-old than to nine-year-old girls.

In the second place, we may be concerned about children's participation in the production of pornography not simply because the harm that may come to them may be different from the harm that might afflict adults, but also because children lack the capacity to make mature judgments about the harm involved. In this connection it is emotional or psychological rather than physical immaturity that is the crucial consideration. Certainly it is this that provides the rationale underlying the prohibition of statutory rape and the prescription of minimum ages for marriage and for contractual consent. The relevant concerns here relate more to the social definitions of childhood than to those based on sexual maturity.

That this is not the exclusive basis for concern about children's participation in pornography can be demonstrated by reference to the implausibility of permitting the substitution of adult judgment for that of the child in this context. As to contractual capacity and also to the marriage of minors, we allow adults in a fiduciary relationship to give consent for a child. It is unlikely in the extreme that any Western state would permit adults to give effective consent to the participation of a minor ward in the production of pornography.

The harms so far discussed relate to those children who are participants in the production of pornography. But there is another way in which child pornography might threaten the welfare of children more generally. If the depiction of children in sexually provocative material led to an expansion of the number of persons desiring and seeking children as sex objects, this might lead to an increase in the risk of predation, which could expose children (who were strangers to the original transactions) to harm.

The nature of the harm that concerns us will have consequences in regard to the ways in which we might wish to regulate child pornography. For example, it has been noted that some of the sexually explicit material involved in the discussion of child pornography involves young adult actors (U.S. Department of Justice, 1986:405 n. 70). Public policy relating solely to the protection of child participants in pornographic production might not be concerned with materials in which the participants were adults in social or legal terms. But a policy designed to minimize the appeal of children as sexual objects should be concerned about the harmful impact of material involving childlike actors as well as that involving "real" children.

An analogous point can be made about enforcement priorities in relation to existing stocks of child pornography. A policy emphasizing the horrors and harms of today's children participating in the production of pornography would give relatively low priority to the clearing up of stocks of films, pictures, and postcards of years gone by. Indeed, assuming that the demand for child pornography, however defined, was relatively stable, one way to reduce or limit the demand for fresh pornographic material portraying children might be to tolerate the free availability of existing stocks. But concern that the use of this material might possibly increase the demand for children as sex objects would be more likely to inspire a policy of general prohibition and suppression in which the priority would be to reduce the total amount of such material available of whatever vintage.

In determining these different possibilities we operate far beyond any foundation in existing empirical knowledge or research. Yet one reason for the lack of knowledge and absence of research in relation to such matters is the failure to address questions at this level of specificity. The continued importance of this subtopic for the administration of the criminal law suggests that further attention should be paid to the child as participant in the production of pornography.

Children as objects

It is almost universally agreed that the public-policy considerations that govern the regulation of the audiences of pornography are different when the audience consists of children. Although some of the same considerations that give rise to special concern when children are the subjects of pornography also apply here, the harms that attach to the child as a consumer of pornography are different and merit separate analysis.

In the case of pornography with children as the central subjects, the extent of the practice is, as we have seen, the subject of debate. But there can be no doubt that large numbers of children, particularly those in early and middle adolescence, make up part of the audience for pornography. Some studies of the characteristics of customers of movie theaters and bookstores that offer sexually explicit materials suggest that a substantial majority of customers are males in the twenty-eight- to sixty-year-old range (e.g., U.S. Commission, 1971–72, 4:231). But although middle-aged males may spend more money and be more visible consumers, there is no doubt that exposure to explicit sexual materials that the Johnson Commission found to be "widespread in adolescence" (U.S. Commission, 1970:21) in 1970 is no less extensive today. Part of the special appeal of pornography for young audiences is that it provides a source of information about sexual practice; and this is also a special concern of those who see children as vulnerable and susceptible to harm.

The Williams Committee heard a number of witnesses who saw ways in which pornography might be harmful to children as an audience and reported that "most of our witnesses wished to see children and young persons protected (Home Office, 1979:88). In particular, Dr. Gallwey of the Portman Clinic thought that "a particular experience of exposure to pornography at a time of stress in the child's process of growing up, particularly when trying to evolve an understanding of aspects of life, could be very confusing to a child and, if in constellation with other disturbing factors, could tip the balance towards psychological damage." Dr. Hyatt Williams, by contrast, saw the danger "more in terms of pornography being used by an adult with a view, for example, to homosexual seduction than in relation to pornography being passed around among children" (ibid.:89).

On the other hand, the Williams Committee also reported: "We did hear from some of our expert witnesses a certain caution about just how susceptible children were to such influences . . . and we heard no evidence of actual harm being caused to children. Some witnesses suspected that children would not take very much notice of pornography and that they might be more robust than was commonly assumed" (ibid.:88–89).

The Meese Commission took the view that the exposure of children even to those sexually explicit materials not violent and not degrading was harmful. "We all agree that at least much, probably most, and maybe even all material in this category . . . is harmful when it falls into the hands of children." The commission's report does not cite any expert evidence on this topic but asserts simply that "the near unanimity in society about the effects on children and on all society in exposing children to explicit sexuality in the form of even nonviolent and nondegrading pornographic materials makes a strong statement about the potential harms of this material, and we confidently agree with that longstanding societal judgment" (U.S. Department of Justice, 1986:343, 344–345).

In fact, there is no doubt that children lack both the maturity of judgment and the experiential background in relation to sex that may come with adulthood. Immaturity of judgment may be associated with vulnerability to the attraction of deviant life-styles, to perverse or misguided attitudes, to poor impulse controls, and to distorted values. Lack of an experiential background about sex, which can be an antidote to grandiose and distorted elements in pornographic material, may lead to psychological stress and confusion.

The distinction between immaturity of judgment and lack of experience has implications for the selection of appropriate means of preventing harms associated with exposing children to pornography. If the problem is seen as one of immaturity of judgment, then the only safeguard may be preclusion of the availability of pornography or the substitution of adult judgment as to what should be made available and at what ages. However, concern about childhood vulnerability because of lack of experience or background in the reality of human sexuality might be better addressed, as the Johnson Commission suggested, by increasing the availability of other sources of information, for example, providing "access to adequate information regarding sex, through appropriate sex education" (U.S. Commission, 1970:29), rather than attempting to block channels of pornographic communication.

Indeed, if lack of experience is the problem, the best antidote for the unusual, grandiose, and misleading features of currently available pornography might be realistic, anatomically correct, and humanistic sexually explicit communication. But if the central concern of those troubled about children as consumers of pornography is the sexual stimulation of the young, clearly a more appropriate policy would be aimed at the minimization of the amount of sexually arousing content in the diet of childhood America. The appropriate responses to innocence may thus operate at cross-purposes to the right method of dealing with immaturity.

In considering these different possibilities, the widely different concepts of childhood referred to in the previous section are not merely relevant but extraordinarily important. Public policy regarding childhood exposure to pornography must deal with children of four, seven, nine, and twelve years of age and, if social and legal definitions are applied, with those fourteen and seventeen years of age as well. Risks of different harms and harms of different magnitudes must attend these substantial age variations.

The issue of experiment

There are very few empirical data available on the question of children as consumers of pornography. Very little work has been done and there has been no attempt to expand research in this area in recent years. The Johnson Commission reported that "insufficient research is presently available on the effect of the exposure of children to sexually explicit materials . . . strong ethical feelings against experimentally exposing children to sexually explicit material considerably reduced the possibility of gathering the necessary data and information regarding young persons" (U.S. Commission, 1970:57). Eysenck and Nias, in their survey of experimental and other research into the effects of exposure to violent and pornographic material, report numerous laboratory studies of violence-viewing with child subjects but remark that "children . . . for ethical reasons, have not been involved in laboratory experiments on the effects of pornography" (Eysenck and Nias, 1978:162). The Williams Committee also noted that "for obvious reasons, children have not been involved in laboratory experiments on the effects of pornography" (Home Office, 1979:88).

Neither the Johnson Commission, nor Eysenck and Nias, nor the Williams Committee explain the nature of the "ethical" and "obvious" reasons that preclude the use of child subjects in experimental work or exposure to pornography. Nor does it seem indisputably obvious that the exposure of children to scenes of violence should be seen as perfectly acceptable while their exposure to portrayals of sexual acts must be regarded as unethical. Indeed, an argument could be made for a directly contrary conclusion.

Four hundred years ago, Montaigne remarked the curious paradox that "we boldly utter the words *kill, rob, betray*" but in regard to "the genital act . . . we dare not speak of it without shame" ([Montaigne, [1580–88] 1946:739). More recently, Gershon Legman in his study of censorship, *Love and Death*, asked: "Why this absurd contradiction? Is the creation of life really more reprehensible than its destruction?" (Legman, 1949:94).

In a similar vein, Geoffrey Gorer wrote:

I have never seen it seriously suggested that the literature of murder – detective stories or crime stories – tended to deprave and corrupt, or would incite weak-minded or immature readers into carrying out in reality the activities described in the fantasies. On the contrary, the literature of murder is considered particularly "healthy" and desirable; and in England representatives of all the most respected professions have stated that detective stories are among their favourite reading. Musing about murder is apparently "healthy"; musing about sexual enjoyment is not. No one, it is apparently assumed, will commit a murder because he spends his leisure reading about other people committing murders; but there is a grave danger that people will commit illegal sexual acts because they read pornography. (Gorer, 1961:37)

Yet, although it may not be immediately self-evident, there are reasonable grounds for distinguishing the two types of material and for reluctance to involve children in experiments on the effects of pornography that do not apply in the case of depictions of violence. In the first place, few children today are not familiar, through the media, with the overt presentation of scenes of violence between real and fictional; and few are unable to distinguish between the real world and the fantastic portrayals of violence found in films and comic books. In the laboratory experiments in which they have been involved, they have not been presented with material significantly different from presentations with which they are already probably overly familiar.

Yet explicit portrayals of sexual acts are not as readily available to children, nor do children have a background of experience to enable them to distinguish between reality and fantasy. Dr. Hanna Segal, an expert witness before the Williams Committee, suggested that one of the principal ways in which exposure to pornographic material might be harmful to children derived from the fact that "children learn to overcome their sexual fantasies by looking at behavior in the real world," whereas if their view of the adult world via the medium of pornography confirmed those fantasies, "they were likely to become fixated by them" (Home Office, 1979:89).

With respect to the ethical issues regarding experimentation with children as consumers of pornography, we think that a distinction should be drawn between prepubescent and older children. The absence of experimentation makes some sense among age groups that have low exposure to pornography and do not seek out such materials on their own.

In age groups where exposure to pornography is higher, and where children frequently and successfully seek pornography on their own initiative, controlled experiments that pay careful attention to human subject issues seem justified by the importance of the issues and the less substantial prospect of great harm to the subjects.

Another dimension of this matter relates to the social context in which children receive sexual cues. This must be an important variable in determining the nature and amount of harm they are likely to suffer. The more importance society attaches to the kinds of harm children may suffer sexually, the more significant those harms tend to become. Thus, many of the traumas arising from the sexual abuse of children owe a great deal to the stigma attached by society to the acts involved: a stigma that, as in some cases of adult rape, is projected onto the victim.

Thus, one could argue that if adults were to treat the process of victimization in cases of child sexual abuse as less of a stigmatizing event and more as the kind of misfortune that is a not uncommon feature of life, and one that can be overcome, the experience might be less traumatic for many child victims. Analogously, a social context in which the existence of pornography is acknowledged and generally accepted by adult society might enable children to adjust more easily to their personal experience with it. We are unaware of any cross-cultural research that has addressed issues of this nature but such studies might provide valuable information.

Child pornography and social values

There is another objection to child pornography that, while not decisive on public policy grounds, is important enough and distinctive enough to merit separate discussion. It can be argued that the portrayal of the sexual use of children tends to corrupt the moral values of a community in a way distinct from, and more troublesome than, either the social effects of pornography generally or even of the degradation of women that is associated with much pornography.

This "moral climate" point is distinguishable from concern about the advertisement of children as sexual objects increasing the amount of predation on children. For the toleration of the sexual use of children may have negative consequences quite apart from any increase in the rate of child sex victimization. And the notion that a society is corrupted by its toleration of child pornography can also be distinguished from the view that all pornography is morally corrupting. Although it has been asserted that everything which is pornographic is also exploitative, there seems to be no obvious reason why all explicit depictions of sexual activity designed to arouse the sexual appetites of an audience should necessarily involve exploitation.

With regard to the argument that pornography is of its nature degrading to the status of women (MacKinnon, 1987:158–162), the contrast between adult women and children as portrayed in pornography may be significant. Pornographic material that portrays the consent to, and pleasure in, sexual activity of female participants may be sheer fantasy and may degrade by suggesting that adult women might behave in ways they should not or do not behave. One may argue that pornography of this sort is inherently misleading in relation to the desires and intentions, actions and reactions, of women. The "central conceit" in the pornographic film *Deep Throat*, says Catharine MacKinnon, is "that we get pleasure in ways we do not" (MacKinnon, 1987:128). But as long as we are willing to grant women a capacity to consent, there is nothing inherently forcible and in *that* sense exploitative about the portrayal of adult women in pornography.

The child's lack of capacity to consent makes it possible to argue that *all* portrayals of the sexual use of children constitute an exploitation that is the moral equivalent of force, no matter if the child involved is pictured as enjoying participating in the pornographic fantasy. If we take seriously distinctions based on capacity to consent, the whole category of child pornography represents the celebration of exploitation.

The contrast between the use of adult women and children in pornography throws light on two other child pornography issues. One involves the definition of childhood that proponents of this view would employ, and the other relates to the question of whether actual children must be the subjects of sexual use for the pornography in question to be socially harmful.

As to the definition of "child," the recent history of the definition of children for the purpose of consent is not without irony. Of the three definitions of "child" just discussed, biological, social, and legal, the legal boundary between childhood and adulthood is both the most arbitrary basis for distinguishing the capacity to consent and also the most frequently used.

Almost no one would doubt that eight-, ten-, and eleven-year-olds lack a meaningful capacity for consent in relation to sex. The problem cases in the troubled career of the crime of statutory rape have involved "legal" children who were well into sexual maturity and possessed a substantial degree of sexual sophistication. In this way, the use of high-legal-age categories such as twenty-one tends to obscure a moral issue that is of considerable importance for younger children.

The "moral climate" problem is not an automatic justification for censorship. It bears repeating that a high regard for free expression counsels against attempts to prohibit communications merely because they foster bad attitudes. We live in a society that rightly tolerates the advocacy of racial discrimination and political violence, as long as no clear and present danger of the attitudes generated being manifested in conduct is the proximate consequence of the communication. Thus, prohibiting the portrayal of the sexual use of children should be based on the risk of child victimization rather than on concern about general community values.

It might not do, however, to regard the issue as resolved; as the Williams Committee put it in relation to children, "there is only a small area of pornographic activity which is not covered by the law on sexual offences" (Home Office, 1979:90). It may be the case that most of the sexual acts portrayed would be unlawful if the actors employed were children. But many less explicit poses by children may stimulate a pedophile audience. And the use of young-looking actors, makeup, and special effects raises questions of the celebration of exploitation that should not be ignored. To overlook them is to take a short cut that obscures an inquiry relevant to the special problem of child pornography.

Criminal law enforcement of child protection

We here discuss aspects of using the criminal law for child protection in an environment where pornographic communication by, for, and about adults is generally permitted. The topics dealt with include child pornography as victimless crime; the distinction between child consumption of, and participation in the production of, pornography as occasions for criminal law enforcement; the extent to which minors should be punished as part of a regulatory scheme; and the need for both the grading of offenses and the selection of appropriate penalties.

Child pornography as victimless crime

There are two contrasting definitions of victimless crime, only one of which would include most instances of the involvement of children in pornography. The most common definition, derived from John Stuart Mill and according to which such crimes have no other victim than the perpetrator, who harms only himself (Mill, [1859] 1975:10–11), does not really apply in this context. Even if children consent to being used in, or exposed to, pornographic communication, their immaturity could nonetheless render them victims in Mill's sense.

But another concept of victimless crime defines it as referring to "crimes [that] lack victims, in the sense of complainants asking for the protection of the criminal law" (Morris and Hawkins, 1970:6). In light of this definition, all of the consumption of pornographic material by willing children, and a substantial amount of child participation in the production of pornography, would be victimless crime. Most children will not complain to the authorities. Law enforcement has to be proactive and organized on the traditional vice-squad model to enforce child-specific bans on consumption.

There are two further contemporary developments that hinder official attempts to restrict child pornography: the deregulation of adult pornography as an industry and the loosening of restrictions on midadolescents who run away from home and seek to live autonomous lives in the American city.

It is not merely that adult pornography has been decriminalized in America and many other Western countries that is the problem here; it has also been deregulated. There is little in the way of law enforcement presence in most "adult" bookstores or video-rental agencies. And in many cities there is a substantially reduced police presence, although still an important one, in bars, live sex shows, and the like.

In theory, the trend toward decriminalization of commercial sex could have resulted in more intensive regulation of the manufacture and sale of pornography. That argument is made by proponents of decriminalization of some forms of vice under the rubric of "it is impossible to regulate behavior that is prohibited" (Morris and Hawkins, 1977:21). In fact, however, the formal prohibition of commercial sex had already evolved into a de facto regulatory scheme in most American cities: a regulatory arrangement that might have made it easier to police special problems such as the exploitation of young children than when further deregulation took place.

Decriminalization has not led to the extensive development of noncriminal law regulation for two reasons: First, the classification of pornographic material as communication creates in the United States a strong presumption against any regulatory control as constituting censorship. Second, once the police are removed as an agency concerned with observing and regulating the commercial sex industry, there are no other public agencies with the incentive or the capacity to take their place. So that a more laissez-faire attitude toward some aspects of pornographic production and consumption by adults diminishes the will and ability of law enforcement to keep children and pornographic communication in separate worlds.

Just as it is more difficult to use traditional vice-control powers to regulate pornography as a way to protect children, it is also increasingly difficult to use the special legal classification of children and the quasi-parental power of the state over them to protect them from exposure to, or even participation in the production of, pornography.

Traditional powers to lock up status offenders, allegedly for their own good, allowed the police and juvenile courts considerable control over truants, runaways, vagrants, and the insubordinate, at least in theory. Removing the power to arbitrarily lock up the young also removed leverage on the part of the police to protect juveniles from real dangers. In effect, the decriminalization of status offenses has also led to the deregulation of youth.

The police, deprived of the power to lock children up, have often staged a strategic withdrawal; many no longer regard themselves as responsible for the welfare of fifteen- and sixteen-year-olds. Other public agencies lack the incentives and resources to fill the gap.

The withdrawal from the coercive regulation of adolescence can be justified because the costs of regulation – in dollars, in liberty, and, most importantly, in youth welfare – exceeded their benefits. But withdrawal of the use of coercive state power has not been costless. The dangers of exercising immature judgment on the streets of major urban areas, living in squalor, and risking disease and death are quite real (Zimring, 1982:61–75).

Consumption versus participation

While the factors just described hinder law enforcement of both the consumption of, and participation in the production of, pornography by the young, the opportunities for enforcement and the prospects for effectiveness differ markedly in relation to these two aspects.

Put simply, the prospects for enforcing a ban on the consumption of pornography by adolescents who wish to do so are minimal. The prospects for enforcing criminal prohibition of child participation in commercial sex and newly produced pornography are much better, particularly for younger children. The prospects for restricting the availability of pornographic material involving children or childlike subjects come somewhere between these two poles.

With respect to children as pornography consumers, the task of keeping millions of pornographic communications out of the hands of millions of children seems hopeless. As we shall show, the severe punishment of the children if caught would be perverse. The notion of punishing only those who make available, or facilitate the availability of, pornography to other children is little better. Most who aid and abet minors in obtaining access to pornography are themselves minors. And many of the remainder are relatively blameless adults who would, in effect, be punished for their own use of pornography or for failing to effectively keep children away from materials intended for adult use.

The situation parallels the one pertaining to tobacco and alcohol. The decision to deregulate for adults guarantees a high level of availability for older children and adolescents. But the prospects for some forms of control are probably less discouraging than this analysis implies. Most of the children who cannot be denied access to pornography are the older and more enterprising young, whose exposure to pornography is less problematic than with the very young or the especially naive.

Further, the extremely limited amount of research available on the effects of pornography does not suggest any harm to children as consumers of pornography comparable to what might be expected from their direct participation in commercial sex. It seems likely that the best policy to adopt in restricting the consumption of pornography by children is a relatively relaxed one without the call for rigorous enforcement or publicized show prosecutions as an attempt to compensate for the futility of the overall effort.

Better prospects exist for enforcing the prohibition of child participation in the production of pornographic books and films, although there are limits. Children from midadolescence onward who are willing participants in the exercise are difficult to remove from the street and will usually be unavailable as complaining witnesses against their corrupters. Much of their participation in movies or employment as photographic models may be beyond the reach of law enforcement.

But the live-sex segment of the industry, particularly if it involves public display or the licensed sale of alcoholic beverages, is often the subject of police scrutiny. And police supervision of bars can make proprietors quite vigilant about age gradations. Whether this can be regarded as a wholly desirable youth-protection policy depends on the extent to which it diminishes the involvement of the young in the commercial sex business, rather than driving adolescents into less visible and less desirable branches of the industry.

For younger children, their appearance alone may operate as a red-flag warning that will reinforce regulatory powers. Purveyors of commercial sex are not unaware of the opprobrium attached to the employment of the young in this area, as well as likelihood of more intensive law enforcement and heavier penalties. Moreover, for very young children, the runaway population from which participants can be recruited is smaller.

The prohibition of the use of children in live displays in public places does not present major enforcement problems. Films, books, and magazines can also be confiscated, although never as fast as they can be reproduced. Yet the relative rarity of unambiguous child pornography, which the Meese Commission acknowledged (saying "there now appears to be comparatively little domestic commercial production of child pornography" [U.S. Department of Justice, 1986:409]), may not be so much due, as the commission thought, to the success of "major law enforcement initiatives" as to the fact that the demand for the product has never been as great or as elastic as the more vocal protesters against this "major horror" have believed.

The punishment of children

One issue highlighted by the consideration of child pornography as victimless crime is the extent to which it is appropriate to punish children for placing their own interests in jeopardy or for jeopardizing the interests of other children. In considering this question, it might also be useful to distinguish between punishing a child for engaging in self-jeopardization and punishing minors for the exploitation of other minors.

It is never appropriate to use either the criminal law or the delinquency jurisdiction of the juvenile court to punish minors severely solely because they put themselves at risk. To do so would be to make assumptions about personal responsibility in deciding punishments that are inconsistent with the ideas about responsibility that led to, and are inherent in, the definition of the offense. Lesser punishments may be predicated on partial responsibility. But secure confinement as punishment for self-jeopardy appears to us to be nonsensical.

If the punishment of minors for putting themselves at risk is unjustified, what about the exercise of state power based on the minor's need for protection rather than on the concept of blameworthiness? This was, and is, the basis of the "status offenses" jurisdiction of the juvenile court; and it has not been totally repudiated.

The problem is that substantial amounts of punishment have been imposed in the guise of nonpunitive child protection. And the one effective control on this tendency is the limitation, on child-protection grounds, of the degree of physical control that can be exercised over adolescent subjects. Long-term secure confinement should be restricted to cases involving the kind of extreme danger that justifies civil commitment. Short-term secure confinement might be permitted as a means of crisis intervention, but it involves the risk of misuse or manipulation by the police and the courts.

The problem of the minor who is responsible for the sexual exploitation of other minors is distinguishable from self-jeopardization, but not in an absolute fashion. The paradigm case of the sexual exploitation of children involves not only incapacity on the victim's part but the assumption of a greater capacity on the part of those responsible for the offense. Something of the same problem involved in punishing the child victim counsels against punishing one fifteen-year-old for exploiting the immaturity of another fifteen-year-old with respect to either commercial or noncommercial sexual practices.

The punishment of minors for the exploitation of other minors might be limited to cases where either physical force was used or there were clear differences in age or capacity. The punishment of a sixteen-year-old for the exploitation of a twelve-year-old is much more clearly justifiable than the punishment of two sixteen-year-olds for mutual exploitation. As a threshold matter, we should require some significant difference in capacity before permitting the punishment of one minor for the exploitation of another. Once that threshold is passed, moreover, an inquiry into the extent of the overreach would be relevant to the selection of the appropriate punishment in such cases.

The criminal jurisprudence of child pornography

The foregoing discussion of the punishment of children is just one of many specific issues that require consideration in relation to the use of criminal sanctions in regulating the involvement of children in pornography and commercial sex. A great many questions regarding the definition and gradation of sexual offenses involving children have received little attention and practically no critical scrutiny. It is almost as though child pornography were a homogeneous harm, so that there was no need to devote serious consideration to the definition of offenses in this area.

In fact, given the tendency for criminal prohibitions to be enacted with enthusiasm and buttressed with inflated penalty scales, the opposite is the case. It is essential that careful thought be given to issues of definition and gradation. Among the key issues are the following:

Is a single grade of offense involving participation in the commercial sexual exploitation of a child sufficient? Or should a higher grade of offense be provided for cases involving younger children, with proportionately lesser penalties being provided for the exploitation of children closer to the borders of adult status? (See Zimring, 1982, 1987.)

Should aggravated penalties be provided for cases involving the use of force?

Should there be mitigation of punishment in cases involving the admittedly imperfect consent of minor victims? Or should the consent of a minor only warrant mitigation when the victim is an older child and when the victim and offender are relatively close in age and capacity?

To what extent should the scale of a commercial child pornography operation be regarded as relevant to the moral blameworthiness of actors in it and the eligibility of offenders for larger penalties? The production of ten child-pornographic films may be regarded as more culpable than the production of one such film; but should the distribution of ten copies of the same film be regarded as more serious than the distribution of one or two? And if so, to what extent and why?

We cannot here even outline a complete jurisprudence of child pornography. Instead we wish to demonstrate that if this matter is to be taken seriously, such questions as these cannot be ignored. And some attempt to construct or formulate a principled basis for sentencing those who exploit children in this manner is a necessary feature of taking child pornography seriously.

On the boundaries of childhood

Just as we do not propose to offer a detailed jurisprudence for the sentencing of those convicted of the sexual exploitation of children, neither shall we attempt a definitive analysis of the appropriate age boundaries that should be prescribed in applying the criminal law to the sexual exploitation of children. Instead we offer two general guidelines that should govern the determination of those boundaries.

First, asking questions about the age at which children are sufficiently mature to make responsible decisions about participation in pornographic production is the wrong way to go about defining the boundaries for criminal prohibition. There is a sense in which no age is old enough for such decisions, and no child or young adult has the experience to make those decisions until he or she has made them. More importantly – and the victimless crime category is again instructive here – the point in adolescence at which criminal prohibitions cease to be useful is when they begin to do more harm than good. And that typically is long before the targets of predation reach anywhere near their full maturity.

Second, it is clear that no single age boundary can usefully span the great variety of issues involved in the regulation of sexual communication and children. If exposure to pornographic material is to be made criminal, it should be so only in relation to young children, with the maximum age certainly no higher than thirteen or fourteen. Sexual conduct is quite different from sexual communication, and there is no reason why the criminal law should not prohibit sexual practices of adults with fourteen- or fifteen-year-olds even if such minors are over the age at which pornographic communication to them ceases to be criminal. Finally, there would be nothing wrong with a scheme of regulation that set the age of consent for participation in commercial sexual activity higher – say at eighteen years of age – than for noncommercial sexual conduct. We think this may be both compatible with, and justifiable in, a situation where a society has completely decriminalized participation in commercial sex by adults.

The specific age boundaries just suggested are, like all age boundaries, largely arbitrary, although the scheme itself both in the distinctions drawn and in the kind of gradation involved is not in itself arbitrary but based on empirical observation. Moreover, it is clearly at this level of specificity that any useful analysis of the problems presented in this chapter must proceed.

Conclusion

We do not intend this chapter as a final statement of the manifold issues of pornography and childhood. Our aim is to help build an agenda for discussion, analysis, and research. In an area known for passionate emotions and frequent political posturing, the need for detached policy assessments is not always obvious. But the case against government by sentiment has this important element: Child welfare is apt to suffer in the absence of reasoned discourse.

8

Pornography in perspective: social response in the noncensoring society

This chapter attempts to break down a false antithesis that has dominated debate about social policy toward pornography; it also discusses a range of policy options available to governmental and to nongovernmental entities in responding to pornography. The false antithesis is the notion that there are only two possible collective responses to pornography as a social issue: the imposition of censorship, or the toleration of anarchy. Those who have sought to use government power to minimize the possible effects of pornography have usually assumed that the only effective way of controlling the social damage believed to be caused by pornography is a system of prior restraint enforced with substantial criminal penalties.

Here we explore the possibilities of a middle path. After reviewing some of the reasons for the bipolar terms of the debate about pornography, we discuss some of the control strategies that private groups can use in responding to the challenge of available pornography as well as appropriate roles for local, state, and federal government other than censorship.

In adopting the assumption that the only alternative to censorship is passivity and limitless tolerance, the opponents of pornography have had the support of many of those groups in society opposed to the censorship of pornographic material. The opponents of censorship rarely speak of collective alternatives to censorship because they do not regard the free availability of pornography as causing any problems.

It is rare that a commentator acknowledges that pornography presents a social problem that could justify some kind of collective response, and yet he or she opposes censorship because that particular remedy is more dangerous than the social ill it is supposed to cure. Those who advise the use of regulatory strategies rather than criminal prohibition in relation to such things as drug abuse and commercial sex do not usually consider or propose strategies of regulation as an option for pornographic communication.

There are a number of explanations for this. First, many observers have concluded from the absence of the kind of evidence of harmful effects discussed in Chapter 4 that it has been demonstrated that pornography is harmless. That is erroneous, of course. Both the Johnson Commission and the Williams Committee distinguish between a verdict of not proven and a positive certification of harmlessness. And they render only the former, and only in regard to the consumption of pornography by adults. Further, both of the U.S. commissions and the Williams Committee endorsed the restriction of pornographic communications involving children as either consumers or participants in the production of pornography.

Another reason why the antithesis between censorship and inaction has been accepted is the widely endorsed assumption that the only collective response worth considering is some form of governmental action and that governmental action will inevitably take the form of censorship and suppression. No doubt justification for this distrust of government can be found both in the past and even in the quite recent history of governmental intervention in this area.

Yet the possibility of a more limited governmental role seems to be a topic worth exploring. Moreover, there seems to be no reason to assume that any intervention by nongovernmental entities must necessarily be ineffectual. Indeed, this is quite inconsistent with that we know about the current mechanism for the distribution of pornography through mainstream economic institutions.

We do not propose in this chapter to endorse any program designed to "solve" the problem of pornography. We wish simply to explore some of the policy options available in a society where the government does not censor sexually explicit books, photographs, motion pictures, videotapes, or records either because these items are sexually explicit or because they are intended to arouse their audiences sexually.

Some concerns expressed about the free availability of pornographic material to adults are: the corruption or exploitation of children; the dissemination and reinforcement of sexist and violently sexist attitudes among both children and adults; and the inability of individuals and families to live their lives in a pornography-free environment. In our view, all of these concerns are genuine and have some basis in fact, but only the first two justify any substantial collective intervention. Moreover, only the first calls for reliance on the use of the criminal law. The general moral climate seems too ephemeral a threat to justify specific collective actions. Attitudes seem best combated by exposure and counterargument in the free market of ideas. If these judgments are correct, it is clearly advisable to explore other less drastic and also unofficial responses that might prove effective or at least ameliorative in countering the attitudinal threat of sexist pornography.

One other preliminary point should be made. We do not mean to suggest that any of the problems identified are completely soluble, or anywhere close to that, by the use of the mechanisms we discuss. Adolescents seem quite capable of obtaining considerable quantities of pornographic material even when governments impose strict censorship on the sexually explicit for all citizens. Lesser measures will almost by definition provide greater opportunities for evasion. Living with pornography will necessarily involve living with many of its negative consequences. The most that rational policy can hope to achieve, and should seek to achieve, is improvement at the margin.

If the problems associated with pornography are not completely soluble, they are also not of momentous social importance. The corruption and exploitation of children are major social problems, but pornography makes a small contribution to child endangerment when compared with problems such as drugs, poverty, sexual abuse by intimates, malnutrition, and inadequate schooling. Much pornography is symptomatic of attitudes toward women and toward sex that do not inspire pride in the social order. But it would be a mistake to confuse one symptom of sexism with a larger and more diffuse pathological process.

The larger social policy reflected in the absence of censorship is significant in the context of the relationship between government and the individual citizen. But the fact that there is easy access to *Debbie Does Dallas* is not a very important feature of contemporary America. Indeed, it is evident that the more successfully a society copes with free access to sexual communication, the less important the subject becomes. America will have reached a real milestone in its social development when it is no longer regarded as necessary to appoint blue-ribbon commissions to inquire into, and make recommendations regarding, what the general citizenry ought to be permitted to read or view. It is not, however, inconsistent with this ordering of the priority of problems in the United States in the 1990s to regard the problems generated by the free availability of pornography to adults as worthy of some attention.

The promotion of perspective, rather than any detailed program, is the principal objective of this chapter. Yet such a perspective is best illustrated by talking about how, respectively, citizen groups, industry, and government cope with pornography in a noncensoring society.

Social control in the private sector

Before discussing some of the control options available to business and citizen groups, it will be useful to rehearse some of the changes noted in Chapter 3 in relation to the distribution of pornography in the United States; and to discuss some of the vulnerabilities to social pressure that current structures may present.

In a situation we can call "pure criminalization," those who produced and distributed pornography would be involved in no other business and have no particular interest in the nature of their reputation in society at large. The customers of the pornographic supplier would either have no large stake in preserving a good reputation or would make every effort to insulate their social identities from their activities as consumers of pornography.

Under these circumstances, the principal means of social control of pornographers would have to be physical restraint exercised by the agencies of criminal law enforcement: the police, the courts, and the jails. One aspect of this social control would be the stigmatization of the roles of both producer and consumer of pornography, and thus to some extent the restriction of demand. This would probably not curtail supply, however, because even if 99 percent of the population were dissuaded from entering the pornography business, the remaining 1 percent would without difficulty maintain an adequate supply of pornographic material.

The pure model of pornography as crime has never existed in the United States or any other Western country. The producers and sellers of pornography may have been regarded as deplorable or even perverted, but not as criminal in the way in which robbers or car thieves are regarded as criminal. The consumers of pornography were always better integrated into society than the crime model would suggest, and were thus more vulnerable to opprobrium and social censure. Thus, the low social esteem in which the consumers and producers of child pornography are held is as firmly fixed in the penal institutions as anywhere else in the world.

When we modify the paradigm of pornography as crime in the direction of creating bonds between the general society and the parties to transactions in pornographic material, we can examine opportunities for means other than physical restraint to affect the nature of the market for pornography. If consumers of pornography are strongly influenced by community values, those values will to some extent shape their preferences and thus the character of the demand for pornography. If vendors of pornography sell other things as well as pornography, they will be sensitive not simply to the demands of their customers for pornographic goods but also to the tastes and requirements of their other customers.

Moreover, if vendors identify themselves as subscribing to the mores and values of the general community, they will be vulnerable to moral appeals as well as to market pressures: a combination that is notably more effective than moral pressures operating alone. How distributors respond to these pressures will help determine the character of the market in pornographic material.

Finally, if the producers of pornographic products make other goods as well, they, too, might be subject to market pressures that will affect the character and quality of the pornographic materials they produce. The ideal situation in regard to responsiveness to social pressure would be one in which pornography was produced by major motion picture studios, distributed by large grocers and department stores, and visibly consumed by church deacons.

The actual situation is currently somewhere between that image and the pure criminalization model specified at the start of this section. And the extent of the economic integration of pornography into the mainstream of commercial activity has resulted in some increased susceptibility by both distributors and consumers to social pressures. In this situation lies the potential for both industry self-regulation and community influence, which has not been sufficiently recognized.

Recognizing that the activity and the industry of sexually explicit communication is inextricably bound up with the larger world of industry and commerce, we can consider some of the existing bases for social control as well as the major strategic choices confronting those concerned about the effects of pornography. The basic strategic choice is between influencing the contents of sexual communication – which is best achieved when sexually explicit communication is a mainstream activity – and reducing the volume of that type of communication, which is best achieved by driving supply and demand for it away from mainstream economic institutions, news racks, and general retail outlets, and back under the larger society's counter.

That strategic choice, in its governmental form, led to the slogan "it is impossible to regulate behavior that is prohibited" (Morris and Hawkins, 1977:21). It was suggested there, that rather than attempt absolute prohibition, it would be better and easier to affect the content and context of goods or services by making them subject to regulation and control. Attempts to prohibit all or most pornography might make it more difficult selectively to stigmatize egregiously sexist or violent material. Prohibition would have this effect by making those at the place of distribution for pornography much less concerned about the attitudes and tastes of the average citizen than is the general retail merchant who sold sex magazines before prohibition. Mainstream retailers are susceptible to boycott. Retailers who do not sell soft drinks, milk, or eggs, but solely pornography, will have no economic stake in staying on the good side of either Anita Bryant or Gloria Steinem.

The toleration of sexually explicit merchandise in mainstream retail outlets may foster the capacity to influence the content of that material, but it does so at a cost. If such material is available in the local convenience store, if *Debbie Does Dallas* is as available as Disney for videocassette rental, anyone who wants pornography can get it, and in abundant supply. As indicated in Chapter 7, we do not mean anyone over twenty-one or over eighteen; we mean anyone with sufficient curiosity, some money, and an ordinary level of guile. Thus, pornography cannot be made freely available in mainstream retail channels for adults and be made scarce for adolescents. When a product is durable and used at home, as with books, magazines, and videocassettes, selective prohibition for the young is not possible. Pornographic communications confined to on-site consumption, as in theaters and peep shows, provide a somewhat better prospect for age-specific prohibitions, but these are also of declining importance in the current market.

This aspect of the choice that has to be made regarding vice regulation is summed up in an inversion of the original Morris and Hawkins slogan: "It is impossible to prohibit what you regulate." The counteraphorism refers not only to the market availability of what is regulated but permitted in normal retail channels, but also to the fact that what is regulated is to some extent legitimated by those who seek to regulate. The ambiguity of the very term "license," which means both "authorization by law to do something" and "excessive, undisciplined freedom," brings out the nature of the problem.

The saga of the 7-Eleven stores

The strategic trade-off involved here is one that affects quasi-public institutions as well as governmental efforts. This trade-off should concern those who set the policies of private sector bodies, such as citizen groups and commercial associations.

The issue is well illustrated by the saga of sex magazines and the 7-Eleven stores, the largest group of food stores under single ownership or sponsorship in the United States. The Southland Corporation, which owns and franchises them, has a greater aggregate stock value than any other food retailer, in part because it also owns the Citgo Oil Company. During the years before 1986 when some sexually explicit magazines were being sold in 7-Eleven stores, an important share of total gross sales of those stores was generated by magazine and newspaper sales – probably under one-fifth of total sales; but much less than this total could be attributed to magazines in general or to sexually explicit magazines in particular.

Yet the 7-Eleven stores did have sexually explicit magazines on display, and the presence of these magazines in their inventory was not of trivial significance, either economically or in terms of the availability of the magazines they carried. It is semantically redundant but logically important here to emphasize that the essence of convenience stores to their customers is convenience. The 7-Eleven stores rarely engage in price competition, except with other convenience stores. But the majority of them are open twenty-four hours a day for impulse purchasers, never have long queues at the check-out, and have almost everything that they sell prominently displayed and easily accessible.

Nothing that costs money could be more openly available to the public than the products featured by 7-Eleven stores – a point well known to manufacturers of cigarettes, soft drinks, and dairy products, to distributors of groceries, novelties, and sundries, and to the executive staff of the Meese Commission on pornography. Less well understood, however, are the strategic choice implications of selective pressure on sexually explicit publications as opposed to the actual campaign removing mainstream soft-core sex magazines from 7-Eleven shelves. For the success of the campaign to achieve general divestiture of sexually explicit material from 7-Eleven stores may have generated some elements of a Pyrrhic victory.

The Meese Commission staff campaign to remove sexually explicit magazines from mainstream retail stores gave it overtones of both governmental blackmail and censorship. Such problems do not, however, infect all organized pressure campaigns. Consider the women's groups who threatened a boycott of 7-Eleven stores because of concern with the sexist content of many magazines, or the parental and women's groups particularly concerned with violent pornography. There does not seem to be anything ethically wrong with this tactic.

A victory for the antipornographers over *Playboy* and *Penthouse* in 7-Eleven stores probably would have the following effects:

Diminution in the sales of sexually explicit magazines not only in 7-Eleven and other convenience stores, but in the aggregate.

Diminution in the competitive advantages of *Playboy*, *Penthouse*, and other soft-core publications over their harder-core competitors.

Diminished influence, or potential influence, of such pressure groups over the contents of *Playboy* and *Penthouse*.

As to the first point, there seems little doubt that the successful removal of the periodicals in question from the shelves of 7-Eleven stores will decrease the aggregate sales of soft-core periodicals. Certainly many customers who used to stop expressly to buy *Playboy* and *Penthouse* at 7-Eleven stores will now buy the magazine of their choice at other stores or newsstands, so that one cannot assume that all of the sales will be lost to the magazine owners or the industry. But many of those sales dollars will have come from the pockets of impulse buyers who were primarily customers for beer or milk. Such sales may be transformed into impulse purchases of other reading materials, snack foods, or nothing.

If, on the other hand, 7-Eleven stores also carry some of the detective magazines that worried at least one of the Meese Commissioners as being "sources of sexually sadistic imagery" (U.S. Department of Justice, 1986:68), the victory over smut may be qualified. There could be a negative displacement effect at 7-Eleven stores, not to the *National Enquirer* or to beef jerky but rather to precisely the kind of material the antipornography group would wish to have restricted or suppressed.

It may be important to recognize some other possible negative consequences of such campaigns. Part of the competitive advantage *Playboy* and

Penthouse used to have over raunchier publications like *Hustler* and *Screw* was that they could find distribution in 7-Eleven stores, whereas the latter could not. If, as a consequence of the successful campaign aimed at the mainstream outlets, customers are diverted from 7-Eleven stores to other outlets, they will therefore be more likely to end up as purchasers of the harder-core publications available at more specialized pornographic outlets.

Further, if the hostility of the pressure groups is viewed by the publishers of *Playboy* and *Penthouse* as unconditional, any potential influence by those groups over the content of the magazines may be lost. We have already mentioned and will presently discuss how, because of the sensitivity of publishers like Hugh Hefner to charges of exploiting violent pornography, outside influence was effectively used in the early 1980s to affect the content of his publications. To declare unconditional war on smut is to lose the capacity to negotiate with the enemy on other than hostile terms. On the other hand, negotiation for changes in some of the content of pornography might imply a kind of license to the enterprise that many of the most politically effective pressure groups in this area would consider unthinkable. It may be that less stark or monolithic strategies on the part of nongovernmental groups would require new players.

There is one other implication of the strategic trade-offs we have been discussing. Groups opposed to one or several aspects of particular patterns of pornography will have to impose a more specific sense of priority on their objectives if they are to make rational strategic choices. Being against smut is an inadequate guide to determining whether it is a good idea to have three fewer copies of *Playboy* sold because the local 7-Eleven does not carry it, but one more copy of *Hustler* fall into the hands of a 7-Eleven customer who wanders elsewhere to buy a sex magazine. Is the acceptance of pornographic representations that are both demeaning and silly, but not vicious, too high a price to pay for discouraging the most egregious examples of sex and gratuitous violence? This is a level of specificity one rarely, if ever, encounters in current discussions of social action against pornography.

Against this background it may be useful to examine two possible private sector mechanisms that could influence the nature or character of pornography as well as the way in which it is distributed: industry self-regulation and organized citizen group action.

Industry self-regulation

Any prospect of industry self-regulation for pornography might seem improbable for a number of reasons. As pointed out in Chapter 3 and as the Johnson Commission made clear, "a monolithic 'smut' industry does not exist; rather there are several distinct markets and submarkets which distribute a variety of erotic materials" (U.S. Commission, 1970:7). There are many different producers and distributors and considerable variation in terms of media, content, and manner of distribution. Frequently those involved in a particular medium for sexually explicit communication will have more in common with those employed in the same medium being used for nonsexual communication than with the producers of other types of pornography. Thus the sales manager of *Playboy* may have as much in common with his or her opposite number at *Good Housekeeping* as with the producers or distributors of sexually explicit films.

Yet another reason why industry self-regulation might seem unlikely in the production and distribution of pornography is the outlaw tradition and socially marginal status of most producers of sexually explicit material and of many who distribute it at the retail level. The idea of a group of pornographic producers or distributors setting out to impose minimum ethical standards might seem almost as incongruous as the notion of a group of muggers forming a craft guild. Yet there are reasons to believe that self-regulation already plays an important role in the marketing of much sexually explicit material in the United States and that, with sufficient incentive, mainstream distributors of sexually explicit material could be induced to adopt a more self-conscious pattern of self-regulation.

It appears that the prospects for self-regulation are hopeful for mass-market magazines, dim for hard-core books, and substantial for mass-distribution adult films for theatrical exhibition.

There is at present no association of pornographic magazine publishers in America, but three aspects of the soft-core sex magazine industry have made major magazine publishers sensitive to objections to particular kinds of material. First, those magazines use regular channels of distribution and are aware that the threat or actuality of consumer boycott could deny them sales channels they would rather retain. Second, a major source of revenue for the majority of soft-core magazines is advertising and this provides an important incentive to avoid content that would mobilize citizen action to reduce advertising. Third, the existence of the outlaw tradition in pornographic publishing has engendered an appetite for legitimacy on the part of some publishers. Hugh Hefner wants to be remembered as a philosopher; certainly not as a sexist or an advocate of sexual violence.

Of course, not all sexually explicit magazines depend on mainstream advertising revenue or rely on general magazine distribution channels; nor are the majority of them published by would-be philosophers. But the existence of these incentives creates the potential for changes in the content of individual magazines and the possibility of the formation of special interest trade groups. Rational and creative publishers might well hire psychologists to evaluate and screen the material to be published. While nothing like the Good

Housekeeping Seal of Approval is likely to be awarded in this field, it is not altogether unlikely that some publishers might agree to a set of prohibited themes or effects in sexually explicit publications.

This would involve a clash with the outlaw tradition and there would, of course, always be a market for the outlaw machismo of a magazine like *Hustler*. But under appropriate market conditions, a set of ethical standards for many sexually explicit magazines is by no means unthinkable. It is also possible that magazine distributors could establish and enforce standards to the same effect if they only distributed publications in compliance.

There is in existence no association of the publishers of pornographic books, and here the prospects for effective self-regulation do not seem strong. Such books do not depend on mass-market sales in the way that soft-core magazines do. Moreover, they do not depend on advertising revenue or mass-distribution channels. Thus, while major trade book publishers might be dissuaded from entering the field or might conform to any industry standards that come to be established, there would be strong competition to achieve lowest-common-denominator status in the dirty-book industry.

The prospects for self-regulation in the film industry are substantially better. To begin, probably 75 percent of those consumer dollars spent to view movies because of their sexual content buy tickets to general release theaters to view mainstream movies. And this is true of some of the problematic films with themes combining sex and violence, as seen in previous chapters. These films are also subject to an extremely elaborate rating system and this system could without difficulty be fine-tuned to create consequences for particular types of combination of sex and violence or for films involving the outrageous degradation of women.

With regard to hard-core pornographic films, it is notable that there already exists the Adult Film Association of America (AFAA), which represents two hundred of the producers, distributors, and exhibitors of sexually explicit film and videotape cassettes. The AFAA has its own guidelines, which state:

1. That films of adult subject matter will be produced for and exhibited to adult audiences and that persons not of legal age will not be admitted.
2. That the definition of an "adult" is that designation set by the constituted authorities of the community, but in no event any person under the age of eighteen years.
3. That we will produce and exhibit only films that are in conformity with the Free Speech provisions of the Constitution of the United States of America.
4. That we will respect the privacy of the general public in our advertising and public displays.
5. That we in no manner will condone, produce, or exhibit child pornography in any form.

John Weston, counsel to the AFAA, testified to the Meese Commission that films made with unconsenting adults and children, as well as material depicting bestiality and excrement, would be regarded as "off limits" by the AFAA (U.S. Department of Justice, 1986:1382). There seems to be no reason why a somewhat more detailed code could not be developed. At present, unlike the Motion Picture Association of America with its rating system enforced if necessary by legal action, the AFAA has no enforcement mechanism to ensure that the guidelines are followed. Although the producers of such material would no doubt be sensitive to reduced distribution channels for nonconforming products, that disincentive would be more likely to affect the producers of high-budget movies shot on film that need to reach mass markets than the far cheaper movies shot directly on videotape – the garage-as-studio genre of moviemaking.

Pressure groups and citizen action

The Meese Commission was the only one of the three bodies we have been considering to have devoted substantial attention to citizen action and private sector pressure groups. It did so for the same reason that its discussion of private citizen group action is predictable. The thirty-eight-page treatment of the subject in the Meese Commission report (U.S. Department of Justice, 1986:1313–1350) describes the marching orders of a citizen army in a War Against Smut. Pressure on government is the keynote of the campaign. The list of fourteen action items for the citizen campaign includes pressure on the police and legislatures, court watching, and lobbying for more intensive use of the criminal law. Consumer boycotts of pornography vendors and parental monitoring of rock lyrics are mentioned only in passing. The section is an agenda of citizen action directed at increasing pressure toward censorship rather than damage control in a noncensoring milieu.

The implicit link between citizen action in this field and calls for censorship may be one reason why neither the Johnson Commission nor the Williams Committee considered organized citizen groups as a positive element in the social response to pornography. Yet there is no necessary connection between the rejection of censorship and opposition to the organization of citizen groups, or to attempts to establish standards, or to selective boycotts of the producers and distributors of objectionable material (see U.S. Department of Justice, 1986:419–425).

Regarding two types of pornography – that involving specific negative stereotypes of women and that containing high levels of violence – there might be a useful role for women's groups or parents' groups to play other than that of exerting pressure for censorship. This could involve using expert panels in a tactic we shall call "negative endorsement," as well as picketing and consumer boycotts designed to influence the nature of sexually explicit material distributed through mainstream channels. The strategy would be to isolate particularly egregious forms of pornography, to make a credible case for their harmfulness, and to attempt to mobilize consumer opinion against distributors who continued to carry the offending material.

The first step in this process could be the recruitment of experts to inform as well as give credibility to a group's judgment about particular harm. If panels of psychologists and psychiatrists with claims to expertise in the area of sexual communication were willing to single out a particular motion picture, videotape, or magazine, a credible case for its specially harmful or objectionable character might be made. The use of experts to single out negative examples avoids the problems of implicit endorsement in licensing. It is utopian to envisage Parent Teacher Associations giving a seal of approval to any explicit sexual depiction likely to arouse adolescent audiences sexually. Any element of implied endorsement would thus probably frighten citizen groups away from the screening of magazines, movies, or tapes. But singling out highly negative examples would be consistent with the image requirements of women's groups, child protection groups, and others who would wish neither to endorse nor to censor all sexually explicit material. This is the comparative advantage of a negative endorsement approach.

Using the threat or actuality of consumer boycott is not illegal nor need such tactics necessarily give rise to serious ethical problems. Just as citizen groups have been urged to boycott grapes in the context of an agricultural labor organizing campaign without encountering any legal difficulties, the boycotting by citizen groups of businesses directly involved in the production and distribution of sexually explicit materials presents no legal problems.

Insofar as ethical problems arise, what is problematic is not the concept of a boycott but the proximity of the boycotted product and entity to the alleged social harm. A boycott of 7-Eleven stores because they sell *Playboy* is close enough to the primary boycott model to be justified. Calling for a boycott of the products of the R. J. Reynolds Tobacco Company because the company advertises in *Playboy* seems to involve a more tenuous connection between culpable behavior and the economic target. An attempt to organize a boycott of the products of the R. J. Reynolds Tobacco Company because the company allowed its products to be sold by stores that also sold *Playboy* would clearly be well beyond the pale, a secondary or tertiary boycott with little ethical foundation.

But it seems probable that a boycott strategy will have trouble with the hazards of imprudence long before it runs the risk of overstepping its ethical limits. It is very easy for such crusaders to appear silly to large segments of the general public, unless the targets for protest are chosen very carefully; and credibility here may be of substantial importance in the long run if social attitudes toward particular kinds of pornography are to be influenced. Credible and well-conducted campaigns that isolate the violent and the especially degrading need not add to the allure of those materials for psychologically normal persons. They could break down the "blue nose" reputation and image of all groups concerned with the social impact of pornography; and this could be a major step toward rational discussion of the matter and away from polarized debate exclusively concerned with censorship.

All these tactics are possible but not necessarily the best use of the time and effort of concerned citizens. It would be unwise to overestimate the likely impact of such activity, or to suggest that contemporary pornography merits the resources required to conduct campaigns of this kind. Perhaps the best argument against this type of citizen action has nothing at all to do with the ethical aspect of boycotts but rather concerns the other social problems competing for the time and attention of citizens. The threat of nuclear war, the destruction of our environment, the abuse of children, and the problems of deserted wives with families all seem much more worthy candidates for organized citizen concern, particularly for citizens with a special interest in the protection of children or the plight of women.

Thus, even if citizen action against pornography is a worthwhile idea, it may lose out in the free marketplace of competing social problems to a host of other more pressing problems. Nevertheless, the threat of citizen action combined with increasing public recognition of such issues as violence and gender degradation in the media might provide sufficient impetus for the type of industry response just mentioned. And this could occur without the creation of highly organized pressure groups as continuing participants in formal negotiations.

Governmental responses

The basic point to be made about governmental response in this field is that the decision to live in a noncensoring society may complicate as well as simplify the question of the most appropriate role for government. Censorship, prohibition, or suppression enforced with all the power of government are relatively simple and straightforward basic strategies, although rarely completely successful. But matters become more ambiguous when censorship as a general strategy of control has been rejected, and yet some aspects of explicit sexual communication are still regarded as legitimate governmental concerns.

State and local government

The major responsibility for the regulation of pornography should rest, as it now does, on state and local government with the principal emphasis at the municipal level – for three reasons. First, to the extent that what the Supreme Court has referred to as "community values" should influence the extent and nature of regulation, the community is no larger than a town or city. In the United States, the national and state governments preside over communities only in a very broad sense of that term. Second, because time, place, and manner regulation is an accommodation between the interests of those who want sexual communication to be freely available and those who are annoyed or offended by open public commerce in such material, how this balance is struck at particular times and particular places is best determined at the local level. Third, to the extent that the police will be part or the whole of the regulating authorities, it is municipal police who will be better suited to this task than state troopers or the FBI.

Rather than discuss detailed regimes of time, place, and manner regulation, it is best to approach the topic of state and local regulation by illustrating and defining the permissible field of choice. With respect to public advertising, the interests in avoiding involuntary exposure and the protection of children and youth would seem to justify the restriction of most public advertising content beyond the announcement of the availability of sexually explicit materials. Community sentiments may also forbid access for such announcements to publicly owned facilities normally used for advertisements. Moreover, if the sale of pornography to the young is to be a criminal offense, the advertisement of pornographic material in or on public facilities used especially by the young can also be restricted.

As to the spatial regulation of the availability of pornography, there may be an important distinction to be drawn between materials intended only for home consumption and those suited for consumption on or near business premises. The sale or rental of items for home consumption does not seem to be a proper candidate for zoning regulation. Possibly, as with liquor stores, local authorities might prohibit the presence of pornographic outlets within a stipulated distance from elementary and secondary schools. But other than restrictions on advertising display, no zoning regulations seem justified.

At the other extreme lies the zoning regulation of commercial sex. This seems a highly attractive candidate for zoning in communities that choose to regulate rather than prohibit the sale of sexual satisfaction. Those commercial enterprises that sell both sexual arousal and sexual satisfaction through pornography would, on an a fortiori basis, appear to be even more eligible for this sort of regulation.

Those establishments that provide for consumption of pornography on their premises might also be restrictively zoned. One basis for a distinction drawn here between home-consumption and on-premise pornography is a doctrine that could be called "sexual nuisance." Commercial establishments providing for on-site consumption of pornographic communication seek to sexually arouse their patrons. It seems reasonable in the circumstances for legislative bodies to conclude that the immediate environs of such establishments would be significantly at risk from acts of prostitution and what has been called "public lewdness." However, whereas this conclusion may be justified in relation to establishments where pornographic communication is consumed on site, the same considerations do not necessarily apply to the regulation of establishments involved only in the sale of pornographic materials for home use.

The risk a neighborhood runs from home-use establishments is no more than the risk of having what many would regard as questionable characters attracted to the area. This is probably not sufficient to justify exclusion from general commercial districts that permit the sale of goods like package liquor. There is a significant difference between the attraction of persons of questionable character and the sexual arousal of persons who are thereafter discharged into the immediate neighborhood of the establishment. It could be argued that the case for zoning restriction is as strong or stronger for establishments providing only on-site stimulation than for those providing both pornographic stimulation and commercial sex; patrons who have just had both may be less of a hazard on their way out of the vicinity than customers who have been sexually aroused but not satisfied.

The foregoing illustrates some of the criteria relevant to determining limits to regulation short of censorship and suppression. In this connection, four general points can be made. First, the free-expression interest in sending and receiving pornographic communication differs in context from the interest in sending and receiving other types of communication. Second, not all types of pornographic communication generate the same social consequences. In fact, the difference between a videocassette rental transaction for home consumption and the on-site display of a film in a peep show or in an "adults only" theater can be of critical importance even though exactly the same film is involved in both cases. Third, although these considerations may justify certain levels of regulation, they do not justify a policy of unlimited restriction. Nor are local authorities obliged to go to the limits in imposing regulations and controls. Unfortunately, it is not unlikely that this may happen, and that in some communities regulations amounting to total prohibition may be imposed. This leads to the fourth point: that policies purporting to provide time, place, and manner regulations, for the purpose of child protection, for example, may in many communities be enforced in such a way as to seriously inhibit, if not suppress, the availability of pornographic communication for adults. In many American communities it is likely that intervention by institutions such as the local or federal courts, less immediately responsive to pressures from religious or secular interest groups, may be necessary to maintain a noncensoring policy.

In defining the permissible field of choice in regard to state and local regulation of pornographic communication, one matter seems to pose a difficult question: whether pornography featuring "deviant" sexual behavior may be subject to special restrictions even if what is called "normal" pornography is not. The difficulty involved is indicated by the use of quotation marks in the preceding sentence. Neither the Johnson Commission nor the Williams Committee defined any borderline between normal and abnormal sexual behavior, although the Meese Commission appears to have envisaged some such distinction.

We noted in Chapter 4 the example given by that commission of "sexually explicit materials that are not violent and not degrading," that is, a "highly explicit photograph of a loving married couple engaged in mutually pleasurable and procreative vaginal intercourse" (U.S. Department of Justice, 1986:342). The commission referred, on the other hand, to "materials that, although undoubtedly consensual and equal, depict sexual practices frequently condemned in this and other societies" (ibid.:338), and also to "paraphilias" defined as "psychosexual disorders where unusual or bizarre imagery or other acts are necessary for sexual excitement" (ibid.:1403–1404).

With regard to this kind of material, the commission reported that "intuitively and not experimentally, we can hypothesize that materials portraying such an activity will either help to legitimize or will bear some causal relationship to that activity itself." But the commission also remarked that "with respect to these materials, therefore, it appears that a conclusion about the harmfulness of these materials turns on a conclusion about the harmfulness of the activity itself. As to this we are unable to agree with respect to many of these activities" (ibid.:338).

In fact, "a conclusion about the harmfulness of these materials" would also depend on whether the commission's intuitions regarding legitimization, or "some causal relationship," were also correct. For those not enamored of the harm principle as employed by the Williams Committee, however, no great leap of faith would be required to reach the conclusion that these materials were harmful.

The Williams Committee did consider the related question of whether it was "necessary to prohibit photographs of acts of buggery" in a situation where, as in England, "heterosexual buggery . . . even between a married couple, constitutes an offence." One problem in this connection was the fact that "what two consenting *male* adults do in private is not by and large the concern of the law" (emphasis added). The committee concluded both that the law should not introduce any "distinction between heterosexual pornography and homosexual pornography" and that "it would be unsatisfactory to introduce any prohibition on pornography which depended just on whether or not the act depicted was against the law" (Home Office, 1979:130–131).

In America the restriction of materials based on their supposed tendency to encourage behavior classified as criminal would in many states encompass both homosexual buggery (or sodomy) and heterosexual buggery (or sodomy). However, if the harm principle is adhered to – apart from harms to those involved in the production of pornography, as in the case of the use of children – the burden of proof in relation to drawing a distinction between "normal" and "abnormal" pornography rests on those who wish to use it as a basis for imposing special restrictions on the latter. Moreover, any proposal for selective censorship in regard to paraphiliac material based on the questionable idea that such behaviors represent "psychosexual disorders" would seem even harder to justify.

The federal role

A further complication in the regulation of pornography is that America has a federal system of government. This involves the distribution of functions and governmental power between different levels of government within the federal system. Political responsibility is not wholly vested in a central authority but is distributed between the federal government on the one hand and state and local authorities on the other. Most aspects of the police power are exercised by state and local government. The federal role in law enforcement is usually secondary.

With respect to the federal government's role in relation to pornographic communication, there might be three functions that are the proper province of various branches of government at the national level:

The passage and enforcement of whatever legislation may be necessary regarding the distribution of pornography in order to prevent the exploitation of children and other special dangers.

The encouragement of, and support for, research into the effects of pornography and the impact of sex education programs on children and young persons.

The enforcement of noncensorship as a national policy when state and local authorities attempt to use residual regulatory powers as tools of censorship.

Federal responsibility should be limited to areas where there is a need for national-level law enforcement, should not be exclusive of state responsibility, and should be modest in scale. Federal customs authorities are better able to control importation than state and local authorities. Some widespread production and distribution networks might call for federal prosecution. It is, however, doubtful that federal police intervention at the first instance is the best way to investigate even federal offenses of this kind. Traditionally we do not employ federal police at the street-enforcement level, with the sole exception of the Drug Enforcement Administration. The substantial costs of deploying federal police on city streets were illustrated by the adventures of the U.S. Treasury during the prohibition era. The comparative advantage in the case of child pornography lies in the larger jurisdiction and prosecution resources available to the federal government.

The function of federal law enforcement in an area such as child pornography should therefore be the provision of relatively modest support for, or aid to, state enforcement and prosecution. Further, in circumstances where uncensored adult pornography is widely available, it would probably be wise to restrict federal prohibition of the exploitation of the young to the unambiguously immature. The current child pornography federal age limit – the eighteenth birthday – is already quite high, extending forward from the commonly accepted boundaries of childhood into youth. And although the young can be exploited well beyond the eighteenth, or for that matter the twenty-first, birthday, high age-boundaries tend to blur the distinction between the exploitation involved in using children in the production of pornography and the harms that may befall all who engage in pornographic performance.

There are, however, noncriminal law aspects of federal responsibility to be considered. Thus research and education, always the scholar's last refuge in public-policy discussions, are as important, or more important, in a noncensoring society than they would be in circumstances where the government attempts to prohibit pornography. Assessing the impact of different kinds of pornography on different kinds of audiences is more important when many of the conceivable combinations of pornography and audience to be found in laboratory experiments will also be frequently found in society at large. The case for adequate and appropriate sex education is reinforced when it is clear that families and governments do not have a shared monopoly of sex education for the young.

With regard to research, the National Institute of Mental Health and the National Science Foundation should support investigations of the impact of violent and other extreme types of pornography on subjects in midadolescence and, in some cases, younger. This can be done with due regard to ensuring effective consent and the protection of the human subjects involved. But it is ludicrous in the extreme when research into the effects of viewing "sexually violent films," reported by the Meese Commission, uses as a stimulus one of Lina Wertmuller's gentler films, *Swept Away* (U.S. Department of Justice, 1986:983), at a time when the same teenagers outside the laboratory are paying their own money to see *Toolbox Murders* and *Texas Chainsaw Massacre*. Researchers and the research enterprise can afford to be bolder.

The availability of pornography is a small and relatively unimportant part of the case for sex education as a public responsibility and for the development of educational materials as a responsibility of the national government. The current epidemics of AIDS and unplanned teenage pregnancy are providing compelling justification for publicly sponsored sexual communication to the young. The point is that educational efforts are also relevant to the defense of children and youth against sexual exploitation and to countering the misinformation and confusion entailed in reliance on pornography as pedagogy.

A contrasting but also important role for national government absent censorship might be the defense of open channels of sexual communication against attempts by state and local authorities to limit the availability of pornography. Such attempts appear to be endemic in state and local politics in the United States. The inclination to grant broad powers in respect of time, place, and manner regulation to local authorities will, if implemented, inevitably generate more cases in which such powers will be manipulated for suppressive ends.

The strategic choices available to federal government are between local option on the liquor-control model and use of federal courts to guarantee free access to some forms of pornography. The pattern in alcohol control is to leave policy to state option. Federal policy on this model would be local option rather than noncensorship, with different states imposing different levels of censorship. This model of power allocation would only be available to the extent that the First Amendment to the Constitution does not impose a substantive policy of noncensorship. Under current constitutional tests, sexually explicit communications that meet our definition of pornography are protected from state and local censorship if they are not found to be obscene, as discussed in Chapter 5. The federal courts will thus be called upon to restrict some of these attempts for the foreseeable future as long as First Amendment protection is continued.

Conclusion

The specific elements of response to pornography just discussed are not as important in our view as two more general points related to the analysis. First, the rejection of censorship does not end all discussion of government policy toward pornography; indeed, the judgments and adjustments that political authorities will be responsible for in a nonsuppression setting will be both more subtle and more complicated than is the battle about censorship.

The second point we would stress is the long-range importance of public attitudes in determining the role of pornography in modern Western countries. As long as censorship is regarded as a viable option, to oppose pornography is to endorse suppression. It is only when this blunt instrument of policy is unavailable that less drastic countermeasures can acquire a constituency.

One reason we have little data on the impact of sustained attempts to stigmatize the use of sexist or violent pornography is that the traditional legal suppression of such materials occupied the field as an antipornography policy. Only recently has the legal availability of this material made public attitudes toward pornography of critical importance. We are thus in the early stages of a social experiment with attitudes toward pornography in a number of Western democracies. The next chapter discusses some possible outcomes of this experiment in the proximate future.

9

Notes toward the future

One way to put current events in context is to project developments in a particular field over a period of ten or twenty years in the future, and to see how the observer's assessment of current events fits with the same observer's sense of this proximate future. That is why this chapter considers future policy toward pornography in the United States. How speculations about the future can serve as a guide to reading current developments might seem mysterious. Would not speculation about the future merely compound the uncertainties associated with assessing the significance of present events?

Yet such speculation over the midrange can put in perspective events that loom large only because they are recent. Last month's report and yesterday's press conference may assume an importance they do not deserve. Viewing recent developments in light of events of the past decade or two imposes one sort of discipline on claiming the present as a turning point. Combining this sense of the proximate past with hypotheses about the probable policies of the 1990s and beyond provides a further corrective.

Three scenarios for the midterm

It would be foolish to offer unqualified or detailed predictions regarding the likely character of future developments in this field. But it seems worthwhile to make some observations regarding possible longer-term trends and developments in both the nature of pornography and the social response to it in the United States. We take up the issue of longer-term trends with a sequence of two exercises. First, in this section we discuss three possible "scenarios" specific to pornography: (1) modest increases in criminal law regulation of photographs and films; (2) increasing participation in the market for sexually explicit communication by the mainstream entertainment industry; and (3) a return to an emphasis on censorship in state and local government.

Each scenario reflects developments already apparent on the American scene in the 1980s. Each is also to some extent inconsistent with the other

218

two. But even if these patterns cannot all develop concurrently, they provide a useful framework for organizing some reflections on possible future trends.

After examining these midterm scenarios, we outline a somewhat broader and less structured conception of the future focused on the year 2002. The Meese Commission reported, "As we in 1986 reexamine what was done in 1970, so too do we expect that in 2002 our work will similarly be reexamined" (U.S. Department of Justice, 1986:226–227). It would be churlish to condemn the third year of the next century to a reexamination of the Meese Commission report or to another national commission on pornography. But a sixteen-year remove from the Meese Report makes a convenient point on which to focus speculation about the future role of sexually explicit communications in society. However, just as competitive skaters are first required to execute "compulsory figures" on the ice before engaging in more creative freestyle routines, midterm scenarios will be discussed before we indulge in concluding reflections that may be colored by wishful thinking.

Divergence between film and the written word

We use the word "film" as a term of art to distinguish material, other than works consisting only of written text, that might be subject to censorship or restriction as being pornographic, including films, videotapes, and perhaps other kinds of pictorial representation as well. We consider this distinction as the basis for a scenario involving a modest tightening of legal controls, for three reasons. First, the distinction between the written word and pictorial representation of sexual activity in magazines, books, and films is an important element in the legal responses of other Western democracies to pornographic material. The Williams Committee, for example, recommended that "the printed word should be neither restricted nor prohibited" (Home Office, 1979:160), while at the same time approving both the censorship of films and restrictions in other areas (apparently contradicting the "harm principle"). This is evidence that the distinction is at least viable.

Second, there is an intuitive appeal to drawing First Amendment distinctions between words and pictorial images and according lesser protection to the latter. In some writing there has been an attempt to buttress the distinction in other ways by suggesting that First Amendment protection does not cover pictorial material because commercial pornographic modeling is a form of prostitution (U.S. Department of Justice, 1986:899–890) and that participants in the production of pornography necessarily violate laws prohibiting prostitution (Edward, 1987:133–138). This kind of distinction appeals even to those who might reject the more extreme argument that "constitutional protection should be accorded only to speech that is explicitly political" (Bork, 1971:20); or the argument that pornographic material is not protected because it lacks communicative content or "falls below [a] minimal threshold of cognitive appeal" (Schauer, 1979; U.S. Department of Justice, 1986:263).

The third reason why this distinction might be significant in the American context is the extreme unlikelihood of a return to attempts to ban any printed matter with sexually explicit content. Evidence of this unlikelihood can be found in the behavior of the Meese Commission and the content of its report. This commission had a stronger representation of antipornographic interests than any of the other national-level governmental inquiries. The failure of that commission to make specific recommendations for the prohibition or suppression of any kind of written material except child-oriented pornography speaks volumes (U.S. Department of Justice, 1986:381–385).

To attempt to anticipate in detail the nature of the separate standards for film and the written word that might receive constitutional blessing from the U.S. Supreme Court would be unjustifiably speculative. Legal doctrine in this area is so fluid that if the Court desires to draw a distinction of this kind, it is unlikely to be much constrained by the nature of its own prior decisions.

Yet even if such a distinction might prove feasible in principle, the effect of its application is another issue. Thus, if it were to result in attempts to impose rigid restrictions on pornographic material in the form of motion pictures, videotapes, and magazines, there would be severe practical problems. There is, first, the matter of currently available supply. The Meese Commission reported that there are "thousands of different video titles currently on the market. *Adult Video News* . . . estimated that 1,700 new sexually explicit videos were released in 1985. It projects this high growth trend will continue" (ibid.:1390). With the use of video recording devices and the present inventory of pornographic films and tapes, six months notice of an impending ban would be sufficient to create an unprecedented abundance of sexually explicit videotapes. Those concerned about the difficulty of enforcing bans on handguns should take heart from the fact that handguns at least do not have the capacity to reproduce themselves.

One further point should be made about any attempt to prohibit, suppress, or withdraw from circulation pornographic films, videotapes, or magazines. There is now a considerable predominantly middle-class constituency habituated to the easy availability of pornography in these forms. Without powerful arguments supported by evidence of social harm acceptable to this constituency, it may be found that what might have been a former consensus in favor of censorship will turn out to be eroded beyond recovery.

In practice, increased scrutiny and more inflexible enforcement of the laws relating to pornographic films and pictorial representations might produce a substantial reduction in the public consumption of pornography but have less impact on in-the-home use of pictorial pornography and sexually explicit videotapes. Thus some of the practical difficulties involved in vigorous enforcement of the law in private homes might lessen the political problems likely to be associated with the prevention of the home use of pornography by the middle class. Even without the special constitutional protection on the order of *Stanley v. Georgia,* in which the Supreme Court held that the First Amendment prohibits making mere private possession of obscene materials a crime (394 U.S. 557, 568 [1971]), it seems likely that still and motion pictures will be available in the home for the foreseeable future.

Decriminalization of production

In Chapter 3 we argued that although some mainstream distribution and retail channels were used to distribute pornography, the producers of hard-core pornography and hard-core pornographic films were still operating as part of an outlaw tradition and regarded as social deviants. One way to illustrate that point is by reference to the kinds of companies and individuals who are not making pornographic products: no motion picture studio, major television producer, or commercial entertainment companies have developed units to produce hard-core pornography.

To some extent this is a matter of semantics. A great many sexually stimulating motion pictures are made by major studios and have attracted audiences for that reason. Nevertheless, there is also a separate industry producing extremely explicit film material of a kind not being produced by the self-defined legitimate film industry. And mainstream film and video companies do not produce what they regard as pornography.

One possible development within the next ten to fifteen years is greater competition on the part of the mainstream entertainment industry for the market now associated with explicitly pornographic material. Some of the economic and social predicates for mainstream participation in the production of soft-core movies or videocassettes are already in place. Videotape rentals have dramatically increased the gross sales of pornographic movies and relocated most rental and sale transactions to the mainstream commercial establishments that major distributors know well. But for the stigma associated with the production and distribution of pornographic material, the comparative advantage in the distribution of explicit sexual material to videocassette-rental agencies lies with those who already distribute other cassettes to the same outlets. Cable television is another arena in which mainstream business enterprises might wish to offer sexually explicit products.

The social stigma associated with renting pornographic films for home use is not as clearly defined as it is in relation to "adult" theaters and peep shows. A significant indication of this is the relatively large number of female renters of such movies at video-rental stores (U.S. Department of Justice, 1986:920).

Probably the laws prohibiting prostitution and the residual stigma will keep major movie producers and distributors out of the business of making pornographic movies themselves. But a major distributor does not need to manufacture films in order to influence the kinds of films made or to obtain a substantial share of the profits that accrue from them. The power to decide which films get widely distributed is the power to influence the nature and variety of sexually explicit material available for home viewing. The same is true with cable operators who choose what materials to display. What distributors will buy and what cable operators will show is what the independent producers will put on tape. Under these circumstances, it is likely that fewer but more expensive pornographic films would be made and there would be at least the possibility of the development of greater diversity of theme and more individual variation in plot and content.

Two points are worth mentioning in relation to this possibility. First, the entry of mainstream economic institutions into more active competition for the pornographic dollar might provide a better indication of what the pornography-consuming public wants and will accept. The market for pornographic communication has always been an imperfect one in a number of significant respects. The criminalization of production has, in fact, both limited the number of people entering the business and narrowed the range of material produced. Reviewing the product available currently leads us to regard the pornographic imagination as almost a contradiction in terms.

The social stigma attached to pornographic movies has also prevented open dialogue about consumer preferences. The deemphasis of the stigma brought about by the development and legitimization of videocassette rentals could help to bring out more specific patterns of demand. This might happen as competition among producers of films and videotapes created a greater ability in the industry to respond to more varied consumer tastes.

The second point is that any development in this direction would depend on the absence of a renewed war on smut. Any major law enforcement initiatives against films or videotapes would probably reverse a trend toward the involvement of mainstream distributors and rental chains as an influence in the pornographic movie market. There is thus a strong likelihood that the threat of restrictive moves against retailers would close off the kind of differential market development we have been discussing.

For those who have complained that pornography has for too long been left to pornographers, competition and diversification would, of course, be a welcome development and seen as beneficial. But under such circumstances, the volume of sexually explicit material consumed would likely be larger than if entry into the market were restricted. The greater availability of pornography can be regarded as a price to be paid for greater diversity. The crude, monotonous, and witless quality of the present-day hard-core pornographic films with the emphasis on what have been called "the mechanistic oil-rig aspects of intercourse" (McGrath, 1985:67), on the other hand, is the price paid for, and the legacy of, criminalization.

A war on smut?

Implicit in the agitation of politicians and citizen groups that both surrounded and was exemplified by the Meese Commission was dissatisfaction with the widespread availability of pornographic materials. It seems clear that many of those who feel in this way would wish to see the criminal law used in a vigorous effort to restrict substantially the availability of pornography. Insofar as such sentiments are widely felt, it must be recognized that one possible scenario for the future of a noncensoring society is its disappearance or dissolution by way of a concerted effort on the part of law enforcement agencies to achieve the suppression of sexually explicit material designed to arouse audiences.

Four points should be made regarding this scenario. First, we have not found any serious discussion of what level of effort by what agencies of government would be required to achieve a major crackdown on pornography. Nor has there been a detailed consideration of what the social and criminal justice effects of such a crackdown would be. The absence of serious consideration of the implications of more vigorous criminal law enforcement, particularly in the Meese Commission Report, is striking and significant.

Both of the other bodies whose work we have reviewed in effect recommended little in the way of increased criminal law regulation as a policy for the future. The Johnson Commission advocated removing restrictions at a time when the availability of pornography was rapidly expanding – essentially approving what it saw as a continuity of trend for American society. The Williams Committee also endorsed the increasing availability of such material in Britain but approved the retention of the existing system of film censorship

The espousal of such essentially noninterventionist policies calls for no assessment of consequences other than appreciation of current conditions. But the apparent endorsement of a "get tough" policy in an attempt to reverse a long-standing trend without any discussion of how the rollback could be achieved or what its consequences might be, is a genuine puzzle. It makes much of the Meese Commission's analysis more a list of complaints about the present than a program for change in the future.

There seem to be no clear precedents for a sustained general crackdown on pornography in the experience of any major American jurisdiction or in that of the Western countries that have also undergone the actual or de facto decriminalization of pornography over the last two decades. Campaigns against public vice have been a recurrent feature of American history but have usually operated at the municipal level. Such campaigns usually involve only the front end of criminal justice systems, with more police raids than prosecutions, and more prosecutions than convictions or jail sentences.

Such efforts tend to be episodic rather than sustained, and public pressure tends to be more pronounced for vice squad–model crackdowns on prostitution than for attempts to restrict the consumption of pornography. More recently, it is the impact of drugs on residential areas rather than other aspects of commercial vice that has concerned the public. Indeed, in most major cities any antipornography drive might have to compete with drug control and antiprostitution initiatives. And there is no evidence to suggest that antipornography agendas could win a battle for scarce law enforcement resources on a sustained basis. In other Western countries, only the legislation banning child pornography serves as recent precedent for a crackdown on pornography. And this effort did not require major changes in law enforcement or, indeed, in the market for pornography.

A third point that should be made about crackdowns is that some quite dramatic effects could be expected even without major investment of law enforcement resources. As we have just seen, relatively mild policy initiatives in relation to video rentals and magazines sales might get mainstream video-rental businesses, chain store booksellers, and major magazine distributors to avoid marginal or risky dealings in sexually explicit materials. Thus, it is possible that some impact in the direction of recriminalization could be achieved on a reasonably modest budget.

But the impact of a low-budget antipornography crusade would be limited and in some cases perverse. Some reduction in the availability of pornographic material could be achieved by deterring mainstream retail merchants and videocassette-rental firms from the rental and sale of pornography. This would make pornography somewhat harder to find for the casual user and genuinely difficult to get in some smaller communities with limited markets for sexually explicit materials.

A low-resource crackdown would also keep nonoutlaw producers out of the business of making movies and tapes and would limit the role of mainstream businesses in providing pornography. The amount of pornography would be less and its availability at least slightly diminished, but there would be less capacity of mainstream groups to influence the forms of pornographic communications, or to reduce the production of sexually violent or especially sexist pornography.

A low-intensity war on smut thus has the potential to fight some of the recent trends in pornography to a stalemate, but has no real potential for removing the sexually violent from general availability or for creating a significant barrier between pornographic materials and teenagers who wish to see them. Viewed against the aims of the groups that endorse them, the potential of a low-budget war on pornography is quite limited.

Thus, the possibility of what can be called a "dynamic stalemate" is far from remote. Indeed, unless the constitutional law of obscenity were altered to allow more film and video censorship, the natural tendency of increased efforts to enforce existing law would be to continue the outlaw tradition of pornographic materials without making a major impact on the availability of such materials in urban areas.

A preview of 2002

The last point to be made about a war on smut scenario is probably the most significant lesson from recent history. There seems to be no great public enthusiasm for any major criminal law crackdown on pornography in the political mainstream of American society in the late 1980s. It is instructive to compare the public and political response to discussion of a war on smut in the summer of 1986 with the response to congressional or presidential calls to a war on drugs one month later. The half-life of pornography as a major public issue after the Meese Commission report's reception was about one month. The amount of legislative attention devoted to pornography is minimal. By contrast, presidential calls for a war on drugs produced omnibus federal drug legislation in Congress within two months and a continuous level of public attention.

In fact, the Meese Commission itself seems to have been more interested in symbolic denunciation than in governmental action with respect to the consumption or production of pornography involving adults. More than half of its total recommendations and a clear majority of its legal recommendations concerned minors. The commission's real agenda with respect to pornography and adults may have been denunciation rather than prohibition; perhaps the public declaration by a government body that violent and degrading pornography is a social evil was a principal aim, rather than the construction of a program of repressive measures designed to have a significant effect on the availability to adults of sexually explicit material. The mission of the Meese Commission was in large part to remove the aura of governmental endorsement that some observers thought the Johnson Commission gave to sexual obscenity.

In a sense, then, the Meese Commission report and its aftermath are more a confirmation of the revolution in the availability of pornographic material than a call to counterrevolution. The commission mounted no attack on "dirty books," apparently recognizing that the era of book banning in the United States has permanently ended. Such recognition is of some significance during a period of social and political conservative renaissance. So, too, is the low political priority accorded by government to action agendas designed to reduce the availability of pornographic magazines, films, and videocassettes. The Meese Commission report seems largely to have completed its rapid journey to join on library bookshelves previous reports on pornography and the reports of other commissions on various national problems. Viewed in historical perspective, the Meese Commission report and its reception seem to have been a confirmation of earlier trends rather than a significant change in the social response to the availability of sexually explicit material.

This is not to say that the public or the government are permanently committed to passivity. Any convincing evidence of a link between particular types of pornography and sexually violent acts might transform what is essentially a laissez-faire attitude into a more active posture. It seems more likely, however, that sexually explicit material will remain widely available in the United States, possibly in greater variety than characterizes the present market. This seems to be the trend throughout the Western industrial world.

Perhaps, also, before the end of the century there will be some development by way of psychological screening or reviewing of the available mass-market sexually explicit films and videotapes. And there might be efforts to encourage the production of sexually explicit material produced and directed by women and designed for consumption by women.

But our best guess about trends in the last decade of the twentieth century is that there will be evolutionary developments rather than revolutionary or counterrevolutionary changes. Moreover, it seems likely that the rate of development will be somewhat slower over the next two decades than it has been in the past twenty years.

A period of gradual evolution and consolidation would certainly be welcome to those who would see diminishing social concern about pornography as a positive good. The last third of the twentieth century may be a period of adjustment to the widespread availability of pornography, a period when conflicts about pornographic communication seem more significant as social issues than will be the case in the longer term. Fascination with smut will never totally abate, for sexuality ever remains an important human concern. But public policy toward pornography may come to be regarded as relatively unimportant. In retrospect, it may well be that both the Johnson Commission and the Meese Commission in the United States and the Williams Committee in Britain will be seen as mileposts on the criminal law's journey into insignificance as an instrument to control sexual communication.

References

Adler, Mortimer J. (1937). *Art and Prudence*. New York: Longmans, Green.

Allen, Walter. (1962). "The Writer and the Frontiers of Tolerance." In J. Chandos, ed., *To Deprave and Corrupt*, pp. 139–52. New York: Association Press.

American Civil Liberties Union. (1986). *Polluting the Censorship Debate*. Washington, D.C.: American Civil Liberties Union.

Baron, L., and Straus, M. A. (1984). "Sexual Stratification, Pornography and Rape in the United States." In N. M. Malamuth and E. Donnerstein, eds., *Pornography and Sexual Aggression*. Orlando, Fla: Academic Press.

——— (1985). "Legitimate Violence, Pornography, and Sexual Inequality as Explanations for State and Regional Differences in Rape." Unpublished manuscript, Yale University.

——— (1986). "Rape and Its Relation to Social Disorganization, Pornography, and Sexual Inequality in the United States." Unpublished manuscript, Yale University.

Beerbohm, Max. (1920). *Seven Men*. New York: Knopf.

Bork, Robert H. (1971). "Neutral Principles and Some First Amendment Problems." *Indiana Law Journal* 47:1–35.

Boyd, Andrew. (1970). "Porno Politics." *The Nation*, November 11, 1970, 452–453.

Brody, Stephen. (1977). *Screen Violence and Film Censorship*. London: Her Majesty's Stationery Office.

Butt, Ronald. (1977). "Stamp It Out: This Abominable Evil of Using Children for Pornography." *The Times* (London), November 24, 1977, 18.

——— (1980). "Pornography: Does a Committee Know Best?" *The Times* (London), June 26, 1980, 16.

Califia, Pat. (1986). "Among Us, Against Us: The New Puritans." In K. Ellis et al., eds., *Caught Looking*, pp. 20–25. New York: Caught Looking Inc.

Canada, Minister of Supply and Special Services. (1985). Report of the Special Committee on Pornography and Prostitution, *Pornography and Prostitution in Canada*. Vols. 1 and 2. Ottawa: Canadian Government Publishing Centre.

Chandos, John. (1962). "Unicorns at Play." In J. Chandos, ed., *To Deprave and Corrupt*, pp. 175–207. New York: Association Press.

Cleland, John. (1749; 1963). *Memoirs of a Woman of Pleasure*. New York: Putnam.

Clor, Harry M. (1971). "Science, Eros, and the Law: A Critique of the Obscenity Commission Report." *Duquesne Law Review* 10:63–76.

Donnerstein, Edward, Daniel Linz, and Steven Penrod. (1987). *The Question of Pornography: Research Findings and Policy Implications*. New York: Free Press.

Duggan, Lisa, Nan D. Hunter, and Carole S. Vance. (1986). "False Promises: Feminist

227

Antipornography Legislation." In K. Ellis et al., eds., *Caught Looking*, pp. 72–88. New York: Caught Looking Inc.

Dworkin, Andrea. (1981). *Pornography: Men Possessing Women*. New York: Putnam.

——— (1985). "Against the Male Flood: Censorship, Pornography, and Equality," *Harvard Women's Law Journal* 8:1–29.

Edward, Bruce E. (1987). "Prostitution and Obscenity: A Comment upon the Attorney General's Report on Pornography." *Duke Law Journal* 1987:123–139.

Ellis, Kate. (1986). "I'm Black and Blue." In K. Ellis et al., eds., *Caught Looking*, pp. 38–47. New York: Caught Looking Inc.

Ellis, Kate, Barbara O'Dair, and Abby Talmer. (1986). Introduction to K. Ellis et al., eds., *Caught Looking*, pp. 4–8. New York: Caught Looking Inc.

English, Deirdre. (1985). "The Politics of Porn: Can Feminists Walk The Line?" In R. Reynolds, ed., *The Best of Mother Jones*, pp. 49–58. San Francisco: Foundation for National Progress.

Eysenck, H. J., and D. K. B. Nias. (1978). *Sex and Violence in the Media*. London: Maurice Temple Smith.

Feinberg, Joel. (1985). *Offense to Others*. Oxford University Press.

Friedan, Betty. (1986). Statement. In National Coalition Against Censorship, *The Meese Commission Exposed*. New York: National Coalition Against Censorship.

Gallup Poll. (1985). *Newsweek*, March 18, 1985, 58–66.

Geyer, Alan. (1970). "The Temptations of Pornography." *The Christian Century* 87:1339.

Gorer, Geoffrey. (1961). Chapter 3. In C. H. Rolph, ed., *Does Pornography Matter?* London: Routledge & Kegan Paul.

Gosling, Robert. (1961). Chapter 5. In C. H. Rolph, ed., *Does Pornography Matter?* London: Routledge & Kegan Paul.

Haight, Anne Lyon. (1978). *Banned Books: 387 B.C. to 1978 A.D.* New York: Bowker.

Hertzberg, Hendrik. (1986). "Big Boobs." *The New Republic*, July 14 and 21, 1986, 21–24.

Hofstadter, Richard. (1965). *The Paranoid Style in American Politics*. New York: Random House.

Home Office. (1979). *Report of the Committee on Obscenity and Film Censorship* (Bernard Williams, chairman). London: Her Majesty's Stationery Office.

Johnson, Lyndon B. (1966). *Public Papers of the Presidents of the United States: Lyndon B. Johnson, 1965*. Vol. 2. Washington, D.C.: Office of the Federal Register, National Archives and Records Service, General Services Administration.

Johnson, Weldon T. (1971). "The Pornography Report: Epistemology, Methodology, and Ideology." *Duquesne Law Review* 10:190–219.

Kalven, Harry. (1960). "The Metaphysics of the Law of Obscenity." *Supreme Court Review* 1960:1–45.

Kaplan, Abraham. (1955). "Obscenity as an Esthetic Category." *Law and Contemporary Problems* 20:544–559.

Keating, Charles H. (1971). "The Report That Shocked the Nation." *Reader's Digest*, January 1971, 37–41.

Kendrick, Walter. (1987). *The Secret Museum: Pornography in Modern Culture*. New York: Viking.

Kinsey, Alfred C., Wardell B. Pomeroy, Clyde E. Martin, and Paul H. Gebhard. (1953). *Sexual Behavior in the Human Female*. Philadelphia: Saunders.

Kramer, Leonie. (1964). "Matter of Sex." *Quadrant* 29:50–55.

Kronhausen, Eberhard, and Phyllis Kronhausen. (1959). *Pornography and the Law*. New York: Ballantine.

Kutchinsky, Berl. (1983). "Obscenity and Pornography: Behavioral Aspects." In S. Kadish, ed., *Encyclopedia of Crime and Justice*, vol. 3, pp. 1077–1086. New York: Free Press.

La Barre, Weston. (1955). "Obscenity: An Anthropological Appraisal." *Law and Contemporary Problems* 20:536.

Lawrence, D. H. (1959). "Pornography and Obscenity." In D. H. Lawrence, *Sex, Literature, and Censorship*, H. T. Moore, ed. Boston: Twayne.

Legman, Gershon. (1949). *Love and Death*. New York: Hacker Art Books.

Levi, Albert William. (1959). "The Value of Freedom: Mill's Liberty (1859–1959)." *Ethics* 70:37–46.

Lewis, C. I. (1929). *Mind and the World Order*. New York: Scribner.

Lockhart, William B. (1971). "The Findings and Recommendations of the Commission on Obscenity and Pornography: A Case Study of the Role of Social Science in Formulating Public Policy." *Oklahoma Law Review* 24:209–23.

Lockhart, William B., and Robert E. McClure. (1954). "Literature, the Law of Obscenity, and the Constitution." *Minnesota Law Review* 38:295–395.

(1955). "Obscenity in the Courts." *Law and Contemporary Problems* 20:587–607.

(1960). "Censorship of Obscenity: The Developing Constitutional Standards." *Minnesota Law Review* 45:5–121.

Loken, Gregory. (1986). "The Federal Battle Against Child Sexual Exploitation: Proposals for Reform." *Harvard Women's Law Journal* 9:105–134.

McGrath, Peter. (1985). "New Themes and Old Taboos." *Newsweek*, March 18, 1985, 67.

MacKinnon, Catharine A. (1987). *Feminism Unmodified: Discourses on Life and Law*. Cambridge, Mass.: Harvard University Press.

Malamuth, N. M. (1983). "Factors Associated with Rape as Predictors of Laboratory Aggression Against Women." *Journal of Personality and Social Psychology* 45:432–442.

(1986). "Predictors of Naturalistic Sexual Aggression." *Journal of Personality and Social Psychology* 50:953–962.

Mill, John Stuart. (1859; 1975). *On Liberty*. New York: Norton.

Milton, John. (1644; 1933). *Areopagitica*. Cambridge University Press.

Montaigne, Michel de (1580–88; 1946). "Upon Some Verses of Virgil." In *The Essays of Montaigne*, trans. E. J. Trechman, pp. 733–786. New York: Random House.

Morris, Herbert. (1960). "Verbal Disputes and the Legal Philosophy of John Austin." *UCLA Law Review* 7:27–56.

Morris, Norval, and Gordon Hawkins. (1970). *The Honest Politician's Guide to Crime Control*. Chicago: University of Chicago Press.

(1977). *Letter to the President on Crime Control*. Chicago: University of Chicago Press.

National Coalition Against Censorship. (1986). *The Meese Commission Exposed*. New York: National Coalition Against Censorship.

Packer, Herbert L. (1971). "The Pornography Caper." *Commentary* 51:72–7.

Paul, James C. and Murray L. Schwartz. (1961). *Federal Censorship: Obscenity in the Mail*. New York: Free Press.

Post, Robert C. (1988). "Cultural Heterogenity and Law: Pornography, Blasphemy, and the First Amendment." *California Law Review* 76:297–336.

Proal, Louis. (1900). *Passion and Criminality: A Legal and Literary Study*. Paris: Charles Carrington.

Quennell, Peter. (1963). Introduction to J. Cleland, *Memoirs of a Woman of Pleasure*. New York: Putnam.

Rees, J. C. (1960). "A Re-Reading of Mill on Liberty." *Political Studies* 8:113–129.

Robinson, Richard. (1950). *Definition*. Oxford University Press.

St. John-Stevas, N. (1964). "Prosecutor's Choice." *The Sunday Times* (London), February 16, 1964.

Schauer, Frederick. (1979). "Speech and 'Speech' – Obscenity and 'Obscenity'; An Exercise in the Interpretation of Constitutional Language." *Georgetown Law Journal* 67:899–933.

Shimm, Melvin G. (1955). Foreword. *Law and Contemporary Problems* 20:531.

Silkin, S. C. (1983). Foreword to A. W. B. Simpson, *Pornography and Politics: A Look Back to the Williams Committee*. London: Waterloo.

Simpson, A. W. B. (1983) *Pornography and Politics: A Look Back to the Williams Committee*. London: Waterloo.

Singer, Max. (1971). "The Vitality of Mythical Numbers." *The Public Interest* 23:3–9.

Stengel, Richard. (1986). "Sex Busters." *Time*, July 21, 1986, 12–21.

Stevenson, Charles L. (1944). *Ethics and Language*. New Haven, Conn.: Yale University Press.

Ten, C. L. (1968). "Mill on Self-Regarding Actions." *Philosophy* 43:29–37.

Toynbee, Polly. (1981). "The Williams Committee Worked Hard." *The Guardian*, October 30, 1981, 9.

Tynan, Kenneth. (1970). "Dirty Books Can Stay." In D. A. Hughes, ed., *Perspectives on Pornography*, pp. 109–21. New York: St. Martin's.

U.S. Commission on Obscenity and Pornography. (1970). *Report*. Washington, D.C.: U.S. Government Printing Office.

——— (1971–72). *Technical Reports*. Vols. 1–9. Washington, D.C.: U.S. Government Printing Office.

U.S. Congress. Senate. Committee on the Judiciary. (1977). *The Protection of Children Against Sexual Exploitation Act 1977*. 95th Cong., 2d sess., 1977. S. Rept. 95-438.

U.S. Department of Justice. (1986). *Attorney General's Commission on Pornography Final Report*. Vols. 1 and 2. Washington, D.C.: U.S. Government Printing Office.

U.S. National Advisory Commission on Civil Disorders. (1968). *Report*. Washington, D.C.: The Commission.

U.S. National Commission on the Causes and Prevention of Violence. (1969). *To Establish Justice, To Insure Domestic Tranquility*. Washington, D.C.: The Commission.

U.S. President's Commission on Organized Crime. (1986). *Report to the President and the Attorney General. The Impact: Organized Crime Today*. Washington, D.C.: U.S. Government Printing Office.

van den Haag, Ernest. (1962). "Quia Ineptum." In J. Chandos, ed., *To Deprave and Corrupt*, pp. 109–124. New York: Association Press.

——— (1971). "Research and a Report." *Commentary* 52:30–33.

Vance, Carole S. (1986). "The Meese Commission on the Road." *The Nation*, August 2 and 9, 1986, 76–80.

Weaver, Warren. (1970). "Nixon Repudiates Obscenity Report as Morally Void." *New York Times*, October 25, 1970, 1, 71.

Webster, Paula. (1986). "Pornography and Pleasure." In K. Ellis et al., eds., *Caught Looking*, pp. 30–35. New York: Caught Looking Inc.

Weightman, John. (1979). "On Her Majesty's (Unpaid) Service in the Porn War." *The Observer* (London), December 2, 1979, 10.

Weininger, Otto. (1903; 1975). *Sex and Character*. New York: Putnam.

Williams, Bernard. (1981). *Obscenity and Film Censorship*. Cambridge University Press.

Willis, Ellen. (1986). "Feminism, Moralism, and Pornography." In K. Ellis et al., eds., *Caught Looking*, pp. 54–59. New York: Caught Looking Inc.

Wilson, James Q. (1971). "Violence, Pornography, and Social Science." *The Public Interest* 22:45–61.

Witcover, Jules. (1970). "Civil War Over Smut." *The Nation*, May 11, 1970, 550–553.

Wollheim, Richard. (1973). "John Stuart Mill and the Limits of State Actions." *Social Research* 40:1–30.
Yaffe, Maurice. (1978). "Pornography: An Updated Review (1972–1977)." In Home Office, *Report of the Committee on Obscenity and Film Censorship,* Appendix 5, pp. 235–249.
Zimring, Franklin E. (1982). *The Changing Legal World of Adolescence.* New York: Free Press.
   (1987). "Legal Perspectives on Family Violence." *California Law Review* 75:521–539.

Index

Adult bookstores and sex shops, 50–1, 54
Adult Film Association of America (AFAA), 207–8
advertising, 211
age boundaries: and child pornography, 196–7; and experiments on effects of pornography, 188–9; for pornography performers, 176–7
American Civil Liberties Union (ACLU), and Meese Commission, 16
antipornography ordinance, 141–2
artistic merit, 110–11

behavior and pornography, 74–5, 108
Bible, 163
books and magazines, pornographic, 35; monthly circulation of, 36
Boston, "Combat Zone," 62
boycotts, and citizen action, 209–10

cable and satellite television, 41
Canadian Special Committee on Pornography and Prostitution, x, 25, 175; and feminist perspective on pornography, 153
Casanova's *Mémoires*, 118–19
censorship: alternatives to, 198–217; and citizen action, 208–9; and John Milton, 114; and Johnson and Meese Commissions, xi–xii; versus inaction, as response to pornography, 198–217; and Williams Committee, 128–30
childhood, definitions of, 182–3, 190
child pornography: and age boundaries, 196–7; consumption and participation compared, 192–4; and criminal law protection, 191–6; definitional issues of, 182–3; extent of, 180–2; jurisprudence of, 195–6; and Meese Commission, 61–2; and pornography commissions, 180; and punishment of children, 194–5; and social values, 189–90; as victimless crime, 191; *see also* children
child protection, as punishment, 194–5
children: capacity to make mature judgments, 183–4, 186; as consumers of and participants in pornography, 129–30, 185–7; and experiments on effects of pornography, 187–9; predation on, 184; as subjects in pornography, 179–85; *see also* child pornography
citizen groups, 208–10
civil remedies, for control of pornography, 141–2
clinical and experimental research, and sex crimes, 100–1
commercial sex, 62–6
computer bulletin boards, 43
consumers, of pornography, 52–62; by gender, 53–6; Johnson Commission studies of, 53–62; by sexual orientation, 58–62
crime commissions, 5–6
crime statistics, problems with, 86–7
criminal law, considered by Meese Commission, 140–1
criminal penalties, 139–41

decriminalization of pornography, 72–3, 191–2
definitions of pornography, 25–9, 162–6; as medium–message combination, 157–62; Meese Commission's problems with, 94–5; by radical feminists, 154–63
deregulation of adult pornography, 191–2
Dial-a-Porn Services, and Meese Commission, 42
Dworkin, Andrea, 30, 141, 151–74; *see also* MacKinnon, Catharine

233

erotica: as defined by radical feminists, 151–
2; definitions of, 21–9; impact of, Johnson
Commission panel report on, 82–3
experimental studies on relation of sexual violence and arousal, 103–4
exploitation films, 33

FBI, on organized crime and pornography,
65
federal government, role in pornography regulation, 214–16
Feinberg, Joel, 155
Feminist Anti-Censorship Task Force, 112,
167
feminists: internal debate of, over pornography, 166–7; support for pornography,
166–7
First Amendment: calculus of balance under,
136–7; and censorship, 216; and limits of
public law, 139–44; and pornography,
109–45, 219–20; and radical feminists,
168–9; and Supreme Court, 130–1; and
U.S. pornography commissions, 130–8; *see
also* Supreme Court
free expression: and pornography, 74–5,
110–12; and radical feminists, 170–4; value
of, 125–6

gender inequality, as basis of pornography,
160–1

hard-core pornography: imports from Scandi-
navia of, 37; and Johnson and Meese Commissions, 37–8
Hefner, Hugh, 205
Holbrook, David, 120
homosexuals, 59–60
human personality, development of, 110

Johnson Commission, x, 7–10; and censorship, 119; and classification of sexually explicit materials, 67; and content analysis of
Romance or *Confession* magazine stories,
45–6; criticisms of research, 82–5; and definition of erotica, 22; and definition of pornography, 21–2, 162; drafts of criminal
statutes relating to pornography, 140; and
empirical research, 17–18; and First
Amendment, 132–3; and future trends,
69–73; history of, 9–10; legislative recommendations of, 6–7; members of, 8; model
of relation between pornography and social
harm, 87–8; and obscenity, 21; and pornographic communication as inducement to
sexual action, 117; on pornography and

children, 175; on pornography and organized crime, 64–6; report on traffic and distribution of pornography, 31–73; and
scope of interests of pornography consumers, 46; and Senator McClellan, 9; and
sexual education, 122; and social harm of
pornography, 77–89, 107; specific tasks assigned to, 7–8; *see also* Meese Commission;
pornography commissions; Williams
Committee
judicial scrutiny of pornography, legislative
restrictions on, 135–6

Kutchinsky, Berl: on child pornography,
181; on Scandinavian pornography, 92

legal controls on pornography, 219–21
Lockhart, William B., 8

MacKinnon, Catharine, 141; on women who
support pornography, 169–70; views on
pornography, 151–74; *see also* Dworkin,
Andrea
mail-order sales: and Meese Commission, 37;
of pornography, 36–7
male supremacy: as major theme of pornography, 157–8; reality of and radical feminists, 170
McClellan, John D., 9
Meese Commission, ix–x, 13–16; and American Civil Liberties Union, 16; and censorship, 15; and citizen action against pornography, 208; and classification of sexually
explicit materials, 67–9; conceptual problems of, 106–7; and content of pornography, 47–9; and definition of obscenity, 23;
and definition of pornography, 23–4, 94–5;
and dissociation between research findings
and interpretation, 99–100; and distinction
between pornography industry and mainstream entertainment, 68–9; on experimental studies of sexual violence and arousal,
103–4; and feminist perspective on pornography, 152–3, 162; and First Amendment,
132, 134–5, 137; and future trends, 69–73;
history of, 14–16; and lack of interest in
pornography consumers, 134–5; lawsuits
against, 15–16; mandate of, 13; members
of, 13–14; on *Miller* test, 131; and pornographic communication and promotion of
moral decay and sexual action, 116–17,
118, 121; and pornographic motion pictures, 34–5; on pornography and children,
175–87; on pornography and organized
crime, 64–6; and public attitudes toward

pornography, 98; public reaction to, 14–15; Recommendation 38, 176–7; recommendation 45, 178; Recommendation 53, 179; recommendations for legislative action on child pornography, 176–9; and research on pornography's harm, 94–107, 108; and restrictive regulation of pornography 142–4; on sex offenders and pornography, 99; and summary descriptions of selected pornography, 47–8; and symbolic denunciation of pornography, 225–6; and term "erotica," 24; and volume of pornography, 30–1; and war on smut, 223–4; and Williams Committee definition of pornography, 27–8; *see also* Johnson Commission; pornography commissions; Williams Committee

Memoirs of a Woman of Pleasure (Cleland), 114–15

Mill, John Stuart: *On Liberty*, 110; and victimless crime, 191

Miller test, 130–1

Milton, John, and censors, 114

misogyny, equation of with pornography, 162–4

motion pictures, 32–5

movie-rating system, 33

objectification, 157–61

Obscene Publications Acts, English, 114

obscenity: definitions of, 20–9, 133; and Johnson Commission, 21

paraphilia, 60–1

peep shows, 44

policy: and definitions, 21; prescriptions for, 70; recommendations, on research, 108

pornography: and adolescents, 56–7; and advertising, 211; and artistic merit, 110–11; audience aimed at, 46–7; availability of, xi; behavioral effects of, reasons for studying, 74–5; as cause of crime, 76; and children, 149–50, 175–97; censorship versus inaction in response to, 198–217; and commercial vice, 64–7; as communication, 109–25; compared with regulation of tobacco and alcohol, 193; control of, by civil remedies, 141–2; as crime, pure model of, 200–1; criminal crackdown on, 223–5; decriminalization of, 72–3, 221–3; definitions of, 20–9, 213–14; and degradation of women, 93; demand for, 53; distinction between printed and films, 219–20; effects of, 74–108, 164–6; and experts, 209; exposure to, 49–50, 124–5; and free expression, 74–5, 110–12; and freedom of expression, 109–

45; governmental regulation of, 210–14, 214–16; governmental responses to, 198–217; home as venue of, 50; identity of its consumers, 52–3; industry, size of, in United States, 30–31; judicial standards of, 130–2; and male heterosexuals, 52–6; and misogyny, 162–3; modest tightening of legal controls of, 219–21; and moral values of youth, 121–2, and motion pictures, 32–5; and mysteries compared, 188; and organized crime, 64–6; places of display of, 49–52; policy options in relation to, 198–217; and prostitution, 62–64; as question of power, 168–9; and public law, xi; and rape, 164–5; response of private groups to, 198–217; restrictive regulation of, 142–4; scenarios of future control, 218–25; and sex offenders, 99; sexually provocative aspect of, 27–9; and social harm, 74–108; as source of information about sex, 111–12; and status of women, 151–74; in Sweden, 55; themes of, 45–9; in 2002, 225–6; and U.S. economic mainstream, 70–3; and zoning, 211–12

pornography commissions: and child pornography, 180; comparative impact of lawyers on, 18; and consumers, 18–19; dominant role of legal profession in, 17; and empirical research, 17–18; era of, 3–4; fate of their recommendations, 7; and feminist perspective, 18; and members' backgrounds, 16–19; origins and composition of, 5–19; and pornography industry, 19; reasons for establishing, 6; and selection of members of, 16–19; *see also* Johnson Commission; Meese Commission; Williams Committee

pornography consumers: by age, 56–8; in Canada, 58; scope of interests of, 46; sexual orientation of, 58–62

pornography producers: outlaw tradition among, 206–7; and record keeping, 177–8

private sector, and social control of pornography, 200–10

Proal, Louis, 119

prohibiting behavior, and regulation, 202–3

prostitutes, as pornography performers, 64

prostitution, 63; varieties of, 31

public attitudes toward pornography, 122–4; and Meese Commission, 98

public opinion polls, 98

punishment, and child protection, 194–5

Racketeer Influenced and Corrupt Organization Act (RICO), 140–1

radical feminist critique of pornography,
151–74; and antipornography ordinance,
170–1; and classical liberalism, 171; on experimental research, 165–6; stipulative definition, 155–7
rape, 164–5
red light districts, 62
Renton ordinance, 143–4
retailers of sexually explicit materials, 68–9
romantic novels, as aid to seduction, 119

Salò, 112–13
San Francisco "Tenderloin" district, 62
self-regulation: by pornography industry,
205–8; prospects for in movie industry,
207–8
semicensorship, 141–4
7-Eleven stores, 203–5; and possible effects
of antipornographer's victory, 204–5
Sex and Character (Weininger), 162–4
sex crimes, and availability of pornography,
100–1
sex education, 186–7; federal role in, 215–16
sex newspapers 44–5
sex offenders, 99
sexual arousal, empirical research on, 115
sexual communication, 112–15
sexual explicitness in U.S. society, 68
sexually explicit materials, classification of,
67–9
sexually violent material, and social harm, 95
sexual offense statistics, and availability of
pornography, 100–1
sexual orientation of pornography consumers,
58–62
sexual tastes, pornography catering to, 60–2
Simpson, A. W. B., ix, 114; 174; and offensiveness of pornography, 123; on radical
feminist definition of pornography, 155
social values, and child pornography, 189–90
soft-core magazine industry, 206–7
status offenders, 192
stipulative definitions, 155
subordination–degradation hypothesis, 172–4

Supreme Court: and definition of obscenity,
130–1; and First Amendment, 130–1; and
radical feminist antipornography ordinance, 170–1

Toolbox Murders, 103–4

van den Haag, Ernest, 115
vice, commercial, 62–6
Video Software Dealers Association, survey
of members, 39–41
videotapes, 38–41
violence, lack of definition of, by Meese Commission, 102

war on smut, 223–5
Weston, John, 52; 207–8.
Williams Committee, ix, x, 10–13; and children as consumers of and participants in
pornography, 129–30, 175, 185–6; criteria
for evaluating the harm of pornography
127; and definition of erotic, 23; and definition of obscenity, 22; and definition of pornography, 22–3, 162; and feminist perspective on pornography, 152; and harm
condition, 89–90, 125–6; history of, 11–
13; members of, 11; and offensiveness of
pornography, 123; and pornographic communication and promotion of moral decay
and sexual action, 116, 118, 120–1; reactions of, 12–13; recommendations of, on
censorship of pornography, 128–30; and relation between pornography and sex
crimes, 91–2; and *Salò*, 113–14; selection
of members, 11; and social harm of pornography, 89–94, 90–2, 107–8; standards for
restricting pornography, 127; terms of reference of, 10; views on Johnson Commission
research on social harm of pornography,
84–5; *see also* Johnson Commission; Meese
Commission; pornography commissions

zoning, 211–12.